# A

# LETTER

FROM

# THE KING

TO

# HIS PEOPLE.

TWENTY-FIFTH EDITION.

LONDON·

PRINTED FOR WILLIAM SAMS,

BOOKSELLER TO HIS ROYAL HIGHNESS THE DUKE OF YORK,
1, St. JAMES'S STREET ;

SOLD ALSO BY W. BLACKWOOD, EDINBURGH ;

C. P. ARCHER, BOOKSELLER TO HIS MAJESTY, DUBLIN ;
AND ALL OTHER BOOKSELLERS IN THE UNITED KINGDOM.

MDCCCXXI.

*Carlton Palace, Dec.* 1, 1820.

# THE KING

𝔖𝔢𝔫𝔡𝔰 𝔞𝔩𝔦𝔨𝔢 𝔥𝔦𝔰 𝔪𝔬𝔰𝔱 𝔞𝔣𝔣𝔢𝔠𝔱𝔦𝔬𝔫𝔞𝔱𝔢 𝔤𝔯𝔢𝔢𝔱𝔦𝔫𝔤.

THE liberty of the press does not permit to your King, the possibility of remaining ignorant of passing events, or unaffected by the public agitation: at one and the same time it conveys to me sentiments of satisfaction or grounds of complaint; the promised support of the constitutional, and the threat of the disaffected. My own conduct, the measures of my executive, the state of my kingdom, and the condition of my subjects, are placed before me in as many various, confused, and contradictory positions, as the greater or lesser degree of information, the rivalship of party, the animosity of prejudice, or the insidiousness of faction alternately suggest. In this chaos of contrariety, to me the first great difficulty is, to discover the truth; the next, so to manage the discovery, as to produce from it some sound and dispassionate course of action.

This liberty of the press, in itself a great abstract good, capable alike of being converted into a bane or antidote; and, by discreet and conscientious management, capable also of promoting and effecting immortal benefits to mankind, or inflicting upon them irremediable ills, keeps up at least a constant communication between us, depriving the courtier of the power of concealing from his Sovereign public opinion, and placing him within the effect of inquiry. With such a constant possibility of explanation, a Monarch may be misguided, but cannot be uninformed; he may adopt decisive rules of government, but cannot remain ignorant of their effects.

Although it is presumed that I become acquainted with political occurrences and opinions, solely through the channel of my official advisers, and can only constitutionally address my people through the regular organ of parliament, or of my council; yet, at this momentous crisis, pregnant with evil to our common country, and to me so interesting as a man and a husband, but above all, as the inheritor of my Royal Father's crown, the form and mode of this communication may stand shielded and excused, in the generally anomalous character of the circumstances to which I shall hereafter advert: nor, on so singular an occasion, do I think it derogatory to the dignity of my exalted station, to attempt the dispersion of a mist, in which too many of my subjects have wandered, led on by a generous delusion.

I will not accuse, I do not accuse, of disaffection either to my person or government, *all* who are advocates for the cause of the Queen; for in that cause, I perceive plainly a variety of motives in activity; in the combination of those motives, differing widely from each other, the immediate danger appears to consist: but it is also, from their dis-

cordance, that future tranquillity may be expected.
I am persuaded that, could my subjects upon reflection, be brought to consider the probability of
my being an injured and calumniated Prince, they
would abstain from further insult to the crown inherited from GEORGE THE THIRD. I am also persuaded that public opinion, although forced into
extremes by the goadings of a portion of the daily
press, alike unrestrained by truth, and as devoid
of principle, as lost to the common civilities of society, would soon right itself; when a plain and
simple narrative (such as any man of reasonable
mind might comprehend) should supersede the distorted and tortured facts which have lately pre-
occupied too great a part of the nation.

So many years have elapsed since the period of
my unhappy marriage, that it may not be inexpedient
(indeed, it appears absolutely necessary, in order
to develope certain springs of action) to recall the
times and circumstances in which, and by which,
this event was produced.

The French Revolution was at its height; the
Royal Family of France had been murdered; Holland had imbibed the revolutionary mania, and the
Stadtholder had fled to this protecting country; at
home, a traitorous spirit was actively at work; trials
for high treason had served only to increase the insolence of faction, and foster rebellion; Ireland
was on the verge of open revolt: and every political appearance threatened an attempt upon the constitution of these realms; a dreadful war was raging:
yet, amidst and in the face of all these evils, it was
the wish of my Royal Father to strengthen the succession to the throne of these realms; and the more

especially, as my royal brother of York had been married four years, without the expectation of a family. No moment could be less auspicious than the one chosen. My own inclination was averse to a marriage of expediency; nor need I tell my subjects under what disadvantages a Prince of the Royal Family labours, and more especially the heir-apparent born in the kingdom, in a chance for matrimonial happiness; and for myself, confined by the laws of my country within the limits of the realm, I could never hope to lead my countrymen to the field of battle, in her just wars, or extend my sphere of useful acquirement, by foreign travels, and the personal examination of the customs, manners, and government of other countries. Of the character of their princes and courtiers, I could only learn by intermediate report.

Debarred thus from active employment, and destined to pass my time in royal idleness, surrounded with pleasures at every step, and captivated with beauty, it would not be the most difficult enigma to solve, how I became thoughtlessly extravagant. Notwithstanding I had experienced the generosity of my countrymen, when twenty-four years of age; yet, in nine years after, my debts became again the object of serious consideration. In the midst of a war then raging, expensive beyond all former precedent, and with no glimpse of termination; when monarchy throughout Europe was threatened with annihilation, some powerful and unanswerable motive, or some important and ostensible good, could alone justify the minister of the day, in applying to parliament for the payment of the debts of an extravagant Prince, for such I acknowledge myself to have been.

The justification of the measure was found to be in *my marriage*.

The nation most generously paid my debts, made provision for such marriage, and I became an *expedient* party to the contract. For me there was no escape; the interest of my creditors demanded such sacrifice; a sacrifice of which my heart could only appreciate the extent.

But, although the match was forced, and I was left (unlike my subjects) to no voluntary choice, I had still a right to expect in a Princess of exalted ancestry, and one previously allied to me by relationship, a female of chaste person and uncontaminated taste.

But the morning which dawned on the consummation of this marriage, witnessed its virtual dissolution.

Our daughter, the lamented Princess Charlotte, the child of a fond and admiring nation, was born precisely at the moment prescribed by nature.

Of the causes which led to this immediate separation, which however was for a time most carefully concealed; and concealed, I trust, from no ungenerous feeling on my part, it does not belong to me to detail the explanation. But who beside ourselves was interested in it? Surely the family of the illustrious female in question! Did they complain? Did they remonstrate? Did they demand a restitution of conjugal rights between us? Did they interfere to conciliate, to palliate, to explain? Never. By their silence, then, was I justified in requiring at a proper moment, a more openly avowed separation. *The first wrong was done to me.*

The situation in which my Royal Father

placed towards us both, was one of peculiar delicacy, and requires your particular attention. In-
dependently of his own good and well-intentioned
motives, he could not but feel that I had sacrificed
my happiness to obedience to his will, and to those
urgent and pressing political influences which directed that will. To him, therefore, it must have
been painful to find, that all chance of connubial
connexion was destroyed as soon as formed; it
must also have been painful to him to know, that in
commanding my marriage, he had (however un-
intentionally) clogged my high station with a source
of constant anxiety and unceasing misrepresenta-
tion. Again: as towards the then Princess of
Wales, his late Majesty, my revered Father and
King, could not but have felt, that a marriage so
brought about at his urgent desire, and enforced
upon one positive condition, called forth from him
more especially every increased attention towards
the illustrious female whom he had introduced into
the country; nor could this fatherly attention be
otherwise than the more marked and decisive, on
account of the relationship of that illustrious female
in question to the then Queen of these realms. His
most sacred Majesty was thus doubly and peculiarly
bound to the protection of the interests of this illustrious female, as well as to a gentlemanly forbearance towards a son, through his influence so unexpectedly,
so unusually, and I may add, so unhappily, circumstanced. This line of nice distinction and difficult conduct, so honourably and so nobly adhered to by his
late Majesty, led to the erroneous supposition, that
my honoured and royal parent and myself were at
:e upon this important occasion: but such

was not in the slightest degree the fact; the subject was, as it were, interdicted mutually from our conferences and meetings, and I always honoured my royal parent the more highly for the motives which influenced and marked out the line of conduct he felt himself peculiarly called upon to adopt. His aim was, to soften by every means of alleviation in his power the situation of the Princess; but, at the same time, he was left without cause of accusation against his son's early determination.

Having rested the propriety of my conduct upon the silence of the relatives of the Princess, on an occasion when silence on their part could only have been imposed by a knowledge of the means of justification; and having discovered the principle which generosity and hospitality dictated to my late Father and King in his conduct towards the Princess, I now refer to a letter, dated Windsor Castle, April 30, 1796; which letter has been termed, insolently, unjustifiably, and almost traitorously, a letter of license.

"*It was always competent for the Princess of Wales to demand from me, if she felt herself so justified, the restitution of her conjugal rights.*" That a female of her lofty daring should not have taken such a step, admits a very strong argument in favour of the retiring husband; at all events, it allows of the inference, that there was a domestic and personal cause for separation, to which the parties mutually consented.

This letter of the 30th of April, above alluded to, may be considered as containing the terms of our separation. On this letter, which evidently refers to former conferences and previous communications, and was written to the Princess at her own request, I have but one observation to make, namely,—

" That pending the arrangement for an open and avowed seperation, the then Princess of Wales, through the medium of Lady Cholmoudeley, required *that the separation should be final and conclusive, as to any future particular intercourse, and not to be renewed at any period, even though our child the Princess Charlotte should die.*" To this proposition I assented; by this proposition I have abided, and ever will abide. It is an extra proposition emanating from the Queen; it contains her own terms.

From the moment of this open and avowed separation, *rendered perpetual* by the proposition of her Royal Highness; I can call herself and the kingdom to witness, whether any thing has been withheld from the personal accommodation of the Princess of Wales? Whether a suitable establishment, regulated by herself, was not provided for her comfort? Whether I ever interfered with her arrangements, her society, or her social convenience; in short, I boldly challenge my people to the proof, whether I had ever been guilty of any step, directly, or indirectly, to break in upon that arrangement of tranquillity, and comfortable society, which was the basis of our mutual separation.

This separation between the Princess and myself, partook not in its origin, of the smallest political mixture; it was purely an unhappy but unavoidable domestic occurrence, of which the good manners of both parties might have softened the effect; and in which, strict propriety of conduct, such as befitted the second lady in the land, might have commanded my respect; though an insurmountable obstacle was opposed to any further feeling. During this separation, the Princess of Wales possessed the most uncontrolled choice and command of her own household; she was mistress of her own conduct; was still the wife of the heir-apparent to the throne, and mother of the heiress presumptive. The Princess must have been aware of the superior legal responsibility attached to the high and important rank she held in the empire; and the peculiarity of her situation demanded a greater degree of discretion; painful and singular as was that situation, it was one in which the Princess might have shone with additional splendour, had she maintained a dignified and elegant association.

I am charged by the giddy press and the partisans of the Queen, with having, upon all occasions, besieged her with spies and suborned traducers.

At the period of this separation in 1796, the then Princess of Wales surrounded herself, not with any friends of mine, but with an establishment of her own choice. But suppose, for argument sake, this false assertion to be true; how completely useless would have been the office of those spies and tale-bearers, had the conduct of her Royal Highness given no grounds for their occupation! In such a case, the more closely her Royal Highness had been watched, the more spotless, chaste and unquestionable would her conduct have appeared. Ought it, under any circumstances, even of presumed aggravation, to have been otherwise?

I approach now the period of the first investigation of 1806, which took place *ten years* after the separation; and which carried back its research four years from the date of its report. The very circumstance, that it became necessary to trace *through several years* the conduct of her Royal Highness, allows me fairly to assert that which was the fact; namely,

" that it was not until after tale upon tale had been
in wide circulation for a long period; nor until those
reports assumed the threatening character of high
treason, that I determined to advise with a retired
Lord Chancellor on the measures necessary to be
adopted." Had I been actuated by the foul spirit
attributed to me, I had at that moment an opportunity of gratifying such revenge, by demanding a
public trial instead of a private investigation. The
base political purposes to which the privacy of that
proceeding was subsequently applied, might almost
tempt me to regret that I had not done so : yet I
do not regret it, since the motive was (even at the
very moment of an inquiry becoming legally expedient) to shield the object of it as much as possible
from publicity, I might almost say, to accommodate
her acquittal. Upon this occasion, the reputation
and character of those eminent noblemen, Lords
Erskine, Spencer, Grenville, and Ellenborough,
must first be destroyed, before I can be charged
with provoking *an unnecessary inquiry* into the existence of circumstances which had long been circulating through every rank of society, which were at
the time generally believed to be true, or enveloped
in a mystery far removed from that absence of all
doubtful and suspicious appearances, which should
characterize the conduct of a Princess of Wales.
On this occasion, the same honourable feelings
which had invariably guided the conduct of my
Royal Father and King, inclined him still to shield
and protect her Royal Highness, and to place the
least culpable interpretation upon the circumstances
of that mysterious case. It was the same generous
ing which induced my Royal Father to adopt, as

a previous step, my proposal of a private and confidential inquiry, in a matter, where less considerate conduct might, at, once, have transferred the cause of offence to a public tribunal. Throughout the whole of this affair, her Royal Highness was treated with a delicacy suitable to the peculiarity of her situation, to which every, and the most generous, consideration was paid. Her Royal Highness was aware of it, and *at the moment* felt herself so treated.

Did I, upon this occasion, dissent from the line of conduct recommended to be pursued? No. Did I interfere with the duties of the noble lords commissioners upon the occasion? No. Did I, as a husband, cease to perform the terms of separation, even after the imperious necessity which had devolved upon me as Prince of Wales, of requiring indemnity for the succession to the throne? No. I assert, that in the conflicting duties imposed upon me as a husband, and as Prince of Wales, that when the admonition of my royal parent was deemed sufficient for the occasion, I acquiesced. Nor, on a subsequent occasion, did I hesitate to pay the debts of the illustrious person in question, in her character of my wife. Nay more, I carried still further the spirit of conciliation, and proof of my acquiescence in the result of such investigation, by the subsequent advance to honour and distinction of one of the parties implicated criminally in the charge against the then Princess of Wales. I am, therefore, on that occasion, the avowed approver of the result of the inquiry; and stand convicted, either of being regardless of my own honour, or of being satisfied that the accusation was overstrained.

Before I dismiss this part of my letter, I w

direct the attention of my subjects and countrymen to the rigour of the law, applicable to the wife of the heir-apparent to the throne. An error which, in any female of less distinguished rank, is merely a civil injury, in the wife of the Prince of Wales *is a crime against the nation.* The mere act of offence is in both cases alike; but in the one may be attended with the last penalty, that of death. If, therefore, in any proceedings connected with the case of a prince of Wales, there appears a greater measure of legal harshness, to which our moral feelings are opposed, it should be remembered, that the anomaly is created by the statutes of the realm. I made not the law for myself.

When the Princess of Wales had received the admonitory letter of 1806, no complaint at the time was made by her, either against its justice, or the mode in which the inquiry had been conducted. It was reserved to revive the painful subject seven years after its occurrence; and to attack the proceedings, as well as the intermediate restraint which had been imposed on the intercourse of the Princess with our daughter, in a letter dated early in 1813, addressed to me as Regent of these United Kingdoms. That letter, as containing a matter of complaint deserving of inquiry, was submitted, without regard to the personally offensive remarks contained in it, to several dignitaries of the church and of the law. Upon this second report, the restriction alluded to was still continued, and the aspersions cast upon the testimony of certain witnesses connected with the inquiry of 1806, were pronounced to be *wholly groundless,* and *without the slightest support of Proof.*

It is important for me to draw your attention to

the circumstance, that the two reports were drawn up by noblemen of differing political sentiments, accustomed to constant parliamentary opposition; if therefore from such an ordeal, the proceedings of 1806 have escaped censure, and consequently became stamped with a character of fair and impartial justice, I have a right to demand, and do demand, a full and complete acquittal from all those false and unprincely motives, by which my conduct has been stigmatized; I plead guilty only of one motive, " That of preserving to my daughter her rights, and protecting the purity of succession to the throne of my ancestors."

Had the result of this second report, produced by a set of political reasoners wholly opposed to the first commissioners, varied from the report of such commissioners; had it brought home to the witnes upon the former occasion, any charge of perjury, or have elicited any trace of unworthy motive, or corruptly contrived evidence; it would have been my unavoidable duty as Regent, and the office most pleasing to me as a husband and man, to have revived that inquiry, and have punished the guilty participators in it; and besides, it was at all times open to the Princess *to bring her accusers before the tribunals of her country.* Unless, therefore, every principle of civilized conduct has been violated by me, and I alone have proceeded upon impulses different from all mankind, surely, on my own account, I must have rejoiced at any elucidation which had sprung up, had it been only for the mere selfish purpose *of wiping from myself* the mortification of such recorded aspersions. Was it to be supposed, that I should tamely cover myself with the mantle of my

own shame, could I have had it in my power to
destroy every thread of the garment? I should
have deserved the scorn of the age, and ill merited
the allegiance of my father's subjects, could I have
hesitated one moment in following the minutest ray
which might detect the mystery of 1806, and completely clear her Royal Highness from those
charges.

But from the date of this letter in 1813, the whole
transaction, which had hitherto been treated as a
domestic difference, assumed on the part of the
Princess of Wales a political aspect. To this point
I shall subsequently refer; for the present, there,
fore, I will pass on to the period of her departure to
visit the continent.

Upon this occasion, her Royal Highness addressed her intentions to me, through the medium
of the Earl of Liverpool, in a letter dated the 25th
July, 1814, in which her Royal Highness stated as her
first and her most urgent motive for wishing to retire to the continent, "the restoration of tranquillity
to my mind." Her Royal Highness then goes on to
complain of the indignities and mortification to which
she had been exposed, by being withheld from receiving her nearest relations, and the most intimate
friends of the late Duke of Brunswick, her father;
and alludes to the rupture of the proposed alliance
between our daughter, the Princess Charlotte, and
the Prince of Orange. Her Royal Highness also
pointing out her route, states that she intends to return to Brunswick her native country, and with a degree of uncertainty adds, she may afterwards travel
into Italy and Greece, and proposes certain arrangements as to the disposition of her private pro-

perty. To all these points I subjoin the reply as transmitted through my prime minister, with this one observation, that Lord Liverpool does not *silently* pass over the circumstance of her Royal Highness possessing apartments in a royal palace, (to which her Royal Highness makes no allusion in her letter,) but absolutely states, that such apartments will still be retained for the use of her Royal Highness; thus, if any conscious doubts had existed in the mind of the Princess, and this omission was intended to draw from me any expression as to the length of her stay on the continent, or whether I considered that the departure of the Princess was intended to be permanent, such doubts are clearly removed by the specific allusion of Lord Liverpool to those particular apartments in a royal palace.

Her Royal Highness then leaves England by her own voluntary act, at her own express desire, retaining by the avowed will of the Prince (acting on behalf of the King) a residence, to which, at any time, she might return. There is also a second point in this letter of the Princess, on which I would make one short observation. Her Royal Highness, referring to the mode of disposal of part of her property, uses this expression: "The Princess of Wales hopes the Prince Regent will *grant* this favour, *the last that she will solicit*." I ask, then, is this the language of a wife receiving injuries from a husband; or is it not characteristic of language from a wife to a husband who, though separated from that husband, had ever been accustomed to receive from him every favour and benefit which could with honour be granted! I subjoin the reply alluded to, as it corrects the political points contained in the letter of the Princess.

## Letter of Lord Liverpool to the Princess of Wales, dated the 28th of July, 1814.

" Lord Liverpool has had the honour to receive the letter of her Royal Highness. Having communicated it to the Prince Regent, he has ordered him to inform her Royal Highness that he can have no objection to the intentions of her Royal Highness to effect the design which she announces to the Prince Regent, of returning to her native country, to visit her brother the Duke of Brunswick, assuring her, that the Prince Regent will never throw any obstacle in the way of her present or future intentions as to the place where she may wish to reside.

" The Prince Regent leaves her Royal Highness at liberty to exercise her own discretion as to her abode in this country or on the continent, as it may be convenient to her.

" Lord Liverpool is also commanded, on the part of the Prince Regent, to inform her Royal Highness, that he will not throw any obstacles in the way of the arrangements of her Royal Highness, whatever they may be, respecting the house at Blackheath, which belonged to the late Duchess of Brunswick, or the rest of the private property of her Royal Highness. But that, for reasons rather too long to explain, the Prince Regent will not permit the Princess Charlotte to be ranger of Greenwich Park, or to occupy any of the houses at Blackheath, which her Royal Highness has hitherto occupied.

" Lord Liverpool has also been enjoined, on the part of the Prince Regent, before he closes the letter which he has the honour to send to her Royal Highness, to tell her, in relation to the two articles which her Royal Highness has put in her letter concerning the rupture of the marriage of the Princess Charlotte with the hereditary Prince of Orange, as well as to the reason for which the allied Sovereigns did not, previously to their departure from England, pay their visit to her Royal Highness ; that, as to the first article, Lord Liverpool is commanded by the Prince Regent to inform her Royal Highness, that the Prince Regent is not persuaded that the private considerations of the circumstances in which the Princess is placed, can have been an obstacle to the marriage of the Princess Charlotte. As to the second article, Lord Liverpool is also enjoined, on the part of the Prince Regent, to signify to her Royal Highness, that the Prince Regent never opposed himself to the allied Sovereigns making a visit to her Royal Highness during their stay in London.

" Lord Liverpool has the honour to be, with all esteem and the highest consideration.

" P. S. The Prince Regent can make no difficulties on the subject of the directions which the Princess has the intention of giving as to the house at Blackheath ; neither will the Prince Regent oppose her Royal Highness's retaining the apartments in the Palace of Kensington, in the same manner as she possessed them while in London, for the convenience of herself and suite."

At the period then of the departure of her Royal Highness from the kingdom, the very last communication between us was on my part, that of assuring her, that the residence more particularly occupied by her as a state residence, should be considered as remaining still at her disposal; thus placing a seal of oblivion on the past, and according every thing but personal communication.

Her Royal Highness was enabled to quit England as became her rank, with a suite of her own choice, with zealous friends among that suite, and with every facility afforded her of rendering her stay on the Continent comfortable and convenient. Her public reception at foreign courts naturally depended on, and was regulated by, established etiquette.

I have thus brought down the material circumstances of my unhappy marriage, to the period of the departure of her Royal Highness for the Continent; the transactions in themselves, however unfortunate, are plain and simple, easily understood, and as capable of explanation, when viewed without any selfish tendency to party or faction. The incidents may be thus briefly stated:—

1. Our private separation.

2. Our public separation.

3. The interval between our public separation and the inquiry of 1806.

4. The complaint of the Princess in 1813, as to the restricted intercourse between herself and daughter.

5. The retirement of the Princess to the Continent.

*The first point,* (the reasons of our private separation), it does not become me to explain; her Royal Highness might (if she had so pleased,) have claimed in the proper court, the restitution of her conjugal rights; such a proceeding would have produced an explanation.

*As to the second point,* we separated upon terms mutually understood, and to which the Princess added herself a peremptory condition; those terms have by me been inviolably preserved; as a husband, I enabled my wife to maintain the dignity of her rank and station as Princess of Wales; I visited her separation with no pecuniary privations, but, on the contrary, paid for her, debts exceeding her means of expenditure, to the amount of forty-nine thousand pounds; the government of the country, at the same time, liquidating a further sum of thirty-one thousand pounds.

*As to the third point,* the preceding remarks, in part apply. On the subject of the actual inquiry, I may be allowed to say, that the Prince of Wales is born with certain rights previously created, as a line of duty to be by him fulfilled. The preservation of the chastity of his wife, with a view to the purity of the succession, is one of those duties. When, therefore, in consequence of rumours, too loud and too deep to remain unheard, I demanded an inquiry, as part of the duty of my high birth and national rank, I submitted the case to the responsible ministers of the crown; I acquiesced in the sentence passed upon the termination of the inquiry, and bowed to the decision which had been pronounced by the warm and zealous friend of the Princess, who was judge upon the occasion.

*As to the fourth point,* I endeavoured, by every means in my power, to prevent our disputes from ing a political turn, embarrassing to the government of the country; and I most particularly aimed at preserving, in the mind of the Princess Charlotte, a neutrality on the delicate occasion; the restriction imposed on the intercourse between the Princess and her daughter was connected with the system of her education, which, by law, rested with the Sovereign. When, at a subsequent period, in 1813, the Princess of Wales addressed to me as Regent, a letter alluding to such restriction, and also to the proceedings of 1806, almost grown out of recollection, I submitted such letter to noblemen, differing in political opinion from those who had on the former occasion made a report on the conduct of the Princess; the result of this re-inquiry produced no change, no imputation on the former statements and evidence, and I still continued to consider the whole affair as one of domestic inconvenience, inasmuch as the succession to the throne was pronounced *not to be endangered.*

*As to the fifth point,* upon the retirement of her Royal Highness to the Continent, I continued to the Princess her residence in a royal palace, leaving it as a domicile open to her return; and, I declare, upon my honour as a Prince, that I never, on any previous occasion, threw the slightest obstacle in the way of her Royal Highness's comfort, tranquillity, and domestic arrangement. The affairs of Princes cannot be conducted in the same obscure and unostentatious mode as those of private individuals; to snatch a few moments of private life is, in a Prince, to enjoy real happiness. All the difficulties which have occurred in the case in question have been produced and created, they were not of natural origin, but have been foisted on the original evil by factious persons, seeking to advance their own political purposes. Had not the Princess placed herself avowedly in such hands, many of the mortifications of her situation had been avoided; they would, indeed, have had no existence. Finally, I declare again, upon my honour, that my conduct aimed to keep the whole unhappy affair within the character of a domestic and purely personal misfortune; and it is only by the attempts made by faction, to give it a political complexion, that the attention of the people has been fixed upon it as a national grievance.

I have now, my subjects and fellow-countrymen, gone through the first great division of my letter; I approach the second, I trust, with feelings as a King, suitable to the occasion.

Hitherto I have appeared only as Prince of Wales, and Regent.

\* \* \* \* \* \* \* \*

Her Royal Highness quitted England as Princess of Wales early in August in the year 1814, and in the succeeding November (a short interval of three months), appears *to have consulted my tranquillity*, by furnishing grounds for *a third* inquiry into the propriety of her conduct. After *three years of rumours; a commission* to examine into their truth or falsehood was *a third time* rendered necessary for the honour of the crown of these realms; thus, in both cases, as well in the investigation of 1806, as also in that of 1818, it was not until *years of rumour* had been allowed to rouse suspicions, that any official measures were adopted to inquire into their reality.

Possibly the great error has been, that such rumours were permitted to remain so long without an inquiry. Had spies really surrounded her Royal Highness, the purposes of a commission of inquiry would have been anticipated and rendered unnecessary.

When the powers of my regency merged in the succession to the throne, one of the first duties devolving upon me as a head of the Church, was, " to settle according to the Act of Uniformity, such parts of the Liturgy as were affected by the decease of my venerable Father and King of blessed memory."

How lightly have too many of my subjects thought of the feelings by which their Sovereign must have been influenced upon so solemn an occasion !

How inconsiderately have too many of my subjects viewed this vital act of religion as a mere matter of form, requiring only a dash of the pen !

How narrowly have too many of my subjects confined their sense of this form, within the bounds of custom and precedent!

How blindly have too many of my subjects viewed this act of devotional formulary !

And how completely have too many of my subjects separated the act to be done, from him upon whom fell the most painful duty of its performance !

Behold then, your Sovereign, in the presence of that God to whom all hearts are open; required by the first servant of our holy national Church, to sanction as head of that Church, a formulary, in which the thousands and tens of thousands, and millions of his subjects were to address their prayers, and praises, and supplications to the King of Kings.

Behold him thus situated, called upon to doubt and to decide between his conscience and his feelings, whether his own wife deserved, without hesitation, to be admitted to the high dignity, *de facto*, of Queen of these United Kingdoms. Behold him

thus situated, and himself obliged to decide, no other
authority, according to the laws of the realm, having
power to relieve him from the duty. And why was
I thus called upon to doubt? Because my council,
according to their oaths, which is " to advise for the
King's honour and good of the public, without partiality, through affection, love, meed, doubt, or
dread;" and in performance of their duty, which is
" *to inquire into all offences against the government;*"
had not left me unacquainted with the existence of
a *primâ facie* case, of gross and long-continued adultery, alleged to be committed by the late Princess
of Wales, now *de jure* the Queen.

It became therefore evident, it was unavoidable,
that whenever the Queen thought proper to return
to my kingdom, she must meet this charge, the truth
or falsehood of which remained still to be proved.
My council strictly confined themselves to their
legal duty, *that of inquiring only :* and the features of
that inquiry imposed upon them the painful duty of
placing the Queen in a state of abeyance.

This solemn decision, I may say, this vitally religious act, presented itself to me in two points of
view. Was I, with such knowledge in my possession, to recommend unhesitatingly and specially,
the name of the Queen, to the prayers of the church?
Or was I to leave the name to be inserted when her
Majesty should have wiped off this foul charge of
adultery? In the first case, it might possibly have
fallen to my painful office, again to have expunged the
insertion; and in the second case, it might happily
have been my duty to have supplied the omission.
Which, of the two modes afforded the least probability of future embarrassment? As yet, only it

*primá facie* suspicion of adultery was exhibited against the Queen; I had a right to presume her innocent, I had a right to expect that future circumstances might justify the insertion of her Majesty's name, but such an insertion being a matter of discretion, the words " *and all the Royal Family,*" *did not exclude the Queen.* To have inserted the Queen's name specially, and subsequently to have found myself obliged by the law of the land to expunge it; would, with a great degree of reason, have subjected me to the charge of having first introduced such name, that I might enjoy the malicious triumph of erasing it; thus adding increased harshness to any future sentence. By using the phrase, "and all the Royal Family," *any future alteration,* under any circumstances of substantiated guilt or innocence, *would be rendered unnecessary.* To have inserted the name of the Queen, with a knowledge such as I possessed through my legal council, would, in my opinion, have been contrary to the laws of the kingdom; for among other charges which *might* have been brought forward against the Queen, was, " her probable conversion to the Roman Catholic faith." But to *postpone* the insertion of the name of the Queen, and afterwards to have been called upon to supply the omission, would, to her Majesty, have been a gracious act of acquittal, and restoration to regal honour; and I had a right to hope that such would be the result. Besides, the object and intention of the postponement of this insertion, was most certainly, not with a view to any proceedings against the Queen, but in anticipation of that continuance of mutual separation, which the Queen, in her letter of leave, declared to be " necessary to my future tranquillity."

I will suppose for one moment, the insertion to have been made. Had it been done under concealment from me, of existing circumstances, *my ministers would have been guilty of misprision of treason, and been liable to impeachment.* But as it was done with my knowledge; if ten thousands of ten thousand tongues were to demand of me, to tarnish the crown of your King, I would abandon it to the people rather than commit so great a crime. Whatever may have been the indiscretions of THE MAN, the future historian of England shall never record them as connected with THE KING.

It should not be overlooked, that the alteration of the Liturgy was also to regulate my own public devotion, as well as that of my subjects; should I not then by the special insertion of the name of the Queen, under existing circumstances, have most deservedly subjected myself to a charge of impious and detestable hypocrisy? "You have been praying yourself specially for the Queen, you Royal Hypocrite! whilst you have watched her destruction;" would have been a just and unanswerable accusation against me; an accusation, which, if well-founded, would have rendered the word of the King unworthy of belief.

Those only are the real exclusionists, who do not choose to comprehend the Queen, as implied in the words, " and all the Royal Family."

Had either the religious or legal considerations of this important point permitted me conscientiously to have inserted the name of the Queen in the Liturgy of the Church; all other minor considerations would have had no bearing upon the question; for that which would have been consistent with religion and law, could not have been *contra bonos mores.* I dwell not therefore on the subject, as connected with the morals of the country, but in its consideration, and in all its vital bearings, I cannot but have contemplated the consequences of a Queen charged with high crimes and misdemeanors, sitting upon that throne so lately occupied by the personification of chastity and matrimonial excellence.

Will the virtuous and noble, the high-minded and chaste, the amiable and domestic females of England, adopt the Queen as an example and model worthy of their imitation? Will they pronounce her faultless? Will they compose her court? If I can place the Queen on the throne of my ancestors upon such terms, I am ready to do so. Upon none other, can or ought a Queen to sit upon the throne of pre-eminent England.

I proceed now to the offer of an ample allowance offered to the Queen, provided she continued to remain abroad in the retirement she had voluntarily adopted; and the alternative with which that offer was accompanied. I have pointed out *this trans-action*, and the *suspension in the Liturgy*, as acts which *may appear* to have emanated more immediately from my own personal feelings.

I have previously remarked, that from the period of my becoming Regent, the differences between the Princess and myself had assumed a political character, and been treated by many as a party question.

The companions of my youth, and the distinguished characters with whom, in my earlier years, I had intimately associated, had created in the public mind, a widely-extended, and readily believed opinion, that when the sceptre of my Father should desce to me, I should, from among those associates, ha'

chosen the members of my administration. During the
discussion of the terms of the regency, I was careful
to avoid giving any pledge of the line of policy I
might find it expedient to adopt. A short previous
administration, composed of those political friends
by whom it was conjectured my councils would have
been directed, had enabled me to form some opinion
of their executive talents; and *notwithstanding*, an
overture was made by me to them, to propose an
administration. But when I found the conditions
required would have reduced me to a mere political automaton, of which they were to possess the
key; that not content with forming the administration, they required also, that I should be surrounded
in my household by their adherents, and left to no
choice in the appointment of my own attendants;
when with this, I compared the candour and the
unequivocal absence of all personal feeling with
which the bill creating the Regency was carried by
the then ministry; and above all, the frank, loyal,
and respectful regret which was shewn to the calamity of my revered Parent; and the so immediate
provision made for the resumption by him of the regal
dignity, that it should have pleased Providence so to
have restored him, my Royal Father would have
awakened as if from a dream, and have found himself
unreminded of his affliction; when to this I added
the important consideration, that the flame of freedom was beginning to glimmer in Spain; that the
then administration were prepared to take advantage
of every circumstance favourable to the destruction
of the military tyrant of Europe; and when all
these various considerations were upheld by the
weight of personal character which was contained

in the then cabinet ; I felt sufficiently justified in not suffering former prepossessions to stand for one moment in the way of newly-created duties. I felt that an existing experienced executive, was, at such a time, safer than a theoretical cabinet. I had also a doubt in my own mind, whether, during my Sovereign's life, I ought, as Regent, to adopt the principles of those who had been violently opposed to my Royal Father's measures, or pursue a line of policy unchanged, and such as my King would have continued had he remained the active head of the Empire. This was a feeling of the heart; it was mine.

This, my determination, produced two consequences; 1. A series of unbroken, glorious, and important victories, attended with such results, as the history of the world, within a similar period of time, cannot produce; 2. The conversion of my matrimonial differences into a political attack upon my authority.

From this moment, then, the Queen, by becoming the tool of party, gave to her cause and her conduct a new feature, and an importance which required the vigilant eye of the government.

I have been led into this digression, that the distinction I still endeavoured to uphold between my marital and royal station, might be plainly and easily comprehended. I return now to the consideration of the offer made to the Queen, of an allowance upon certain stipulations; *viz.*, that the Queen should *cease to use* the name and style of Queen of England, and remain abroad, where she had voluntarily seceded.

The period when this determination was de

upon, must not be forgotten; it must not only not be forgotten, but it should be allowed its due weight in the decision of so momentous an affair. It appears almost, indeed, to be overlooked, that I met my first parliament in the month of April, at the very period, and while a set of infuriated, misguided and unhappy culprits were on their trial for a conspiracy to overturn the constitution and government of these realms, of which the commencement was intended to be, the indiscriminate assassination of my cabinet ministers. The general situation of the country, at that precise moment, appears also to have been thrown into the back ground. I cannot better recall those unhappy inauspicious moments, than by repeating again to my subjects the topics addressed to the Lords and Commons in Parliament assembled, upon our first meeting.

*My Lords and Gentlemen,*

" Deeply as I regret that the machinations and designs of the disaffected should have led in some parts of the country, to acts of open violence and insurrection, I cannot but express my satisfaction at the promptitude with which those attempts have been suppressed by the vigilance and activity of the magistrates, and by the zealous co-operation of all those of my subjects whose exertions have been called forth to support the authority of the laws.

" The wisdom and firmness manifested by the late parliament and the due execution of the laws, have greatly contributed to restore confidence throughout the kingdom; and to discountenance those principles of sedition and irreligion, which had been disseminated with such malignant perseverance, and had poisoned the minds of the unwary and ignorant.

" I rely upon the continued support of parliament, in my determination to maintain, by all the means intrusted to my hands, the public safety and tranquillity.

" Deploring, as we all must, the distress which still unhappily prevails among many of the labouring classes of the community, and anxiously looking forward to its removal or mitigation, it is, in the mean time, our common duty, effectually to protect the loyal, the peaceable, and the industrious, against those practices of turbulence and intimidation, by which the period of relief can only be deferred, and by which the pressure of the distress has been incalculably aggravated.

" I trust that an awakened sense of the dangers which they have incurred, and of the acts which have been employed to seduce them, will bring back by far the greater part of those who have been unhappily led astray, and will revive in them that spirit of loyalty, that due submission to the laws, and that attachment to the constitution, which subsist unabated in the hearts of the great body of the people, and which, under the blessing of Divine Providence, have secured to the British Nation, the enjoyment of a larger share of practical freedom, as well as of prosperity and happiness, than have fallen to the lot of any nation in the world."

If to the pending trials alluded to, and this general reference to the state of the kingdom, suffering under severe privations in some of its provinces, are added the numerous cases of treason, libel, and minor political offences under the progressive cognizance of the courts of law; I think my subjects and countrymen will admit, that to such previously existing evils *no addition was wanting to renew internal agitation which was beginning to subside.* The return of the Queen, under the circumstances which she must necessarily meet, was, of all others, calculated to revive that internal agitation; and why was it so calculated? Because the Queen had (as I have previously remarked) given, by her conduct, a political feeling to the differences between us. Had this not been the case, she could not have had, at least she ought not to have had, any motives for her return; or had she any, she ought to have sacrificed them to the welfare of our country.

From 1796 we had been separated, a period now of twenty-four years; disturbed by an almost constant suspicion of her conduct: the Queen had been estranged from Court, our Royal Daughter was no more; and her Majesty had but one duty to perform towards me, " the performance of an agreed separation."

A Queen Consort of England has no political rank, she possesses *in ease* of the Sovereign, certain inherent prerogatives ; those prerogatives are capable of being enjoyed by her, in her absence ; they required not her presence. The presence of the Queen could neither revive trade (languishing in some of its branches), tranquillize the irritation of distress, or conciliate the clamour of faction ; and, indeed, many records of English History hand down to us, the impolitic and dangerous counsels, which have ensued from the interference of Queens Consort in the political contests of the times. Although by way of eminent distinction, the word " Queen" is applicable only to the King's wife, yet, it originally signifies a wife, or woman. A Queen of England (unless Queen in her own right,) is a subject of the King, and can claim no political character from the people ; to her, at a coronation, no oath is administered, and no homage or allegiance offered. The coronation of a Queen is distinct, and subsequent to that of the King ; it is not at all necessary to the accession or title to the throne; and when performed, is a ceremony so performed for the greater honour of the kingly office. It proceeds from the King*.

If, therefore, I am to define the office or duty of a Queen Consort, I might sum it up in a few words, " To give a tone to *the morals* of the country." Does not the late reign furnish an indisputable proof of the truth of this axiom ?

Since then the Queen had deprived herself of the

* Taylor's *Glory of Regality.*

possibility of performing the duties of her station, and her return could produce none of those effects which were so evident during the long reign of my late Royal and revered Parents, could the next object of my solicitude be otherwise, than an attempt, still to treat the long borne separation, as a personal and domestic transaction?

The Queen was growing old, we are both beyond the hey-day of life, and the levities of conduct attributed to her, might now be supposed to have worn or to have been wearing away. Our country required political repose; and, above all, an internal quietude. Had no charge of adultery at all existed, there were sufficient grounds on both sides, for wishing, and for rendering desirable, a continuance of the existing separation.

In private life, what would the friends of a married couple, so long divided as the Queen and myself have been, think of the conduct of a wife, who would wish to return to her husband, under circumstances, such as have occurred between us? Would any female in England so *meanly* conduct herself? Would any husband in England so take back a wife? If he would not, why should your King? If the female would not so return, why should the Queen? You will tell me, "To claim her rights." I reply, that the Queen possesses no political rights; but certain prescribed prerogatives; those prerogatives are legally defined, their value as personal advantages can be ascertained, they can be enjoyed by the Queen, as well absent as present. I have offered her an equivalent. You will tell me, "That *she chooses* to return to our country, and that I have no right to restrain her." The Queen has chosen to return, and by the laws of the realm must she now abide; the Queen is my subject.

If, then, I am asked, " Why did I offer the Queen fifty thousand pounds a year to remain abroad, and cease to use openly the style and title of Queen of England," I answer, " To purchase the tranquillity of my country; to prevent a recurrence of those acts which had seduced so many of my subjects into danger, and to bring them back to that spirit of loyalty, that due submission to the laws, and that attachment to the constitution, which I hope still subsists in the hearts of the great body of my people;" all which I knew would be endangered by the *selfish return of a Queen*, who never can, and never will, sit upon the throne of England whilst George the Fourth wears the crown of his forefathers; until the female nobility shall, in a body, justify him in such act, with their sanction and presence, every other rank of the virtuous and the chaste would coincide.

Before I conclude this subject of an offered pension, I cannot but regret extremely, that the chance of cool and dispassionate deliberation which the Queen might have been disposed to have given to my offer and its alternative, was greatly diminished by the neglect of her Attorney-General, in the delivery of an ultimatum communicated to him in the month of April. Such neglect rendered Lord Hutchinson's communication so much the more sudden, stern, and unexpected. Of the zeal of that gentleman (her Majesty's Attorney-General) no one can entertain a higher opinion than myself; for his own sake, I may be allowed to say, that nothing disgraced his advocacy, but the threat of personal danger held out to the assembled Peers

Peers of the realm. Otherwise, who would not wish
to have a cause so defended ? Had also her Majesty's
Solicitor-General omitted one or two similes in his
declamation, he had also retired from his duty with
more dignity. Upon the grounds of the case I am
silent; but, looking to the conduct of the Lord Chancellor, the differences which existed between the
members of the cabinet; the splendid and argumentative talents of the Opposition, all tending and
working together to elicit truth and produce an impartial judgment; I may fearlessly ask, if, under
such principles and in such an assembly, justice is
not to be found ? I ask, fearlessly, where does she
dwell upon earth ? I view, finally, the pause which
this unhappy affair has taken, as a striking proof of
that inflexible adherence to parliamentary avowals,
which combines the good man with the great minister; and as the performance of the pledge, that
" the Queen should have an equivalent for any and
every obstacle which the anomaly of her case presented in the obstruction of her trial."

I am now drawing towards the close of this my
letter, in the which my faithful subjects and excellent fellow-countrymen will (I trust) agree with
me, not only that the difference existing between
her Majesty and myself arose out of a domestic
cause, and was solely of a domestic nature; but
that all the popular feeling which has been excited,
has arisen from the political misdirection imposed
upon the transaction, a transaction important to the
nation only as it can be connected with their welfare. How that welfare can be promoted by forc-
ing upon a loathing husband an equally loathing
wife, appears to me, a problem in government, not

D

easily to be maintained in argument, or proved by
historical reference. If I am unhappily united to
a bad wife, or the Queen be under the caprice of a
bad husband ; provided those unpleasantries be confined within the limits of our personal conduct, and
are not mixed up with affairs of state, I see then no
impediment to the due constitutional performance
of my duties as King : but on the contrary, if the
people disturb my kingly office, and clog its executive or dignity with an unseasonable family
blister, the chance is that the system of government
may become ill executed, greatly obstructed, or
completely embarrassed. If such is the aim of the
partizans of the Queen, I have then only to declare
this my determination, " That if the claims of the
Queen can make no impression on me *upon their own
merits*, any political association which she may form
to give weight to, or to disguise such claims, will
only call forth from me as your King, a firmer defence of my own rights, which are the rights of the
constitution under which I, the nobles, and the
people, all alike find reciprocal protection."
My people will now (I trust) begin to allow
themselves more clearly to define, and more ac-
curately to preserve the distinction between my
conduct as Prince of Wales, with reference to the
purity of the succession to the throne of my forefathers, and my behaviour as a separated husband.
In the one case, the performance of painful public
duties has devolved upon me, but I feel satisfied
that their unavoidable performance has not been accompanied by uncourteous or vexatious personal
conduct. To the high individual as a separate wife,
every attention has bben invariably paid, and upon

every occasion, money has been at her command for the purposes of comfort, pleasure, or fickleness. Surely, in return for such complete observance of the terms of mutual separation, the Prince of Wales had a right to expect the performance of the only duty remaining to be performed by, and the only one required of, the Princess; namely, " *An unquestionable and unequivocal propriety of conduct.*"

I could not probably fix upon a more convenient or appropriate mode of portraying the consequences of the present public effervescence than by anticipating the sentiments which some historian of my reign may hand down to future ages. I will do this in two ways ; *First,* Upon the supposition, that the Queen (even after what has already occurred,) will be reinstated in all the prerogatives of her rank;" *and secondly,* " That the Queen will remain estranged from the crown."

IN THE FIRST CASE, the historian may be supposed thus to express himself : "George the Fourth, after a Regency of nearly nine years, succeeded to the throne of his venerable and most excellent Father, whose eventful reign had extended beyond the period of any other British Monarch. The brilliant events of the Regency of George the Fourth, unparalleled in history, are already recorded ; his reign commenced amidst domestic losses, (his Brother, the Duke of Kent; having died very suddenly at Sidmouth, in Devonshire, six days only before their Royal Parent) public agitation, and great national distress, attended with all those factious symptoms, which the English History appears almost invariably to record, as a symptom of peace. A month had not elapsed, before a most atrocious conspiracy, aiming no less than at

the indiscriminate assassination of all his Majesty's
Ministers during a cabinet dinner, was detected.
On the twenty-first of April, His Majesty met his
parliament, and in his Royal Speech upon the occasion, alluded to the disquietude and distress of
the kingdom, hinted at their cause, and expressed
a hope, that in the returning loyalty and legal obedience of the people, a remedy for those evils would
be found. The atrociousness of the conspiracy
alluded to, had opened the eyes of the supine, and
alarmed the fears of the timid ; and a more imposing public attitude being consequently produced,
tranquillity was gradually increasing into confidence.
At this moment, it pleased the Queen, (who had
now been separated from her Royal Husband
*twenty-four years*, and had estranged herself from
England for six years,) to return from the continent
under the auspices of *one* Wood, an Alderman of
the City of London. The Queen returned, in the
teeth of a proposition from the administration, that
she should still continue to remain abroad, and not
seek to disturb a connexion so long broken off;
and in defiance of a threat, that judicial proceedings
would follow her landing. The intrepidity of her
conduct was well calculated to please the English
Nation, and this daring and inconsiderate step, (a
step which her own legal adviser pronounced to be
unhappily taken, both as regarded herself, the parliament, the government, and the country) was rendered immediately popular by the epithet of *brave*.
Would any but an innocent woman (said the populace) have thus conducted herself?

'Whilst the Queen was pursuing her journey from
Dover to the metropolis, a royal message was

delivering to parliament ; and papers in sealed bags brought down to both houses    The Queen arrived on the very day on which his Majesty went down to the House of Lords, to give his assent to the first bill passed since his accession.    After various in-effectual delays, in the hope of effecting an arrange-ment, by which the Queen might have again left the kingdom ; the House of Lords proceeded to appoint a secret committee, to examine the documents sent down to them (the House of Commons suspending their proceedings,) and shortly made a report on the same, charging the Queen with an adulterous inter-course with a menial of the name of Bergami, or Pergami, on whom she had conferred, or for whom she had procured, certain titles and orders of dis-tinction. A bill of Pains and Penalties was there-upon brought in by the Earl of Liverpool, after long and elaborate arguments upon the propriety and applicability of the proceeding, had taken place in the House of Peers. The case presented an ano-maly, for no statute existed, applicable to a charge of adultery committed by a Queen of England, *abroad and with a foreigner.* This nice distinction took the offence from within the pale of high treason, for inasmuch as the principal was not amenable to the laws of the country ; consequently, the *particeps criminis* could not be judicially recog-nized by the statutes of treason. Every preliminary of this great measure, was discussed to the very letter, with a degree of eloquence and profound learning which reflected unfading lustre upon the House of Peers, and on the individual noblemen, who led both sides of the debates. The question appeared new, and every aspect of its bearing was

most minutely and rigidly examined; great debate
more particularly took place on the question of
allowing to the illustrious accused, a list of witnesses, as in cases of high treason; when it was at
length decided to open the case, produce the evidence, and allow the Queen an interval, (such as her
counsel should deem requisite) to prepare her
defence. Thus her Majesty was not only supplied
eventually with a list of witnesses; but had the
further guide of their sworn testimony. The Attorney General, (Sir R. Gifford,) opened the case
according to his instructions, and by command of
the House, with little preliminary remark, and
certainly without inflation. Her Majesty's cause
was less upheld by the evidence of the witnesses
against her, (of whom the popular feeling pronounced a pre-judgment of perjury,) than by a deficiency
of refutation on her own part. The Queen was
most ably, most zealously, and most eloquently defended by Messrs. Brougham, Denman, Lushington
and others; and the House bore the license of their
harangues with a noble equanimity of patience.
After hearing both the charge and the defence,
which occupied forty-five days, the House adjourned
two days, before it met to debate the principle of
the bill; which discussion occupied four days. The
second reading was carried by a majority of twenty-
eight, the numbers being *for it* 123, *against it* 95.
During the progress of the measure, several protests were entered on the Journals of the House, in
one of which the Lord Chancellor and the Prime
Minister were directly opposed to each other; a
brother of the King absented himself wholly from
the investigation; a cousin of the King voted against

the measure in all its stages; both the Ministry and
the Opposition were divided amongst themselves,
and intermingled their votes; the preamble of the
bill underwent but little alteration in the committee : and in the clause for pronouncing a divorce
as part of the pains and penalties, all the Cabinet
Ministers, (nine) voted against it. The divorce
clause was however carried by a majority of 67,
there being contents 129, non-contents 62. Most
of the peers who had' till this moment contended
against the principle of the bill in all its stages,
argued (with much plausible appearance of reason)
that since the Queen was virtually pronounced
guilty of an adulterous intercourse, by the votes of
the second reading ; *divorce became the natural conse-*
*quence, as part of the sentence of the bill*, they therefore
voted for it. The third reading of the bill, was
carried on the 10th November, by the small majority
of nine ; the numbers being for it 108, against it 99.

Lord Liverpool, (who had brought in the bill, as
an individual peer, and not as a member of the administration), immediately moved, that " the bill be
read that day six months," alleging the smallness
of the majority, as the motive *.

---

* Bill [as read a third time,] entitled, An act to deprive her
Majesty, Caroline Amelia Elizabeth, of the title, prerogatives,
rights, privileges, and exemptions of Queen Consort of this
realm ; and to dissolve the marriage between his Majesty and
the said Caroline Amelia Elizabeth.
Whereas in the year one thousand eight hundred and fourteen,
her Majesty Caroline Amelia Elizabeth, then Princess of Wales, and
now Queen Consort of this realm, being at Milan, in Italy, engaged
in her service, in a menial situation, one Bartolomeo Pergami, a
foreigner of low station, who had before served in a similar capacity :
And whereas after the said Bartolomeo Pergami had so entered the
service of her Royal Highness the said Princess of Wales, a most un-

The friends of the Queen received this unexpected
reprieve from the bill, after proof of the facts; and
admission of their reality, as a total and complete

---

becoming and degrading intimacy commenced between her said
Royal Highness and the said Bartolomeo Pergami, and her said
Royal Highness not only advanced the said Bartolomeo Pergami to
a high situation in her Royal Highness's household, and received into
her service many of his near relations, some of them in inferior and
others in high and confidential situations about her Royal Highness's person, but bestowed upon him other great and extraordinary
marks of favour and distinction, and conferred upon him a pretended
order of knighthood, which her Royal Highness had taken upon
herself to institute, without any just or lawful authority: And
whereas also her said Royal Highness, whilst the said Bartolomeo
Pergami was in her said service, further unmindful of her exalted
rank and station, and of her duty to your Majesty, and wholly
regardless of her own honour and character, conducted herself towards the said Bartolomeo Pergami, both in public and private, in
various places and countries which her Royal Highness visited with
indecent and offensive familiarity and freedom, and carried on a
licentious, disgraceful, and adulterous intercourse, with the said Bartolomeo Pergami, which continued for a long period of time, during
her Royal Highness's residence abroad; by which conduct of her
said Royal Highness, great scandal and dishonour have been brought
upon your Majesty's family and this kingdom. Therefore, to manifest our deep sense of such scandalous, disgraceful, and vicious conduct on the part of her said Majesty, by which she has violated the
duty which she owed to your Majesty, and has rendered herself unworthy of the exalted rank and station of Queen Consort of this
realm; and to evince our just regard for the dignity of the crown, and
the honour of this nation; we, your Majesty's most dutiful and
loyal subjects, the lords spiritual and temporal, and commons in
parliament assembled, do humbly entreat your Majesty that it may
be enacted; and be it enacted by the King's most excellent Majesty,
by and with the advice and consent of the lords spiritual, and temporal, and commons, in this present parliament assembled, and by
the authority of the same, that her said Majesty, Caroline Amelia
Elizabeth, from and after the passing of this act, shall be, and is
hereby deprived of the title of Queen, and of all the prerogatives,
rights, privileges, and exemptions, appertaining to her as Queen Consort of this realm; and that her said Majesty shall, from and after
the passing of this act, for ever be disabled and rendered incapable
of using, exercising, and enjoying the same, or any of them; and,
moreover, that the marriage between his Majesty and the said
Caroline Amelia Elizabeth be, and the same is hereby, from henceforth for ever, wholly dissolved, annulled, and made void, to all intents, instructions, and purposes whatsoever.

acquittal of her Majesty from all charge of criminality; and proclaimed their sense of her innocence by rejoicings and illuminations; to which the
Lord Mayor of London, two days old in office, gave
his young countenance. Less riot and disturbance,
however, took place than might have been expected; but this was principally owing to the mo-
deration of their antagonists; who (whatever might
be their opinion of the guilt or innocence of the
Queen, and did not consider a happy escape in the
light of an honourable acquittal) were not disposed
to thwart the effect of a delusion which appeared in
many of its features to portray great generosity
and sympathy in supposed sufferings. The Queen
returned thanks in the church of the hamlet of the
parish in which she resided, and a second time on
the 29th of November, at St. Paul's, escorted by
the voluntary association of her friends, and was
received with due civic honour at Temple Bar by
the young Lord Mayor of London. Immense as
was the crowd assembled, judicious regulations,
prompted by the high responsibility which the
young chief magistrate took upon himself on the
occasion, prevented all confusion or accident. The
King had previously adjourned both Houses of Parliament, without a Speech either from the Throne
or by his Commissioners. The Speaker of the
House of Commons was hissed as he proceeded to
follow the Usher of the Black Rod to the House of
Peers; nor did he (there being no Royal Speech,
but merely a command to adjourn) again enter the
House. This mode of separation appeared to the
nation very ungracious, and the disturbed reign of
Charles the First was ransacked for precedents.

But the King could hardly have avoided reference
to the proceedings of the Lords, and the more especially as the Commons had been adjourned, subject to a call of the House, and to meet only for
business, in the event of the Bill of Pains and Penalties coming down to them. On the whole, then,
it appeared better to leave the ungracious mode of
adjournment for explanation till the next Sessions,
when men's minds might have acquired greater
power of discrimination, a quality very seldom in
request on popular occasions.

.Thus far have I brought down (and, I trust, fairly
and dispassionately) the outline of this transaction,
as it 'occurred; and with this outline (which will
serve, as far as it goes, for both speculations, that
of preceding " the restoration of the Queen to all
her prerogatives and her court," and that of still
" restraining her from their enjoyment and exercise,") I go on, in my assumed character of an historian, to observe on the consequences of such opposite results.

First then, the historian may hereafter portray
the consequences of the Queen's restoration to her
prerogatives and court, in the following manner :—

" Whether the ministers mistook the popular clamour for the real feeling of the nation, or were unwilling to resign their seals of office ; or whether
they were intimidated by the examples of Spain,
Portugal, Naples, and Sicily, all at this time changing
their form of government, with more or less of
violence ; they advised the King to feel no impediment to the public reception of the Queen; who,
having now the vantage ground, insisted upon the
insertion of her name in the Liturgy, and the ex-

punging from the Journals of the House of Lords, of all the proceedings connected with her case, as preliminaries to such reception. The first was readily accomplished; to procure the second, the Prime Minister and the Lord Chancellor (two of the most able ministers and upright men of the day) having retired in disgust, every parliamentary finesse was resorted to ; and, at length, with great difficulty, and amid violent debates and mutual recriminations, the point was carried by a majority of one; there being for the expunging 91; against it 90. Bonfires and illuminations, strong beer and roasted beasts were, for a whole week, the order of each successive day; and in so great a joy, few troubled themselves to calculate upon futurity.

" But short was the delirium, and dreadful the consequences.

" The King was laughed at, and pitied as a dupe, the Queen was openly scorned, faction was triumphant, no competent administration could be formed; and monarchy was on the wane. Those who had opposed the Queen, not from vindictive motives, but to justify the honour of the crown, felt no longer an attachment to a bauble undignified with the jewel of female chastity. The court was seldom held; when held, neglected; official levees supplied its place. The higher and respectable ranks of life withdrew within their own pure and virtuous associations; and that intermixture of society which is the true essence of a free government and a virtuous court, no longer existed. Rich, vulgar plebeianism took the lead in public. At foreign courts, the younger branches of the nobility experienced great difficulty of reception, not having chosen to be pre-

sented at their own; but when received at such
courts, it was considered as a matter of especial
favour conceded to their peculiar situation. Thus
was the national character subjected to sarcastic
insult; and thus was the lustre of the Crown of
England obscured; for whatever might have been
the personal faults of its sovereigns, as individuals
no more exempt from human frailty than the humblest of their subjects, but rather more exposed to
their commission; yet the Crown of England had
been entitled, for the last century at least, to the
homage due to unsullied and unquestionable honour.
Such were some of the effects of the Queen's restoration.

" The evil, however, stopped not here; scarcely
had sufficient time elapsed to justify inconsistency,
than the truth of the original charges against the
Queen was loudly revived by that very press which
had forced her innocence down the throats of the
nation. The levellers and jacobins, who lorded
over public opinion, professed to defend their
change, by the discovery of some new evidence
which (said they), had we known before, would
have produced a different opinion. Thus, the very
men who had so conspicuously advocated the cause
of the Queen; who had poured into her ears addresses of congratulatory exultation; who had
headed her processions, and maddened the populace
in her behalf; these very men, who had artfully
drawn her to the very precipice of rebellion against
her husband and King; these men, from whom she
could not but have expected eternal friendship and
never-ending adulation, finding her without influence
or patronage, became within six months, her scorn-

ful foes. These very men, who had provoked the
measure of expunging the whole transaction from
the Records of Parliament, and who would fain have
burnt, in one huge pile, every paper and every
Journal which contained the adulterous evidence,
themselves were the first to direct the same press
which had borne down all opposition against her,
to insult, remind, and mortify her. The reign of
terror had commenced. Such were the effects of
this unaccountable delusion! Such were the consequences of excusing and exalting vice on the frail
plea of political expediency!!

* * * * * * * * * * * * *

I proceed now (still in the character of a prophetical historian) to mark the consequences which might
follow the Queen's continued restriction from the
public exercise of her prerogatives.

" On Friday, the 10th of November, this bill of
Pains and Penalties passed the third reading, when
it was *suspended*, under the form of being read that
day six months, and the Lords adjourned to the 23d,
the day on which the Commons were to meet, to
pursue (if necessary) this important affair. On the
23d both houses met, and were instantly prorogued
by Commission, without any Royal Speech. This
hasty procurement of separation gave great offence
to the Queen's party; the House of Commons being
summoned at the very moment when the Solicitor
General of the Queen was about to communicate to
the House, *a message* from her majesty.

" It was evident that the King could have made
no Speech to the Houses of Parliament, omitting
all reference to the late momentous transaction.
Had his Majesty said, that he regretted the issue

it, he would have committed himself personally, besides being guilty of the most unconstitutional error;
*that of presuming to know a parliamentary proceeding in
transitu,* for as yet the bill was not absolutely abandoned. Had his Majesty, on the other hand, made
a Royal Communication, omitting, as he must necessarily have done, all reference to the bill in question; it might have been inferred, that future proceedings, in any shape, were abandoned; besides,
the interval of adjournment was but for *two* months,
and not *seven or eight,* as usually happens, the bill
having driven the attendance of both houses to a
most unusual lateness. It was deemed therefore
most prudent, to encounter the accusation of an
ungracious prorogation, for so short a period as two
months, rather than be hurried into any hasty
avowal. But had there been no such prudent
ground for the proceeding, it was sufficiently justified by the subsequent conduct of the Queen;
who assumed to herself an authoritative act of
government, having prepared her official adviser
with *a message* to be delivered to the Commons
House of Parliament; a step which might well alarm
the servants of the Crown, and indeed the whole
nation; for it aimed, in the shape of a message, at a
share of the Monarch's power, which the Queen
Consort does not possess, *being only a subject* *. It
is a radical error, for a Queen Consort to call the

* " The Queen hath also many exemptions and minute prerogatives. For instance, she pays no toll, nor is she liable to any
amercement in any Court. But in general, unless where the law
expressly declared her exempted, *she is upon the same footing
in other subjects;* and not his equal: in like manner as in the im-
ial law: ' *Augusta legibus soluta non est.'* " *Blackstone,* cap. 4.
220.

King's people, *her people*, or for the King's subjects
to call themselves the subjects of the King's wife ; it
is a fault of misdirected loyalty. We may call ourselves, by way of courtesy, the Queen's most dutiful
and affectionate *servants* ; but legally and constitutionally we can only be the dutiful and affectionate
*subjects* of ' the King.'

" During the interval between the prorogation and
the meeting of both Houses, the Queen proceeded
to Saint Paul's, continued to receive Addresses of
Congratulation, and renewed unsuccessfully her application for a Royal Residence. But the people
had now time to reflect, to compare, to decide.
John Bull is never long misled, and now discovered
in the case, premature judgments, audacious falsehoods, attempts at intimidation, and unproved assertions ; above all, a complete absence of all those promises of refutation, which had been so lavishly and
so loudly proclaimed ; and the non-performance of
which was the more extraordinary, inasmuch as the
persons who might, if they could, have given such
testimony, were already in England, and at the
Queen's command.

" Upon the meeting of Parliament, the Commons
desired a conference with the Upper House, and
having thereat obtained leave to search the Journals
of the Peers, they became constitutionally acquainted with the late proceedings. They found
therein a sentence of guilt pronounced, which (to
say the least of it,) was tantamount to the effect of a
true bill by a grand Jury.

With this impression upon their minds, the Commons soon felt, that the question was now completely in their own hands. The passing of the

Civil List bill was exactly the period, when their
influence would become apparent: but they previously determined once more to address the Queen,
by the same deputation, which had gone up on a
former occasion. This address commenced by the
firm and dignified assurance of the unshaken attachment of the Commons to the throne, the constitution,
and the altar, and their determination to preserve
them from every attempt of factious anarchy. It
proceeded to express great regret for the past, and
a hope that by conciliatory measures, all further
personal legislation would become unnecessary.
It assured the Queen that she might rely upon the
continued care and attention of the commons;
should her Majesty, by sacrificing some part of her
high claims, be the means of restoring tranquillity to
the public mind. It intimated that some points on
which the Queen had heretofore insisted, might be
the subject of future and favourable consideration ;
but that time was necessary to produce a change,
which should justify their concession ; and it finally
dwelt upon the total impossibility, that even should
the Queen gain the object of her wishes, it would
(under existing circumstances) be attended to her
with happiness or peace of mind."

" In answer to this address, the Queen made but
few remarks; but principally dwelt on the utter
impossibility of quitting a nation, who had treated
her with such unbounded generosity, and espoused
her cause with such enthusiastic ardour; and finally
proposed, that three friends, appointed by herself,
should confer with the deputation of the Commons,
and agree upon a basis for a complete adjustment."
To this it was objected, that the deputation had no

49

such power of treating; but the difficulty was
eventually got over, by their consenting to meet the
friends of the Queen as individuals, and subsequently use their exertions to induce the House to
adopt such a course of conduct, as might result
from the conference; after two meetings it was
eventually agreed, *that the Queen should return to
Saint Omer's, and find herself placed in the same situation,
as she would have been, had her legal advisers delivered
to her Lord Liverpool's communication of April, previously to that made by Lord Hutchinson.*

" This departure was accomplished in so unexpected and in so judicious a manner, as far as the
coast, that until the Queen was saluted by the guns
at Dover, on her embarkation in a Royal Yacht, it
was but just rumoured. The Queen was accompanied by two of her legal advisers, who were met
by two others, on the part of the Crown. The departure of the Queen being made known to the
Parliament, a most gracious vote of thanks was
passed in both Houses; the Commons renewed their
assurances, that they would pay all due attention to
her Majesty's interests. The Civil List bill was expeditiously passed, and a Royal Message brought
down to both Houses by Ministers, in which the
King thanked the Commons for the generous provision made for the Queen's future comfort. Her
Majesty's Attorney-General, also on his return from
Saint Omer's, expressed the Queen's thanks, accompanied by her regret, on leaving England; but
attributing the step she had taken to a thorough
conviction that she could never hope to promote the
happiness of the King; and therefore her next wish
was to contribute to the tranquillity of the Kingdom.

He also adverted to the impaired health of the Queen; and the possibility, that she might not again return to the Country of her adoption.

Thus ended an affair which could not possibly have happened at a more critical moment, for whilst it was proceeding, military revolutions were following one another, through the South of Europe; and that the mania did not extend to England, can be attributed solely to the sound principles of the vast majority of the Kingdom; principles which were daily and hourly assailed, by a venal press; and by a system of the most pernicious, irritating, and base political libels, and personal caricatures. But on this occasion the Constitution floated above, the passions of the people, safe and unhurt as her Navy rides on the turbulent billow, which dashes against Albion's rocky sides.

" Amidst these internal commotions, it pleased Providence to bless the kingdom with a most abundant harvest; so that the winter passed over with much less proportionate privations to the humbler classes of the community. Indeed it may be rather said, that such heavenly bounty, administered by charitable hands and feeling hearts, rendered distress unknown. The following Spring found the whole nation, except certain disappointed speculating politicians, in good humour; and the moment was most judiciously seized to administer to the whole United Kingdom, the oath of allegiance. The ceremony was accompanied by every mark of joy and magnificence; it was indeed a national banquet. ON THE TUESDAY, the magistracy took the oaths in the county towns. ON THE THURSDAY, the population took them in every city, town, and village, in the following manner: Lists had been previously signed, and to each list was prefixed a power by deputation to some person therein named, to take the oath publicly for as many persons as were contained in such list; and by its form, all persons therein subscribed were held to be bound by the oath of allegiance, recited also in such instrument. ON THE SATURDAY, the Army took the oaths, by regiments, squadrons, and detachments, at their individual quarters; and the Navy by fifties, after the form of the general population. This splendid and national rejoicing seemed to annihilate every spark of disaffection.

" In the Autumn, the coronation of his Majesty took place, and the first Act of Grace performed immediately after, was, ' *to expunge from the Journals of the Lords all the accusatory proceedings connected with the Queen of England.*'

" This last step was considered an act of oblivion, and a compliment to the crown." The Queen remained abroad during her life, in conformity with her word of honour."

\*    \*    \*    \*    \*    \*    \*    \*

And now, my faithful subjects, and well-beloved fellow-countrymen, your King takes his leave, recommending the alternative to your attention, and praying to the God and Father of us all, that he will so direct your steps, as to lead both to your temporal and your eternal happiness; praying also that the crown of his forefathers may not be dishonoured on his head, but that mutual love and confidence may render happy both King and People.

My excellent subjects, may God Almighty bless you——Farewell.

GEORGE.

## APOLOGY.

Should the readers of the preceding Letter, have entertained doubt of its authenticity, the Author and Publisher beg leave to satisfy those doubts, by stating, " That it is one of those literary fictions, which can only be justified by a good cause." Indeed they feel so high a degree of veneration for the sacred name of " The King," which, (speaking constitutionally), " Never dies ;" and so anxious a desire, that nothing directly or indirectly should appear to trifle with' its use ; that, previous to their determination to publish, they submitted the. following Question to the opinion of a most eminent Counsel ; which question at once proclaimed the author's motive, and the answer subjoined, contains (we trust) our justification.

## THE QUESTION.

Suppose A. writes a letter entitled " A Letter from the King," and having written and published such Letter, states, in a Postscript annexed that such title was adopted to excite curiosity, and extend its political utility ; and that such Letter was neither directly or indirectly written by the King; will such acknowledgment take the assumption of the King's name, out of any and every statute of *premunire?*

## OPINION.

I am clearly of opinion, that such acknowledgment as is proposed, will take the Letter out of the Statutes of *premunire*. The term and the offence *premunire*, are now merely sounds: but I decidedly think, that the Letter proposed, written in the tone and spirit which is suggested, will not render the writer responsible to *any penalty whatever*.
*Temple, December 4th,* 1820.

Thus far as to the legality of the act; but should our most gracious Sovereign chance to see a Publication thus imputed to him; we beg leave most respectfully to deprecate any sentiment of personal dissatisfaction, which he may feel at our bold assumption; assuring The King, that he does not possess among his people, more disinterestedly loyal subjects, than the Author and Publisher of this Letter.

---

## POSTSCRIPT TO THE FOURTH EDITION.

The Amanuensis of this Letter has heard many observations made on this bold attempt of imputing to his Sovereign the sentiments contained therein. He has taken some pains to discover the feelings of the parties raising objections to it ; as well as of those who consider it a *timely* boldness. He has the satisfaction of finding, that those are most violent against it, who are unable to answer its argument; and those talk insidiously of this abuse of the King's name, who are great admirers and encouragers of caricatures on his person. In some cases, there is also (even among those who think with himself) a scrupulous feeling as to the mode in which his thoughts are conveyed. Such feeling is conscientious and honourable, but on this occasion, *over nice.* The mode adopted was the only one, capable of producing a dispassionate review of the King's case ; it has succeeded beyond the most sanguine expectation, as four editions within a Fortnight testify.

---

## POSTSCRIPT TO THE FIFTH EDITION.

From the moment of deciding upon the bold step of publishing this Letter, it was also determined never to notice any reply, attack, or abuse of it. We are most happy to know, that it has convinced many of the most violent advocates of the Royal Tenant of Brandenburg House, of their injustice towards their noble-minded Sovereign.

THE END.

LONDON:
PRINTED BY WILLIAM CLOWES,
Northumberland-court.

1, *St. James's Street.*

# WILLIAM SAMS,

*HAS LATELY PUBLISHED THE FOLLOWING WORKS:*

A LETTER to the HOUSE OF COMMONS, on the Subject of the Litany, and the Allowance to the Queen. By the Author of the King's Letter to his People, 8vo. 2s.

THE CITY ADDRESS EXPOSED, in a Letter to the Right Honourable the Lord Mayor. By the same, 8vo. 2s.

OCCASIONAL REMARKS on Mr. TENNYSON'S *Observations on the Proceedings against the Queen.* By WESLEY DOYLE, ESQ., 8vo. 1s. 6d.

A FULL EXPLANATION of the Law respecting Prayers for the Queen and the Royal Family. By PROFESSOR CHRISTIAN.

TO-DAY, a POETICAL SATIRE. By ERNESTUS. Second Edition, 8vo.

A COMPLETE TREATISE on ROUGE et NOIR; in which is developed a Practical Method of successfully playing the Game. 2s. 6d.

THE VIEW and other POEMS, by CHANDOS LEIGH. fcap. 8vo. 5s.

ERATO'S LAYS, or LYRICAL POEMS, on Amatory, Satirical, and Incidental subjects, being the Ideas of a Fortnight. Post 8vo. 5s. bds.

OPOLEYTA, or a TALE of IND. A Poem in Four Cantos. By BERTIE AMBROSE, ESQ. Second Edition, 8vo. 6s.

JAMES THE THIRD, King of Scotland, a Tragedy, in Five Acts, 8vo. 3s. 6d.

CATHERINE de MEDICIS, a Tragedy. By the Author of James the Third, 8vo. 3s. 6d.

FASHIONABLE INTRIGUE, or the MATCH MADE UP, A Comedy, in five Acts. By the Same, 8vo.

TOO LATE FOR DINNER, a Farce, in Two Acts. By RICHARD JONES, ESQ. of the Theatre Royal Covent Garden, 8vo. 2s.

THE YOUTHFUL DAYS of FREDERICK the GREAT, a Melo-drama in Two Acts, by WILLIAM ABBOTT, ESQ. of the Theatre Royal Covent Garden, 8vo. 2s.

A CATALOGUE of Two Hundred Popular Works for Instruction and Amusement, may be had of W. SAMS, GRATIS.

An ADDRESS to the IMPERIAL PARLIAMENT upon the PRACTICAL MEANS of gradually ABOLISHING the POOR LAWS, and Educating the POOR systematically; illustrated by an Account of the Colonies of Fredericksoord in Holland, and of the Common Mountain in the South of Ireland. By W. HERBERT SAUNDERS, ESQ.

IN THE PRESS,

A LETTER on our AGRICULTURAL DISTRESSES, their
Causes and Remedies; accompanied with Tables and Copper-
Plate Charts, shewing and comparing the Prices of Wheat, Bread
and Labour, from 1550 to 1821; addressed to the Lords and
Commons. By WILLIAM PLAYFAIR. 5s.

*On the 31st of May next will be published,*

(TO BE CONTINUED MONTHLY,)

No. I. of BRITISH HONOUR and HUMANITY DIS-
PLAYED, and RANK and PROPERTY DEFENDED,
as being beneficial to all classes of Society; containing an account
of those Noblemen and Gentlemen who are particularly attentive
to the welfare and prosperity of their Tenants, Dependants, and
the Poor. Edited by WILLIAM PLAYFAIR.

Printing for William Sams, 1, St. James's Street.

# A

# SECOND LETTER

FROM THE

# KING

TO

# HIS PEOPLE.

FIFTH EDITION.

LONDON·

PRINTED FOR WILLIAM SAMS,

BOOKSELLER TO HIS ROYAL HIGHNESS THE DUKE OF YORK,
1, St. JAMES'S STREET;

SOLD ALSO BY W. BLACKWOOD, EDINBURGH;

C. P. ARCHER, BOOKSELLER TO HIS MAJESTY, DUBLIN;

AND ALL OTHER BOOKSELLERS IN THE UNITED KINGDOM.

MDCCCXXI.

LONDON:
PRINTED BY WILLIAM CLOWES,
Northumberland-court.

# A
# SECOND LETTER

FROM

# THE KING

## TO HIS PEOPLE.

---

*Carlton-Palace, May* 1821.

To all our loving Subjects and Countrymen,

WHEN I last addressed myself to my people, during that factitious irritation of the public mind, which has since been pacified by gradual reflection, I anticipated a procedure of weakness and of wickedness, which would rarely have been paralleled; nor do I find it needful, on my present consideration of past events, to qualify that prediction, however apparently reproachful and severe. So much has been essayed by factious malignity on the one hand, and hazarded by capricious petulance on the other, that violence, inconsistency, and dissension, have sensibly impressed the character of a party, which attempted, under the seducing banners of affected patriotism, to annihilate the moral principles of my realms, to degrade the solemnities of our religion, and to infuse into the bosom of our common country, the most unworthy and pernicious inferences of shallow and constructive casuistry. We have lived in times of the most important political events, both domestic and external. In a per , to

B

ing immortal benefits to mankind, or inflicting upon
them irremediable ills, keeps up at least a constant
communication between us, depriving the courtier
of the power of concealing from his Sovereign
public opinion, and placing him within the effect
of inquiry. With such a constant possibility of explanation, a Monarch may be misguided, but cannot be uninformed ; he may adopt decisive rules of
government, but cannot remain ignorant of their
effects.

Although it is presumed that I become acquainted
with political occurrences and opinions, solely
through the channel of my official advisers,
and can only constitutionally address my people
through the regular organ of parliament, or of my
council ; yet, at this momentous crisis, pregnant
with evil to our common country, and to me so interesting as a man and a husband, but above all, as
the inheritor of my Royal Father's crown, the form
and mode of this communication may stand shielded
and excused, in the generally anomalous character
of the circumstances to which I shall hereafter
advert: nor, on so singular an occasion, do I think
it derogatory to the dignity of my exalted station,
to attempt the dispersion of a mist, in which too
many of my subjects have wandered, led on by a
generous delusion.

I will not accuse, I do not accuse, of disaffection
either to my person or government, *all* who are advocates for the cause of the Queen; for in that
cause, I perceive plainly a variety of motives in
activity ; in the combination of those motives, differing widely from each other, the immediate danger
appears to consist : but it is also, from their dis-

tensions of the factious had misled. My experience of the character of my subjects assured me of
this result; and the king of a great nation may congratulate himself, that in such a calculation, he has
found himself informed of the minds and bosoms of
his people.

At such a season it cannot misbecome the monarch to address the subjects of his realm ; the
informality of such a condescension is readily explained by the novelty of the occasion; the Laws
and all the Powers of the Constitution will protect
the *King;* and surely while presumption and fatuity
assail him as an *individual,* denied the choice of
usual vindication, the high-minded men and females
of his dominion will attend with impartiality, at
least, to the arguments and reasons of the *man.* The
feelings of our nature are the same, but *I* am denied
the reparation which belongs to the meanest of my
people ; to offer insult to the monarch with security,
is in the power of *all* my subjects, I am certain in
the will of very *few:* to sustain it, is the hard condition of the King ; and though thus placed by exaltation beyond the power of his own protection, he
will, at all events, dispel the cloud of falsity and
folly, which would veil the truth of past and present
circumstances.

I feel with pleasure, that it is the essence of a
people, so proverbially and virtually free as those of
England, to adopt a vigorous opposition to every
apparent encroachment on our constitutional immunities ; and that one of the vulgar, though not use
prejudices of the people, is that vigilant suspicion

the powerful, which has always conclusively demonstrated, in its result, the virtue of the suspected party, or the equable operation of our laws on the delinquencies of the noble as well as of the mean. Let not therefore prejudice impose on greatness one further incumbrance than the weight of royalty, and deny the King alone the impartiality of justice, that birth-right co-extensive with his realms.

I can by no means more effectually exhibit to my people the purpose of a faction, and the indiscretion of the Queen, than by adverting to the Letter of her Majesty, bearing date the 7th of August, 1820. The ostentatious boldness of the assertions comprehended in that violent production, was an evidence of desperation, which in the onset was publicly mistaken (indeed it was intended so to be) as the firm assurance of conscious purity. Few of my subjects, who recur to the co-operating circumstances of that time, can fail to discover in each insidious observation, a mockery of noble sentiment and patriotic sympathy, directed at the agitated feeling of some portion of the people of the metropolis and the suffering classes of the distant districts of the kingdom. The freedom of the press had been endangered by treasonous and irreligious tracts, which tended equally to subvert the altar and the throne. The fallacious reasonings of impious men were industriously scattered through the realm, and the work of demoralization was profanely urged, as the best preparatory measure, to ensure the dissolution of civil order, and the introduction of an anarchy uctive both of Church and State. The dignity of the bench invaded; the sacredness of our religion ridiculed; the equal operations of the law ascribed to the adjudication of dependent judges; the implication of individuals of vulgar popularity and incendiary principles; were either present to the observation, or fresh on the remembrance, of the public. Two men, ever wildly in quest of popular clamour, and enamoured of illegal declamation, affecting a spirit of independence, and evolving sentiments of turbulent assurance, had made themselves, in the opinion of a misguided class, the objects of the public interest.

By the common artifice of palpable aggression, at which no Government of strength or virtue could connive, they affected to undergo a grievous mar_tyrdom to conscience: and having duly calculated that chastisement would wait on outrage, they endeavoured to conciliate the voices of the disaffected, and to claim the suffrage of confiding folly, which thought itself defended, at the very time that it was manifested and cajoled. A band of dissolute and idle men, the unfortunate disciples of a doctrine long disseminated by the captious discontent of some Utopian theorists, had so far fostered the pernicious tenets of their apostles, that the perpetration of a crime, almost unknown to England, was digested, by which the ministers of my government were to have fallen by the hands of desperate assassins. Need I expatiate on the expedients which were requisite, at this alarming crisis, to arrest the progress of immorality, and disarm the evil dispositions of those abandoned and deluded men, who were addressing, without scheme or rational pretext, their public and their secret homilies, to every ignorant, desperate, unhappy, and credulous outcast of society? Need I labour to refute those trite and superficial prelections of false economy and radical amendment, which originated in perverse contradiction to practical benefit, and have now become the ridicule, the very laughing-stock, of almost all their earlier proselytes? To deter the preceptors of this methodized insanity from the propagation of *their* vicious theories, to repress the vehement excitement which the spell words of *radicalism, innovation,* and *reform* had created ; and to preserve from their contagious principles, the sane and salutary parts of my dominion, the prompt application of the powers of government was effectually and charitably adopted. Provisional acts of legislature, of consummate wisdom and indispensable expediency, adapted to the pressing exigency of the times, and frustrating, by their comprehensive and restrictive tendency, the evasive ambiguity of evil-doers, received from the supporters of all *other* innovation, a character of obloquy and hyperbolical denunciation. The *preservation* of the Constitution of the kingdom was denounced as a *violation* of the Constitution, and the reviling jargon of radical alarmists, was employed to stimulate the thoughtless and unwary to acts of outrage on their patient and resolute preservers. The vacillating conduct of the Queen at St. Omers; the mysterious deportment of her Majesty's legal adviser; and, ultimately, the abrupt determination of her

Majesty to come to England, ensured the effectuation
of a preconcerted plan ; she arrived on the shores
of the kingdom, apparently deserted ; placed in a
condition imposing to the public mind : the effect
was obvious, and the evident unkindness of her reception was to attract interest and compassion to the
digested scenes of the ensuing tragi-comedy.

Ignorant as the people were of what had been
the usage of the Queen abroad, and what had been
her usage of the King, and of the honour of this
pre-eminent and glorious country, the hasty pre-
dilection of the people was one of those magnani-
mous demonstrations, which, however erroneous at
the time, exhibited, in all its force and bearing,
the chivalrous enthusiasm of a great and valiant
country. And happy, my countrymen and people, too happy, had your King been, could that
generous sentiment have been justifiably continued
to the Queen on the test of scrutiny ; by that
impartial public inquiry, to which the Ministers of
your Sovereign were, officially and dutifully, bounden
to cite the first illustrious, female personage of his
dominion !! I will not descend to notice the varied,
the incessant, the tumultuary methods used to pre-
possess the public sentiment, altogether uninformed,
in favour of the Queen ; to confer on me a myriad
of disgraceful calumnies essentially opposed to all
the peculiar moral feelings of our country, and to
effect a presumptuous anticipation of the finding of
the House of Lords ; machinations of the most illiberal and *ex-parte* character, generative alike of
prejudice and misinformation ; in brief, a perfi-

dious tissue of enormous falsities and unimportant truths, from which uncandid sophisters might hope, with trivial facts to warrant monstrous falsehoods, and to establish specious premises for argumentative equivocation.

Having thus noticed the condition of the kingdom immediately antecedent to the arrival of the Queen in England, I shall proceed to lay before you an inquisitive analysis of the style and motives of the Letter of her Majesty. It may be in the remembrance of the people, that I communicated no instructions to the Earl of Liverpool, " *to make any communication to her Majesty in consequence of her Letter.*" To that Letter and its tenor, I by no means condescend, at present, TO REPLY : but, the dispassionate examination of its contents, may afford to the community at large, sufficient evidence of the intention and the hopes conceived by her Majesty, to effect, by the temporary embarrassments of my Government, an issue which it was utterly impossible to attain, except by the deliberation and decisive wisdom of my Parliament. For, even in those momentous times of popular vicissitude, which carry their alternate influence to a monarch's heart, I will rule by conscience, for the good and glory of the realm. I would still consult the reverence due to the example of my royal parents ; I will imitate, if I am unable to attain, the excellence of their remembered virtues ; duty, even at the sacrifice of popular affection, should govern me unshaken in the prosecution of my people's welfare ; and, though faction should achieve delusions painful to the Monarch, the solemn functions of my royal office would lead me to persist, and even rather fall, with honour, from my station, than disgrace the British throne by one unkingly compromise of selfish fear.

I said that I would analyze the Letter of the Queen. The evidence adduced before the House of Lords is fresh in the remembrance of my people. Let me, therefore, urge specifically on their notice, the pompous inchoation of that specimen of chaste effrontery. The King is charged with " *an unpar-ralleled and unprovoked persecution, which, during a series of years has been carried on against the Queen, under the name and authority of his Majesty.*" This unhesitating calumny, so uniform with every other part of that disingenuous and immodest document, is aptly stated as the harbinger of her embodied injuries The Queen proceeds: " It is not without a great sacrifice of private feeling that I now, even in the way of remonstrance, bring myself to address this letter to your Majesty. But, bearing in mind that royalty rests on the basis of public good; that to this paramount consideration all others ought to submit; and, *aware of the consequences that may result from the present unconstitutional, illegal, and hitherto unheard-of proceeding ;* with a mind thus impressed, I cannot refrain from laying my grievous wrongs once more before your Majesty, in the hope that the justice which your Majesty may, by evil-minded counsellors, be still disposed to refuse to the claims of a *dutiful, faithful, and injured wife,* you may be induced to yield to con-

siderations connected with the honour and dignity
of your crown, the *stability* of your throne, *the
tranquillity of your dominions, the happiness and safety
of your just and loyal people, whose generous hearts
revolt at oppression and cruelty, and especially when
perpetrated by a perversion and a mockery of the laws.*"

I might, in the first instance, assume the language
of an illustrious and long-departed nobleman, and answer to the imputation of " *persecution under my royal
authority and name*," by saying, that the charge is too
ridiculous to be refuted, and deserves only to be mentioned that it may be despised. On reference to recent facts, it hardly will be pleaded, by even the compassionate admirers of the Queen, that any considerable portion of private feeling was likely to be
sacrificed by her Majesty, either in her address to
me, or to ' *my* ' people. The uncontroverted moral
axiom, which her Majesty admits in deference to our
enlightened polity, but ill appears before the turbid
and prophetic menaces of a conditional revolt; before " *the consequences that may result from the present
unconstitutional, illegal, and hitherto unheard-of proceedings,*" the " *considerations connected with the stability of
my throne, and the tranquillity of my dominions;*" and the
" *oppression and cruelty perpetrated by a perversion and
a mockery of the laws.*" England, Scotland, and Ireland, have heard or seen the solemn, the deliberate
considerations of the aristocracy; I therefore leave
to them the painful commentary, which their King
will not apply, to the inflated " claims of duty, faith,
and injury."—But that the nation may duly estimate
the latent objects in the contemplation of the Queen

and her pragmatic faction, I will call the steady observation of every separating and combining intellect
to the likely influence of their inflammatory innu-
endoes. I can with difficulty think that any party in
my realm could hope to awe, by such extended
threats, the *Monarch, or the servants of his Govern-
-ment ;* but I can readily suppose, that such allure-
ments were extended to the reposing class of baffled
*democrats*, whom exemplary penalties had recently
diverted from pernicious plans; and that they affected to evoke from the retirement of contrite depravity some few restless spirits of a questionable
penitence. That the Queen should have imputed
to the Lords an intended perpetration of oppressive cruelty, by the " perversion and mockery
of law," asserts an estimation of their House
which I shall not descend to controvert. Can
it be incumbent on the King to establish a defence for his Imperial Parliament, or Commons
House; or rather would it be compatible with decency to meet an accusation on the legislative body
of the Constitution, in refutation of such errant,
such captious impeachments ; of impeachments so
associated, and so preferred ? Having thus ex-
plored the leading paragraph of her Majesty's Letter,
I would ask the mass of all the people, who have
read or heard the evidence produced before the
House of Lords ; yes, even those whose sceptical
refinements would exonerate the Queen from the
specific guilt alleged against her; What is the pur-
port, what the object, of that bold defiance and
casuistical lamentation pervading the inception of
her Letter to her husband? I would adjure him by

his conscience, by his love of country, by his hope
in God, and thus adjured myself, I could most
solemnly declare, the object was vindictive, not conciliatory, subversive of, and not conducive to, the
tranquillity and safety of my people.

The ensuing paragraph of the Letter of the Queen
is of a more occult and enigmatical description.
It would, however, very pointedly insinuate that
the tenacious feminality of her Majesty forbears to
bring to light the real causes of our domestic separation. That sentiments of delicacy should guide
the conduct of the Queen, is doubtless creditable
to her Majesty; but that concealment is desirable
to me or to my deportment, on that unfortunate
occasion, I distinctly and positively, to all my people,
do deny. I solicit from the Queen no favours of
suppression, and should conceive her Majesty the
dupe of an unseasonable remission, if from delicacy
to *my* demeanour, she neglected the paramount duty
of establishing the propriety of her *own*. The
figurative charge of " *driving a wife from beneath my
roof with an infant in her arms,*" is rather too imaginary to enter into the prosaic gravity of serious
accusation, and will be scarcely entertained by
those indulgent beings of condolence, whose affected sympathy has recently so much enlarged
the teeming objects of her Majesty's complaints.
That my separation from her Majesty " was a sentence pronounced on her without a cause assigned,"
might have been delicately requited on her part,
by the inviolable, the honourable taciturnity which
has governed me. I shall not indulge in any scrutiny of sentiment, however elegantly turned or

pathetically associated ; but the disturbance of sanctified remembrances so dear to a paternal breast, might well, on such a point as this, be spared ; in that departed object of my own and of the nation's love, their hope and mine is lost for ever; it was the will of God, and I have bowed in resignation. If the memory of early virtue can atone for the desolation of the best of earthly hopes, such melancholy consolations are reserved for the internal communion of an afflicted spirit; and, may it henceforth please Heaven, while the unhappy father is providing for the peace of his beloved people, that at least the recesses of affectionate retirement may not be profaned, by 'factious intercessions in the name of one so beloved while living, and now so revered in immortality !

The three succeeding paragraphs convey a body of invective, which, compounded of generalities, and derived from the incoherent and conflicting rumours to which loquacity, exaggeration and misconception give a being, are only to be met on contradictions equally diffuse and comprehensive. It would be needless to point out to a discerning people, that particularity of accusation is, to the accuser and the accused, the certain and most candid method of conviction or acquittal ; specific charges must be specifically met; but imputations of so general and vague a nature as those collectively set forth against me by her Majesty, arise from the evident anxiety of a molested spirit, willing to embody accusations too insubstantial to be met, and too untrue to be refuted, and which the prejudice, or the prep session, of an agitated public may possibly assume as the mitigated statement of a person who would hint her injuries, but not declare their name.

The seventh paragraph of the Letter I discuss, is one of those surprising instances of froward pertinacy, which so perniciously revolts against discretion, and discovers the capricious vanity of an assumed but an untenable position. My people know the noble Lords who constituted in the year 1806, the Inquiry into the conduct of the, then, Princess of Wales. Those names alone will vindicate the purity of that Inquiry, But can it be possible to a personage of such illustrious descent, of such exalted rank, and such immaculate pretensions as the Queen, to *triumph* in the issue of that inquiry, and to dwell with an exulting smile on the *qualified* result of its proceedings. What lady in the realm would dare to glory in such imperfect exculpations of suspected error, or vaunt the issue of a scrutiny, which, however leniently and delicately set, implies at least the dangerous approaches of impurity. " This evasion of the law and justice," such is the phrase her Majesty employs, might well have lowered the plumes of any prince, to whom the hard alternative was left, of vitally invading all the dearest interests of Britain, or of bearing under mute conviction, the audacious obloquy, with which presumption, shamelessness, and base ingratitude requited his forbearance. Her Majesty proceeds to eulogize my royal father, of blessed and immortal memory. In such praises, I and all my people heartily and fervently concur.

Nor could I, the successor to his vacant throne, have more devoutly proved my reverence for the best of kings, than by deferring to that wise selection of ministerial power, which had, under the principles of his irresoluble government, maintained the glory of his kingdom against the world in arms, and ultimately led the larger states of Europe to the demolition of that despotic tyranny, which had subdued and desolated the greater part of civilized mankind. In the sacrifice of private friendship to the paternal love and duty which I bear my people, have I not foregone the dearest happiness of social life, denied to none but me? Could I have been insensible, in the critical conjuncture of the affairs of Europe, when, owing to the calamity of my blessed father, I was called to the discharge of his suspended functions, of the superior efficacy of a practical administration to one of untried theory? And how could I have compensated any national calamity, which might have been produced by a capricious hazard of reputed but unascertained capacity? The character of my administration will never justify the rash invective of her Majesty; more than ever, at the present crisis, do I see the need of vigilant, determined, and experienced statesmen. The generous spirit of my people can uplift the powerful supremacy of Britain against the leagued attempts of *foreign* enemies; but there are latent foes *within*, who would disseminate despondency and discontent. The condition of the people must be gradually ameliorated; the establishment of universal satisfaction cannot be magically

## Letter of Lord Liverpool to the Princess of Wales, dated the 28th of July, 1814.

" Lord Liverpool has had the honour to receive the letter of her Royal Highness. Having communicated it to the Prince Regent, he has ordered him to inform her Royal Highness that he can have no objection to the intentions of her Royal Highness to effect the design which she announces to the Prince Regent, of returning to her native country, to visit her brother the Duke of Brunswick, assuring her, that the Prince Regent will never throw any obstacle in the way of her present or future intentions as to the place where she may wish to reside.

" The Prince Regent leaves her Royal Highness at liberty to exercise her own discretion as to her abode in this country or on the continent, as it may be convenient to her.

" Lord Liverpool is also commanded, on the part of the Prince Regent, to inform her Royal Highness, that he will not throw any obstacles in the way of the arrangements of her Royal Highness, whatever they may be, respecting the house at Blackheath, which belonged to the late Duchess of Brunswick, or the rest of the private property of her Royal Highness. But that, for reasons rather too long to explain, the Prince Regent will not permit the Princess Charlotte to be ranger of Greenwich Park, or to occupy any of the houses at Blackheath, which her Royal Highness has hitherto occupied.

" Lord Liverpool has also been enjoined, on the part of the Prince Regent, before he closes the letter which he has the honour to send to her Royal Highness, to tell her, in relation to the two articles which her Royal Highness has put in her letter concerning the rupture of the marriage of the Princess Charlotte with the hereditary Prince of Orange, as well as to the reason for which the allied Sovereigns did not, previously to their departure from England, pay their visit to her Royal Highness ; that, as to the first article, Lord Liverpool is commanded by the Prince Regent to inform her Royal Highness, that the Prince Regent is not persuaded that the private considerations of the circumstances in which the Princess is placed, can have been an obstacle to the marriage of the Princess Charlotte. As to the second article, Lord Liverpool is also enjoined, on the part of the Prince Regent, to signify to her Royal Highness, that the Prince Regent never opposed himself to the allied Sovereigns making a visit to her Royal Highness during their stay in London.

" Lord Liverpool has the honour to be, with all esteem and the highest consideration.

" P. S. The Prince Regent can make no difficulties on the subject of the directions which the Princess has the intention of giving as to the house at Blackheath ; neither will the Prince Regent oppose her Royal Highness's retaining the apartments in the Palace of Kensington, in the same manner as she possessed them while in London, for the convenience of herself and suite."

parent propriety, which even ordinary parents must discover in such control; but viewing the Princess Charlotte as the heiress-apparent to the Crown, that restriction seemed prescribed by reasons far more cogent, than the need of domestic dispositions; for reasons, which the King must conscientiously have felt himself officially bounden to respect, in honour and duty to that nation which, with the permission of God, his daughter would have one day ruled. To revive the discussion of that important point, the King would have to recall considerations of no peculiar satisfaction to the Queen; the act was neither personal nor wanton, but purely of a moral and political essence; the King cannot abandon the incontrovertible authorities which acquiesced in its incumbent rectitude; and every retrospective consideration assures him of the indispensable necessity and justice of that provision.

Far be it from my hope to deny the Queen to have possessed the natural affection of so dear and close a tie; but let the people ask, when my beloved daughter was no more, should that calamity, so mutual to the Queen and to myself, have shed a gloom of chastening sorrow on our hearts and minds; should that calamity have wooed us to the solitude of pious resignation, and have bowed us down in sorrow at so deep a visitation of afflicting Providence? The Queen asserts, " this was the moment chosen to redouble her persecutions." When then, how circumstanced and how surrounded was the Queen, to be by any means, by rights; such a proceeding would have produced an explanation.

*As to the second point,* we separated upon terms mutually understood, and to which the Princess added herself a peremptory condition; those terms have by me been inviolably preserved; as a husband, I enabled my wife to maintain the dignity of her rank and station as Princess of Wales; I visited her separation with no pecuniary privations, but, on the contrary, paid for her, debts exceeding her means of expenditure, to the amount of forty-nine thousand pounds; the government of the country, at the same time, liquidating a further sum of thirty-one thousand pounds.

*As to the third point,* the preceding remarks, in part apply. On the subject of the actual inquiry, I may be allowed to say, that the Prince of Wales is born with certain rights previously created, as a line of duty to be by him fulfilled. The preservation of the chastity of his wife, with a view to the purity of the succession, is one of those duties. When, therefore, in consequence of rumours, too loud and too deep to remain unheard, I demanded an inquiry, as part of the duty of my high birth and national rank, I submitted the case to the responsible ministers of the crown; I acquiesced in the sentence passed upon the termination of the inquiry, and bowed to the decision which had been pronounced by the warm and zealous friend of the Princess, who was judge upon the occasion.

*As to the fourth point,* I endeavoured, by every means in my power, to prevent our disputes from taking a political turn, embarrassing to the government of the country; and I most particularly aimed at preserving, in the mind of the Princess Charlotte, a neutrality on the delicate occasion; the restriction imposed on the intercourse between the Princess and her daughter was connected with the system of her education, which, by law, rested with the Sovereign. When, at a subsequent period, in 1813, the Princess of Wales addressed to me as Regent, a letter alluding to such restriction, and also to the proceedings of 1806, almost grown out of recollection, I submitted such letter to noblemen, differing in political opinion from those who had on the former occasion made a report on the conduct of the Princess; the result of this re-inquiry produced no change, no imputation on the former statements and evidence, and I still continued to consider the whole affair as one of domestic inconvenience, inasmuch as the succession to the throne was pronounced *not to be endangered.*

*As to the fifth point,* upon the retirement of her Royal Highness to the Continent, I continued to the Princess her residence in a royal palace, leaving it as a domicile open to her return; and, I declare, upon my honour as a Prince, that I never, on any previous occasion, threw the slightest obstacle in the way of her Royal Highness's comfort, tranquillity, and domestic arrangement. The affairs of Princes cannot be conducted in the same obscure and unostentatious mode as those of private individuals; to snatch a few moments of private life is, in a Prince, to enjoy real happiness. All the difficulties which have occurred in the case in question have been produced and created, they were not of natural origin, but have been foisted on the original evil by factious persons, seeking to advance their own political purposes. Had not the Princess placed herself avowedly in such hands, many of the mortifications of her situation had been avoided; they would, indeed, have had no existence. Finally, I declare again, upon my honour, that my conduct aimed to keep the whole unhappy affair within the character of a domestic and purely personal misfortune; and it is only by the attempts made by faction, to give it a political complexion, that the attention of the people has been fixed upon it as a national grievance.

I have now, my subjects and fellow-countrymen, gone through the first great division of my letter; I approach the second, I trust, with feelings as a King, suitable to the occasion.

Hitherto I have appeared only as Prince of Wales, and Regent.

\* \* \* \* \* \* \* \*

Her Royal Highness quitted England as Princess of Wales early in August in the year 1814, and in the succeeding November (a short interval of three months), appears *to have consulted my tranquillity*, by furnishing grounds for *a third* inquiry into the propriety of her conduct. After *three years of rumours,* *a commission* to examine into their truth or falsehood was *a third time* rendered necessary for the honour of the crown of these realms; thus, in both cases, as well in the investigation of 1806, as also in that of 1818, it was not until *years of rumour* had been allowed to rouse suspicions, that any official measures were adopted to inquire into their reality.

Possibly the great error has been, that such rumours were permitted to remain so long without an inquiry. Had spies really surrounded her Royal Highness, the purposes of a commission of inquiry

totally removed, by provisions of attested prudence,
it became a topic of affected triumph to the advocates of insecurity, that the powers of Government
were uselessly arrayed to preserve subordination in
the people. It would be a prostitution of the
powers of reason, to meet by serious argument the
multiform perplexities of hypothetical pretension,
which still attempt to urge the preference of speculative possibilities to the real welfare so substantially secured by measures of precautionary foresight.

I have stated on a previous occasion, that I had
hoped the absence of the Queen, of whose proceedings I was still informed, would have enabled
me to confine her conduct within the pale of a domestic, personal calamity; to secure to myself and
to the nation the advantage of tranquillity, the
ample convenience of the Queen was regularly, I
may add, munificently afforded; I rationally thought
the Queen would see the obvious interest of her
secession from the artful solicitations to political
significance; and, that to have declined the opportunity of national disturbance, (which, as we have
recently perceived, is at the influence of all notorious political offenders, however high or low), would
indeed have manifested, on one occasion, that interest in the national benefit which her Majesty affects
to feel so profoundly upon all. I entertained the
more ardently this hope as I readily foresaw, that
without benefit to the cause which had expressly
brought her Majesty to my dominions, she would
be assumed as an imposing instrument, in the ha

thus situated, and himself obliged to decide, no other
authority, according to the laws of the realm, having
power to relieve him from the duty. And why was
I thus called upon to doubt? Because my council,
according to their oaths, which is " to advise for the
King's honour and good of the public, without partiality, through affection, love, meed, doubt, or
dread;" and in performance of their duty, which is
" to inquire into all offences against the government;"
had not left me unacquainted with the existence of
a primá facie case, of gross and long-continued adultery, alleged to be committed by the late Princess
of Wales, now de jure the Queen.

It became therefore evident, it was unavoidable,
that whenever the Queen thought proper to return
to my kingdom, she must meet this charge, the truth
or falsehood of which remained still to be proved.
My council strictly confined themselves to their
legal duty, that of inquiring only : and the features of
that inquiry imposed upon them the painful duty of
placing the Queen in a state of abeyance.

This solemn decision, I may say, this vitally religious act, presented itself to me in two points of
view. Was I, with such knowledge in my possession, to recommend unhesitatingly and specially,
the name of the Queen, to the prayers of the church?
Or was I to leave the name to be inserted when her
Majesty should have wiped off this foul charge of
adultery? In the first case, it might possibly have
fallen to my painful office, again to have expunged the
insertion; and in the second case, it might happily
have been my duty to have supplied the omission.
Which, of the two modes afforded the least probability of future embarrassment? As yet, only a

*primâ facie* suspicion of adultery was exhibited against the Queen; I had a right to presume her innocent, I had a right to expect that future circumstances might justify the insertion of her Majesty's name, but such an insertion being a matter of discretion, the words " *and all the Royal Family,*" *did not exclude the Queen.* To have inserted the Queen's name specially, and subsequently to have found myself obliged by the law of the land to expunge it; would, with a great degree of reason, have subjected me to the charge of having first introduced such name, that I might enjoy the malicious triumph of erasing it; thus adding increased harshness to any future sentence. By using the phrase, "and all the Royal Family," *any future alteration,* under any circumstances of substantiated guilt or innocence, *would be rendered unnecessary.* To have inserted the name of the Queen, with a knowledge such as I possessed through my legal council, would, in my opinion, have been contrary to the laws of the kingdom; for among other charges which *might* have been brought forward against the Queen, was, "her probable conversion to the Roman Catholic faith." But to *postpone* the insertion of the name of the Queen, and afterwards to have been called upon to supply the omission, would, to her Majesty, have been a gracious act of acquittal, and restoration to regal honour; and I had a right to hope that such would be the result. Besides, the object and intention of the postponement of this insertion, was most certainly, not with a view to any proceedings against the Queen, but in anticipation of that continuance of mutual separation, which the Queen, in her letter of leave, declared to be "necessary to my future tranquillity."

I will suppose for one moment, the insertion to have been made. Had it been done under concealment from me, of existing circumstances, *my ministers would have been guilty of misprision of treason, and been liable to impeachment.* But as it was done with my knowledge; if ten thousands of ten thousand tongues were to demand of me, to tarnish the crown of your King, I would abandon it to the people rather than commit so great a crime. Whatever may have been the indiscretions of THE MAN, the future historian of England shall never record them as connected with THE KING.

It should not be overlooked, that the alteration of the Liturgy was also to regulate my own public devotion, as well as that of my subjects; should I not then by the special insertion of the name of the Queen, under existing circumstances, have most deservedly subjected myself to a charge of impious and detestable hypocrisy? " You have been praying yourself specially for the Queen, you Royal Hypocrite! whilst you have watched her destruction;" would have been a just and unanswerable accusation against me; an accusation, which, if well-founded, would have rendered the word of the King unworthy of belief.

Those only are the real exclusionists, who do not choose to comprehend the Queen, as implied in the words, " and all the Royal Family."

Had either the religious or legal considerations of this important point permitted me conscientiously to have inserted the name of the Queen in the Liturgy of the Church; all other minor considerations would have had no bearing upon the question; for that which would have been consistent with religion and law, could not have been *contra bonos mores.* I dwell not therefore on the subject, as connected with the morals of the country, but in its consideration, and in all its vital bearings, I cannot but have contemplated the consequences of a Queen charged with high crimes and misdemeanors, sitting upon that throne so lately occupied by the personification of chastity and matrimonial excellence.

Will the virtuous and noble, the high-minded and chaste, the amiable and domestic females of England, adopt the Queen as an example and model worthy of their imitation? Will they pronounce her faultless? Will they compose her court? If I can place the Queen on the throne of my ancestors upon such terms, I am ready to do so. Upon none other, can or ought a Queen to sit upon the throne of preeminent England.

I proceed now to the offer of an ample allowance offered to the Queen, provided she continued to remain abroad in the retirement she had voluntarily adopted; and the alternative with which that offer was accompanied. I have pointed out *this transaction*, and the *suspension in the Liturgy*, as acts which *may appear* to have emanated more immediately from my own personal feelings.

I have previously remarked, that from the period of my becoming Regent, the differences between the Princess and myself had assumed a political character, and been treated by many as a party question.

The companions of my youth, and the distinguished characters with whom, in my earlier years, I had intimately associated, had created in the public mind, a widely-extended, and readily believed opinion, that when the sceptre of my Father should descend to me, I should, from among those associates, have

chosen the members of my administration. During the
discussion of the terms of the regency, I was careful
to avoid giving any pledge of the line of policy I
might find it expedient to adopt. A short previous
administration, composed of those political friends
by whom it was conjectured my councils would have
been directed, had enabled me to form some opinion
of their executive talents; and *notwithstanding*, an
overture was made by me to them, to propose an
administration. But when I found the conditions
required would have reduced me to a mere political automaton, of which they were to possess the
key; that not content with forming the administration, they required also, that I should be surrounded
in my household by their adherents, and left to no
choice in the appointment of my own attendants;
when with this, I compared the candour and the
unequivocal absence of all personal feeling with
which the bill creating the Regency was carried by
the then ministry; and above all, the frank, loyal,
and respectful regret which was shewn to the calamity of my revered Parent; and the so immediate
provision made for the resumption by him of the regal
dignity, that it should have pleased Providence so to
have restored him, my Royal Father would have
awakened as if from a dream, and have found himself
unreminded of his affliction; when to this I added
the important consideration, that the flame of freedom was beginning to glimmer in Spain; that the
then administration were prepared to take advantage
of every circumstance favourable to the destruction
of the military tyrant of Europe; and when all
these various considerations were upheld by the
weight of personal character which was contained

in the then cabinet;. I felt sufficiently justified in
not suffering former prepossessions to stand for one
moment in the way of newly-created duties. I felt
that an existing experienced executive, was, at such
a time, safer than a theoretical cabinet. I had also
a doubt in my own mind, whether, during my Sovereign's life, I ought, as Regent, to adopt the
principles of those who had been violently opposed
to my Royal Father's measures, or pursue a line
of policy unchanged, and such as my King would
have continued had he remained the active head of
the Empire. This was a feeling of the heart; it was
mine.

This, my determination, produced two consequences; 1. A series of unbroken, glorious, and
important victories, attended with such results, as
the history of the world, within a similar period of
time, cannot produce; 2. The conversion of my
matrimonial differences into a political attack upon
my authority.

From this moment, then, the Queen, by becoming
the tool of party, gave to her cause and her conduct
a new feature, and an importance which required
the vigilant eye of the government.

I have been led into this digression, that the distinction I still endeavoured to uphold between my
marital and royal station, might be plainly and
easily comprehended. I return now to the consideration of the offer made to the Queen, of an allowance upon certain stipulations; *viz.*, that the Queen
should *cease to use* the name and style of Queen of
England, and remain abroad, where she had voluntarily seceded.

The period when this determination was decided

upon, must not be forgotten; it must not only not be forgotten, but it should be allowed its due weight in the decision of so momentous an affair. It appears almost, indeed, to be overlooked, that I met my first parliament in the month of April, at the very period, and while a set of infuriated, misguided and unhappy 'culprits were on their trial for a conspiracy to overturn the constitution and government of these realms, of which the commencement was intended to be, the indiscriminate assassination of my cabinet ministers. The general situation of the country, at that precise moment, appears also to have been thrown into the back ground. I cannot better recall those unhappy inauspicious moments, than by repeating again to my subjects the topics addressed to the Lords and Commons in Parliament assembled, upon our first meeting.

*My Lords and Gentlemen,*

" Deeply as I regret that the machinations and designs of the disaffected should have led in some parts of the country, to acts of open violence and insurrection, I cannot but express my satisfaction at the promptitude with which those attempts have been suppressed by the vigilance and activity of the magistrates, and by the zealous co-operation of all those of my subjects whose exertions have been called forth to support the authority of the laws.

" The wisdom and firmness manifested by the late parliament and the due execution of the laws, have greatly contributed to restore confidence throughout the kingdom; and to discountenance those principles of sedition and irreligion, which had been disseminated with such malignant perseverance, and had poisoned the minds of the unwary and ignorant.

" I rely upon the continued support of parliament, in my determination to maintain, by all the means intrusted to my hands, the public safety and tranquillity.

" Deploring, as we all must, the distress which still unhappily prevails among many of the labouring classes of the community, and anxiously looking forward to its removal or mitigation, it is, in the mean time, our common duty, effectually to protect the loyal, the peaceable, and the industrious, against those practices of turbulence and intimidation, by which the period of relief can only be deferred, and by which the pressure of the distress has been incalculably aggravated.

"I trust that an awakened sense of the dangers which they have incurred, and of the acts which have been employed to seduce them, will bring back by far the greater part of those who have been unhappily led astray, and will revive in them that spirit of loyalty, that due submission to the laws, and that attachment to the constitution, which subsist unabated in the hearts of the great body of the people, and which, under the blessing of Divine Providence, have secured to the British Nation, the enjoyment of a larger share of practical freedom, as well as of prosperity and happiness, than have fallen to the lot of any nation in the world."

If to the pending trials alluded to, and this general reference to the state of the kingdom, suffering under severe privations in some of its provinces, are added the numerous cases of treason, libel, and minor political offences under the progressive cognizance of the courts of law; I think my subjects and countrymen will admit, that to such previously existing evils *no addition was wanting to renew internal agitation which was beginning to subside.* The return of the Queen, under the circumstances which she must necessarily meet, was, of all others, calculated to revive that internal agitation; and why was it so calculated? Because the Queen had (as I have previously remarked) given, by her conduct, a political feeling to the differences between us. Had this not been the case, she could not have had, at least she ought not to have had, any motives for her return; or had she any, she ought to have sacrificed them to the welfare of our country.

From 1796 we had been separated, a period now of twenty-four years; disturbed by an almost constant suspicion of her conduct: the Queen had been estranged from Court, our Royal Daughter was no more; and her Majesty had but one duty to perform towards me, " the performance of an agreed separation."

A Queen Consort of England has no political rank, she possesses *in ease* of the Sovereign, certain inherent prerogatives ; those prerogatives are capable of being enjoyed by her, in her absence ; they required not her presence. The presence of the Queen could neither revive trade (languishing in some of its branches), tranquillize the irritation of distress, or conciliate the clamour of faction ; and, indeed, many records of English History hand down to us, the impolitic and dangerous counsels, which have ensued from the interference of Queens Consort in the political contests of the times. Although by way of eminent distinction, the word " Queen" is applicable only to the King's wife, yet, it originally signifies a wife, or woman. A Queen of England (unless Queen in her own right,) is a subject of the King, and can claim no political character from the people ; to her, at a coronation, no oath is administered, and no homage or allegiance offered. The coronation of a Queen is distinct, and subsequent to that of the King ; it is not at all necessary to the accession or title to the throne; and when performed, is a ceremony so performed for the greater honour of the kingly office. It proceeds from the King*.

If, therefore, I am to define the office or duty of a Queen Consort, I might sum it up in a few words, " To give a tone to *the morals* of the country." Does not the late reign furnish an indisputable proof of the truth of this axiom ?

Since then the Queen had deprived herself of the

---

* Taylor's *Glory of Regality.*

possibility of performing the duties of her station, and her return could produce none of those effects which were so evident during the long reign of my late Royal and revered Parents, could the next object of my solicitude be otherwise, than an attempt, still to treat the long borne separation, as a personal and domestic transaction ?

The Queen was growing old, we are both beyond the hey-day of life, and the levities of conduct attributed to her, might now be supposed to have worn or to have been wearing away. Our country required political repose ; and, above all, an internal quietude. Had no charge of adultery at all existed, there were sufficient grounds on both sides, for wishing, and for rendering desirable, a continuance of the existing separation.

In private life, what would the friends of a married couple, so long divided as the Queen and myself have been, think of the conduct of a wife, who would wish to return to her husband, under circumstances, such as have occurred between us? Would any female in England so *meanly* conduct herself? Would any husband in England so take back a wife ? If he would not, why should your King? If the female would not so return, why should the Queen? You will tell me, " To claim her rights." I reply, that the Queen possesses no political rights ; but certain prescribed prerogatives; those prerogatives are legally defined, their value as personal advantages can be ascertained, they can be enjoyed by the Queen, as well absent as present. I have offered her an equivalent. You will tell me, " That *she chooses* to return to our country, and that I have no right to restrain her." The Queen has chosen to return, and by the laws of the realm must she now abide; the Queen is my subject.

If, then, I am asked, " Why did I offer the Queen fifty thousand pounds a year to remain abroad, and cease to use openly the style and title of Queen of England," I answer, " To purchase the tranquillity of my country; to prevent a recurrence of those acts which had seduced so many of my subjects into danger, and to bring them back to that spirit of loyalty, that due submission to the laws, and that attachment to the constitution, which I hope still subsists in the hearts of the great body of my people;" all which I knew would be endangered by the *selfish return of a Queen*, who never can, and never will, sit upon the throne of England whilst George the Fourth wears the crown of his forefathers; until the female nobility shall, in a body, justify him in such act, with their sanction and presence, every other rank of the virtuous and the chaste would coincide.

Before I conclude this subject of an offered pension, I cannot but regret extremely, that the chance of cool and dispassionate deliberation which the Queen might have been disposed to have given to my offer and its alternative, was greatly diminished by the neglect of her Attorney-General, in the delivery of an ultimatum communicated to him in the month of April. Such neglect rendered Lord Hutchinson's communication so much the more sudden, stern, and unexpected. Of the zeal of that gentleman (her Majesty's Attorney-General) no one can entertain a higher opinion than myself; for his own sake, I may be allowed to say, that nothing disgraced his advocacy, but the threat of personal danger held out to the assembled Peers

Peers of the realm. Otherwise, who would not wish
to have a cause so defended? Had also her Majesty's
Solicitor-General omitted one or two similes in his
declamation, he had also retired from his duty with
more dignity. Upon the grounds of the case I am
silent; but, looking to the conduct of the Lord Chancellor, the differences which existed between the
members of the cabinet; the splendid and argumentative talents of the Opposition, all tending and
working together to elicit truth and produce an impartial judgment; I may fearlessly ask, if, under
such principles and in such an assembly, justice is
not to be found? I ask, fearlessly, where does she
dwell upon earth? I view, finally, the pause which
this unhappy affair has taken, as a striking proof of
that inflexible adherence to parliamentary avowals,
which combines the good man with the great minister; and as the performance of the pledge, that
" the Queen should have an equivalent for any and
every obstacle which the anomaly of her case presented in the obstruction of her trial."

I am now drawing towards the close of this my
letter, in the which my faithful subjects and excellent fellow-countrymen will (I trust) agree with
me, not only that the difference existing between
her Majesty and myself arose out of a domestic
cause, and was solely of a domestic nature; but
that all the popular feeling which has been excited,
has arisen from the political misdirection imposed
upon the transaction, a transaction important to the
nation only as it can be connected with their welfare. How that welfare can be promoted by forc-
ing upon a loathing husband an equally loathing
wife, a        to me, a problem in government, not

easily to be maintained in argument, or proved by
historical reference. If I am unhappily united to
a bad wife, or the Queen be under the caprice of a
bad husband ; provided those unpleasantries be confined within the limits of our personal conduct, and
are not mixed up with affairs of state, I see then no
impediment to the due constitutional performance
of my duties as King : but on the contrary, if the.
people disturb my kingly office, and clog its executive or dignity with an unseasonable family
blister, the chance is that the system of government
may become ill executed, greatly obstructed, or
completely embarrassed. If such is the aim of the
partizans of the Queen, I have then only to declare
this my determination, " That if the claims of the
Queen can make no impression on me *upon their own*
*merits*, any political association which she may form
to give weight to, or to disguise such claims, will
only call forth from me as your King, a firmer defence of my own rights, which are the rights of the
constitution under which I, the nobles, and the
people, all alike find reciprocal protection."

My people will now (I trust) begin to allow
themselves more clearly to define, and more ac-
curately to preserve the distinction between my
conduct as Prince of Wales, with reference to the
purity of the succession to the throne of my forefathers, and my behaviour as a separated husband.
In the one case, the performance of painful public
duties has devolved upon me, but I feel satisfied
that their unavoidable performance has not been accompanied by uncourteous or vexatious personal
conduct. To the high individual as a separate wife,
every attention has bben invariably paid, and upon

every occasion, money has been at her command for
the purposes of comfort, pleasure, or fickleness.
Surely, in return for such complete observance of
the terms of mutual separation, the Prince of Wales
had a right to expect the performance of the only
duty remaining to be performed by, and the only
one required of, the Princess; namely, " *An unquestionable and unequivocal propriety of conduct.*"

I could not probably fix upon a more convenient
or appropriate mode of portraying the consequences of the present public effervescence than by
anticipating the sentiments which some historian of
my reign may hand down to future ages. I will do
this in two ways; *First,* Upon the supposition, that
the Queen (even after what has already occurred,)
will be reinstated in all the prerogatives of her rank;"
*and secondly,* " That the Queen will remain estranged
from the crown."

IN THE FIRST CASE, the historian may be supposed
thus to express himself : "George the Fourth, after a
Regency of nearly nine years, succeeded to the throne
of his venerable and most excellent Father, whose
eventful reign had extended beyond the period of any
other British Monarch. The brilliant events of the
Regency of George the Fourth, unparalleled in history, are already recorded ; his reign commenced
amidst domestic losses, (his Brother, the Duke of
Kent, having died very suddenly at Sidmouth, in
Devonshire, six days only before their Royal Parent)
public agitation, and great national distress, attended
with all those factious symptoms, which the English
History appears almost invariably to record, as a
symptom of peace. A month had not elapsed, before
almost atrocious conspiracy, aiming no less than at

the indiscriminate assassination of all his Majesty's
Ministers during a cabinet dinner, was detected.
On the twenty-first of April, His Majesty met his
parliament, and in his Royal Speech upon the occasion, alluded to the disquietude and distress of
the kingdom, hinted at their cause, and expressed
a hope, that in the returning loyalty and legal obedience of the people, a remedy for those evils would
be found. The atrociousness of the conspiracy
alluded to, had opened the eyes of the supine, and
alarmed the fears of the timid ; and a more imposing public attitude being consequently produced,
tranquillity was gradually increasing into confidence.
At this moment, it pleased the Queen, (who had
now been separated from her Royal Husband
*twenty-four years*, and had estranged herself from
England for six years,) to return from the continent
under the auspices of *one* Wood, an Alderman of
the City of London. The Queen returned, in the
teeth of a proposition from the administration, that
she should still continue to remain abroad, and not
seek to disturb a connexion so long broken off;
and in defiance of a threat, that judicial proceedings
would follow her landing. The intrepidity of her
conduct was well calculated to please the English
Nation, and this daring and inconsiderate step, (a
step which her own legal adviser pronounced to be
unhappily taken, both as regarded herself, the parliament, the government, and the country) was rendered immediately popular by the epithet of *brave*,
Would any but an innocent woman (said the populace) have thus conducted herself?
Whilst the Queen was pursuing her journey from
Dover to the metropolis, a royal message was

delivering to parliament ; and papers in sealed bags
brought down to both houses   The Queen arrived
on the very day on which his Majesty went down to
the House of Lords, to give his assent to the first
bill passed since his accession.   After various in-
effectual delays, in the hope of effecting an arrangement, by which the Queen might have again left the
kingdom ; the House of Lords proceeded to appoint
a secret committee, to examine the documents sent
down to them (the House of Commons suspending
their proceedings,) and shortly made a report on the
same, charging the Queen with an adulterous intercourse with a menial of the name of Bergami, or
Pergami, on whom she had conferred, or for whom
she had procured, certain titles and orders of distinction.   A bill of Pains and Penalties was there-
upon brought in by the Earl of Liverpool, after long
and elaborate arguments upon the propriety and
applicability of the proceeding, had taken place in
the House of Peers.   The case presented an anomaly, for no statute existed, applicable to a charge
of adultery committed by a Queen of England,
*abroad and with a foreigner.*  This nice distinction
took the offence from within the pale of high
treason, for inasmuch as the principal was not
amenable to the laws of the country ; consequently,
the *particeps criminis* could not be judicially recog-
nized by the statutes of treason.  Every preliminary
of this great measure, was discussed to the very
letter, with a degree of eloquence and profound
learning which reflected unfading lustre upon the
House of Peers, and on the individual noblemen,
who led both sides of the debates.  The question
appeared new, and every aspect of its bearing was

most minutely and rigidly examined; great debate more particularly took place on the question of allowing to the illustrious accused, a list of witnesses, as in cases of high treason; when it was at length decided to open the case, produce the evidence, and allow the Queen an interval, (such as her counsel should deem requisite) to prepare her defence. Thus her Majesty was not only supplied eventually with a list of witnesses; but had the further guide of their sworn testimony. The Attorney General, (Sir R. Gifford,) opened the case according to his instructions, and by command of the House, with little preliminary remark, and certainly without inflation. Her Majesty's cause was less upheld by the evidence of the witnesses against her, (of whom the popular feeling pronounced a pre-judgment of perjury,) than by a deficiency of refutation on her own part. The Queen was most ably, most zealously, and most eloquently defended by Messrs. Brougham, Denman, Lushington and others; and the House bore the license of their harangues with a noble equanimity of patience. After hearing both the charge and the defence, which occupied forty-five days, the House adjourned two days, before it met to debate the principle of the bill; which discussion occupied four days. The second reading was carried by a majority of twenty-eight, the numbers being *for it* 123, *against it* 95. During the progress of the measure, several protests were entered on the Journals of the House, in one of which the Lord Chancellor and the Prime Minister were directly opposed to each other; a brother of the King absented himself wholly from the investigation; a cousin of the King voted against the measure in all its stages; both the Ministry and the Opposition were divided amongst themselves, and intermingled their votes; the preamble of the bill underwent but little alteration in the committee: and in the clause for pronouncing a divorce as part of the pains and penalties, all the Cabinet Ministers, (nine) voted against it. The divorce clause was however carried by a majority of 67, there being contents 129, non-contents 62. Most of the peers who had' till this moment contended against the principle of the bill in all its stages, argued (with much plausible appearance of reason) that since the Queen was virtually pronounced guilty of an adulterous intercourse, by the votes of the second reading; *divorce became the natural consequence, as part of the sentence of the bill*, they therefore voted for it. The third reading of the bill, was carried on the 10th November, by the small majority of nine; the numbers being for it 108, against it 99.

Lord Liverpool, (who had brought in the bill, as an individual peer, and not as a member of the administration), immediately moved, that " the bill be read that day six months," alleging the smallness of the majority, as the motive *.

---

* Bill [as read a third time,] entitled, An act to deprive her Majesty, Caroline Amelia Elizabeth, of the title, prerogatives, rights, privileges, and exemptions of Queen Consort of this realm; and to dissolve the marriage between his Majesty and the said Caroline Amelia Elizabeth.
Whereas in the year one thousand eight hundred and fourteen, her Majesty Caroline Amelia Elizabeth, then Princess of Wales, and now Queen Consort of this realm, being at Milan, in Italy, engaged in her service, in a menial situation, one Bartolomeo Pergami, a foreigner of low station, who had before served in a similar capacity: And whereas after the said Bartolomeo Pergami had so entered the service of her Royal Highness the said Princess of Wales, a most un-

The friends of the Queen received this unexpected reprieve from the bill, after proof of the facts; and admission of their reality, as a total and complete

---

becoming and degrading intimacy commenced between her said Royal Highness and the said Bartolomeo Pergami, and her said Royal Highness not only advanced the said Bartolomeo Pergami to a high situation in her Royal Highness's household, and received into her service many of his near relations, some of them in inferior and others in high and confidential situations about her Royal Highness's person, but bestowed upon him other great and extraordinary marks of favour and distinction, and conferred upon him a pretended order of knighthood, which her Royal Highness had taken upon herself to institute, without any just or lawful authority: And whereas also her said Royal Highness, whilst the said Bartolomeo Pergami was in her said service, further unmindful of her exalted rank and station, and of her duty to your Majesty, and wholly regardless of her own honour and character, conducted herself towards the said Bartolomeo Pergami, both in public and private, in various places and countries which her Royal Highness visited with indecent and offensive familiarity and freedom, and carried on a licentious, disgraceful, and adulterous intercourse, with the said Bartolomeo Pergami, which continued for a long period of time, during her Royal Highness's residence abroad ; by which conduct of her said Royal Highness, great scandal and dishonour have been brought upon your Majesty's family and this kingdom. Therefore, to manifest our deep sense of such scandalous, disgraceful, and vicious conduct on the part of her said Majesty, by which she has violated the duty which she owed to your Majesty, and has rendered herself unworthy of the exalted rank and station of Queen Consort of this realm ; and to evince our just regard for the dignity of the crown, and the honour of this nation ; we, your Majesty's most dutiful and loyal subjects, the lords spiritual and temporal, and commons in parliament assembled, do humbly entreat your Majesty that it may be enacted ; and be it enacted by the King's most excellent Majesty, by and with the advice and consent of the lords spiritual, and temporal, and commons, in this present parliament assembled, and by the authority of the same, that her said Majesty, Caroline Amelia Elizabeth, from and after the passing of this act, shall be, and is hereby deprived of the title of Queen, and of all the prerogatives, rights, privileges, and exemptions, appertaining to her as Queen Consort of this realm ; and that her said Majesty shall, from and after the passing of this act, for ever be disabled and rendered incapable of using, exercising, and enjoying the same, or any of them ; and, moreover, that the marriage between his Majesty and the said Caroline Amelia Elizabeth be, and the same is hereby, from henceforth for ever, wholly dissolved, annulled, and made void, to all intents, instructions, and purposes whatsoever.

acquittal of her Majesty from all charge of criminality; and proclaimed their sense of her innocence by rejoicings and illuminations; to which the
Lord Mayor of London, two days old in office, gave
his young countenance.  Less riot and disturbance,
however, took place than might have been expected; but this was principally owing to the mo-
deration of their antagonists; who (whatever might
be their opinion of the guilt or innocence of the
Queen, and did not consider a happy escape in the
light of an honourable acquittal) were not disposed
to thwart the effect of a delusion which appeared in
many of its features to portray great generosity
and sympathy in supposed sufferings.  The Queen
returned thanks in the church of the hamlet of the
parish in which she resided, and a second time on
the 29th of November, at St. Paul's, escorted by
the voluntary association of her friends, and was
received with due civic honour at Temple Bar by
the young Lord Mayor of London.  Immense as
was the crowd assembled, judicious regulations,
prompted by the high responsibility which the
young chief magistrate took upon himself on the
occasion, prevented all confusion or accident.  The
King had previously adjourned both Houses of Parliament, without a Speech either from the Throne
or by his Commissioners.  The Speaker of the
House of Commons was hissed as he proceeded to
follow the Usher of the Black Rod to the House of
Peers; nor did he (there being no Royal Speech,
but merely a command to adjourn) again enter the
House.  This mode of separation appeared to the
nation very ungracious, and the disturbed reign of
Charles the First was ransacked for precedents.

But the King could hardly have avoided reference
to the proceedings of the Lords, and the more especially as the Commons had been adjourned, subject to a call of the House, and to meet only for
business, in the event of the Bill of Pains and Penalties coming down to them.  On the whole, then,
it appeared better to leave the ungracious mode of
adjournment for explanation till the next Sessions,
when men's minds might have acquired greater
power of discrimination, a quality very seldom in
request on popular occasions.

Thus far have I brought down (and, I trust, fairly
and dispassionately) the outline of this transaction,
as it 'occurred; and with this outline (which will
serve, as far as it goes, for both speculations, that
of preceding " the restoration of the Queen to all
her prerogatives and her court," and that of still
" restraining her from their enjoyment and exercise,") I go on, in my assumed character of an historian, to observe on the consequences of such opposite results.

First then, the historian may hereafter portray
the consequences of the Queen's restoration to her
prerogatives and court, in the following manner :—

" Whether the ministers mistook the popular clamour for the real feeling of the nation, or were unwilling to resign their seals of office ; or whether
they were intimidated by the examples of Spain,
Portugal, Naples, and Sicily, all at this time changing
their form of government, with more or less of
violence ; they advised the King to feel no impediment to the public reception of the Queen ; who,
having now the vantage ground, insisted upon the
insertion of her name in the Liturgy, and the ex-

punging from the Journals of the House of Lords, of
all the proceedings connected with her case, as preliminaries to such reception. The first was readily
accomplished; to procure the second, the Prime Minister and the Lord Chancellor (two of the most able
ministers and upright men of the day) having retired in disgust, every parliamentary finesse was resorted to ; and, at length, with great difficulty, and
amid violent debates and mutual recriminations, the
point was carried by a majority of one; there being
for the expunging 91; against it 90. Bonfires and
illuminations, strong beer and roasted beasts were,
for a whole week, the order of each successive day;
and in so great a joy, few troubled themselves to.
calculate upon futurity.

" But short was the delirium, and dreadful the
consequences.

" The King was laughed at, and pitied as a dupe,
the Queen was openly scorned, faction was triumphant, no competent administration could be
formed, and monarchy was on the wane. Those
who had opposed the Queen, not from vindictive
motives, but to justify the honour of the crown, felt
no longer an attachment to a bauble undignified with
the jewel of female chastity. The court was seldom
held; when held, neglected; official levees supplied
its place. The higher and respectable ranks of life
withdrew within their own pure and virtuous associations; and that intermixture of society which is
the true essence of a free government and a virtuous
court, no longer existed. Rich, vulgar plebeianism
took the lead in public. At foreign courts, the
younger branches of the nobility experienced great
difficulty of reception, not having chosen to be pre-

sented at their own; but when received at such
courts, it was considered as a matter of especial
favour conceded to their peculiar situation. Thus
was the national character subjected to sarcastic
insult; and thus was the lustre of the Crown of
England obscured; for whatever might have been
the personal faults of its sovereigns, as individuals
no more exempt from human frailty than the humblest of their subjects, but rather more exposed to
their commission; yet the Crown of England had
been entitled, for the last century at least, to the
homage due to unsullied and unquestionable honour.
Such were some of the effects of the Queen's restoration.

" The evil, however, stopped not here; scarcely
had sufficient time elapsed to justify inconsistency,
than the truth of the original charges against the
Queen was loudly revived by that very press which
had forced her innocence down the throats of the
nation. The levellers and jacobins, who lorded
over public opinion, professed to defend their
change, by the discovery of some new evidence
which (said they), had we known before, would
have produced a different opinion. Thus, the very
men who had so conspicuously advocated the cause
of the Queen; who had poured into her ears addresses of congratulatory exultation; who had
headed her processions, and maddened the populace
in her behalf; these very men, who had artfully
drawn her to the very precipice of rebellion against
her husband and King; these men, from whom she
could not but have expected eternal friendship and
never-ending adulation, finding her without influence
or patronage, became within six months, her scorn-

ful foes. These very men, who had provoked the measure of expunging the whole transaction from the Records of Parliament, and who would fain have burnt, in one huge pile, every paper and every Journal which contained the adulterous evidence, themselves were the first to direct the same press which had borne down all opposition against her, to insult, remind, and mortify her. The reign of terror had commenced. Such were the effects of this unaccountable delusion! Such were the consequences of excusing and exalting vice on the frail plea of political expediency!!

. . * . * . * . * . * . * . * . * . * . *

. I proceed now (still in the character of a prophetical historian) to mark the consequences which might follow the Queen's continued restriction from the public exercise of her prerogatives. ·

· "On Friday, the 10th of November, this bill of Pains and Penalties passed the third reading, when it was *suspended*, under the form of being read that day six months, and the Lords adjourned to the 23d, the day on which the Commons were to meet, to pursue (if necessary) this important affair. On the 23d both houses met, and were instantly prorogued by Commission, without any Royal Speech. This hasty procurement of separation gave great offence to the Queen's party; the House of Commons being summoned at the very moment when the Solicitor General of the Queen was about to communicate to the House, a *message* from her majesty.

· "It was evident that the King could have made no Speech to the Houses of Parliament, omitting all reference to the late momentous transaction. Had his Majesty said, that he regretted the issue of it, he would have committed himself personally, besides being guilty of the most unconstitutional error; *that of presuming to know a parliamentary proceeding in transitu*, for as yet the bill was not absolutely abandoned. Had his Majesty, on the other hand, made a Royal Communication, omitting, as he must necessarily have done, all reference to the bill in question; it might have been inferred, that future proceedings, in any shape, were abandoned; besides, the interval of adjournment was but for *two months*, and not *seven or eight*, as usually happens, the bill having driven the attendance of both houses to a most unusual lateness. It was deemed therefore most prudent, to encounter the accusation of an ungracious prorogation, for so short a period as two months, rather than be hurried into any hasty avowal. But had there been no such prudent ground for the proceeding, it was sufficiently justified by the subsequent conduct of the Queen; who assumed to herself an authoritative act of government, having prepared her official adviser with *a message* to be delivered to the Commons House of Parliament; a step which might well alarm the servants of the Crown, and indeed the whole nation; for it aimed, in the shape of a message, at a share of the Monarch's power, which the Queen Consort does not possess, *being only a subject* *. It is a radical error, for a Queen Consort to call the

---

* "The Queen hath also many exemptions and minute prerogatives. For instance, she pays no toll, nor is she liable to any amercement in any Court. But in general, unless where the law has expressly declared her exempted, *she is upon the same footing with other subjects;* and not his equal: in like manner as in the imperial law: ' *Augusta legibus soluta non est.*' " *Blackstone*, cap. 4. page 220.

King's people, *her people*, or for the King's subjects
to call themselves the subjects of the King's wife ; it
is a fault of misdirected loyalty.  We may call ourselves, by way of courtesy, the Queen's most dutiful
and affectionate *servants* ; but legally and constitutionally we can only be the dutiful and affectionate
*subjects* of ' the King.'

   " During the interval between the prorogation and
the meeting of both Houses, the Queen proceeded
to Saint Paul's, continued to receive Addresses of
Congratulation, and renewed unsuccessfully her application for a Royal Residence.  But the people
had now time to reflect, to compare, to decide.
John Bull is never long misled, and now discovered
in the case, premature judgments, audacious falsehoods, attempts at intimidation, and unproved assertions ; above all, a complete absence of all those promises of refutation, which had been so lavishly and
so loudly proclaimed ; and the non-performance of
which was the more extraordinary, inasmuch as the
persons who might, if they could, have given such
testimony, were already in England, and at the
Queen's command.

   " Upon the meeting of Parliament, the Commons
desired a conference with the Upper House, and
having thereat obtained leave to search the Journals
of the Peers, they became constitutionally acquainted with the late proceedings.  They found
therein a sentence of guilt pronounced, which (to
say the least of it,) was tantamount to the effect of a
true bill by a grand Jury.

   With this impression upon their minds, the Commons soon felt, that the question was now completely in their own hands.  The passing of the

Civil List bill was exactly the period, when their influence would become apparent: but they previously determined once more to address the Queen, by the same deputation, which had gone up on a former occasion. This address commenced by the firm and dignified assurance of the unshaken attachment of the Commons to the throne, the constitution, and the altar, and their determination to preserve them from every attempt of factious anarchy. It proceeded to express great regret for the past, and a hope that by conciliatory measures, all further personal legislation would become unnecessary. It assured the Queen that she might rely upon the continued care and attention of the commons; should her Majesty, by sacrificing some part of her high claims, be the means of restoring tranquillity to the public mind. It intimated that some points on which the Queen had heretofore insisted, might be the subject of future and favourable consideration; but that time was necessary to produce a change, which should justify their concession; and it finally dwelt upon the total impossibility, that even should the Queen gain the object of her wishes, it would (under existing circumstances) be attended to her with happiness or peace of mind."

"In answer to this address, the Queen made but few remarks; but principally dwelt on the utter impossibility of quitting a nation, who had treated her with such unbounded generosity, and espoused her cause with such enthusiastic ardour; and finally proposed, that three friends, appointed by herself, should confer with the deputation of the Commons, and agree upon a basis for a complete adjustment." To this it was objected, that the deputation had no such power of treating; but the difficulty was eventually got over, by their consenting to meet the friends of the Queen as individuals, and subsequently use their exertions to induce the House to adopt such a course of conduct, as might result from the conference; after two meetings it was eventually agreed, *that the Queen should return to Saint Omer's, and find herself placed in the same situation, as she would have been, had her legal advisers delivered to her Lord Liverpool's communication of April, previously to that made by Lord Hutchinson.*

" This departure was accomplished in so unexpected and in so judicious a manner, as far as the coast, that until the Queen was saluted by the guns at Dover, on her embarkation in a Royal Yacht, it was but just rumoured. The Queen was accompanied by two of her legal advisers, who were met by two others, on the part of the Crown. The departure of the Queen being made known to the Parliament, a most gracious vote of thanks was passed in both Houses; the Commons renewed their assurances, that they would pay all due attention to her Majesty's interests. The Civil List bill was expeditiously passed, and a Royal Message brought down to both Houses by Ministers, in which the King thanked the Commons for the generous provision made for the Queen's future comfort. Her Majesty's Attorney-General, also on his return from Saint Omer's, expressed the Queen's thanks, accompanied by her regret, on leaving England; but attributing the step she had taken to a thorough conviction that she could never hope to promote the happiness of the King; and therefore her next wish was to contribute to the tranquillity of the Kingdom.

He also adverted to the impaired health of the Queen; and the possibility, that she might not again return to the Country of her adoption.

Thus ended an affair which could not possibly have happened at a more critical moment, for whilst it was proceeding, military revolutions were following one another, through the South of Europe; and that the mania did not extend to England, can be attributed solely to the sound principles of the vast majority of the Kingdom; principles which were daily and hourly assailed, by a venal press; and by a system of the most pernicious, irritating, and base political libels, and personal caricatures. But on this occasion the Constitution floated above, the passions of the people, safe and unhurt as her Navy rides on the turbulent billow, which dashes against Albion's rocky sides.

" Amidst these internal commotions, it pleased Providence to bless the kingdom with a most abundant harvest; so that the winter passed over with much less proportionate privations to the humbler classes of the community. Indeed it may be rather said, that such heavenly bounty,. administered by charitable hands and feeling hearts, rendered distress unknown. The following Spring found the whole nation, except certain disappointed speculating politicians, in good humour; and the moment was most judiciously seized to administer to the whole United Kingdom, the oath of allegiance. The ceremony was accompanied by every mark of joy and magnificence; it was indeed a national banquet. ON THE TUESDAY, the magistracy took the oaths in the county towns. ON THE THURSDAY, the population took them in every city, town, and village, in the following manner: Lists had been previously signed, and to each list was prefixed a power by deputation to some person therein named, to take the oath publicly for as many persons as were contained in such list; and by its form, all persons therein subscribed were held to be bound by the oath of allegiance, recited also in such instrument. ON.THE SATURDAY, the Army took the oaths, by regiments, squadrons, and detachments, at their individual quarters; and the Navy by fifties, after the form of the general population. This splendid and national rejoicing seemed to annihilate every spark of disaffection.

"In the Autumn, the coronation of his Majesty took place, and the first Act of Grace performed immediately after, was, ' *to expunge from the Journals of the Lords all the accusatory proceedings connected with the Queen of England.*'

"This last step was considered an act of oblivion, and a compliment to the crown." The Queen remained abroad during her life, in conformity with her word of honour."

\*  \*  \*  \*  \*  \*  \*  \*

And now, my faithful subjects, and well-beloved fellow-countrymen, your King takes his leave, recommending the alternative to your attention, and praying to the God and Father of us all, that he will so direct your steps, as to lead both to your temporal and your eternal happiness; praying also that the crown of his forefathers may not be dishonoured on his head, but that mutual love and confidence may render happy both King and People.

My excellent subjects, may God Almighty bless you——Farewell.

GEORGE.

## APOLOGY.

Should the readers of the preceding Letter, have entertained doubt of its authenticity, the Author and Publisher beg leave to satisfy those doubts, by stating, " That it is one of those literary fictions, which can only be justified by a good cause." Indeed they feel so high a degree of veneration for the sacred name of " The King," which, (speaking constitutionally), " Never dies ;" and so anxious a desire, that nothing directly or indirectly should appear to trifle with its use ; that, previous to their determination to publish, they submitted the following Question to the opinion of a most eminent Counsel ; which question at once proclaimed the author's motive, and the answer subjoined, contains (we trust) our justification.

## THE QUESTION.

Suppose A. writes a letter entitled " A Letter from the King," and having written and published such Letter, states, in a Postscript annexed that such title was adopted to excite curiosity, and extend its political utility ; and that such Letter was neither directly or indirectly written by the King ; will such acknowledgment take the assumption of the King's name, out of any and every statute of *premunire?*

## OPINION.

I am clearly of opinion, that such acknowledgment as is proposed, will take the Letter out of the Statutes of *premunire.* The term and the offence *premunire*, are now merely sounds : but I decidedly think, that the Letter proposed, written in the tone and spirit which is suggested, will not render the writer responsible to *any penalty whatever.*
*Temple, December 4th,* 1820.

Thus far as to the legality of the act ; but should our most gracious Sovereign chance to see a Publication thus imputed to him ; we beg leave most respectfully to deprecate any sentiment of personal dissatisfaction, which he may feel at our bold assumption; assuring The King, that he does not possess among his people, more disinterestedly loyal subjects, than the Author and Publisher of this Letter.

## POSTSCRIPT TO THE FOURTH EDITION.

The Amanuensis of this Letter has heard many observations made on this bold attempt of imputing to his Sovereign the sentiments contained therein. He has taken some pains to discover the feelings of the parties raising objections to it ; as well as of those who consider it a *timely* boldness. He has the satisfaction of finding, that those are most violent against it, who are unable to answer its argument; and those talk insidiously of this abuse of the King's name, who are great admirers and encouragers of caricatures on his person. In some cases, there is also (even among those who think with himself) a scrupulous feeling as to the mode in which his thoughts are conveyed. Such feeling is conscientious and honourable, but on this occasion, *over nice.* The mode adopted was the only one, capable of producing a dispassionate review of the King's case; it has succeeded beyond the most sanguine expectation, as four editions within a Fortnight testify.

## POSTSCRIPT TO THE FIFTH EDITION.

From the moment of deciding upon the bold step of publishing this Letter, it was also determined never to notice any reply, attack, or abuse of it. We are most happy to know, that it has convinced many of the most violent advocates of the Royal Tenant of Brandenburg House, of their injustice towards their noble-minded Sovereign.

### THE END.

LONDON:
PRINTED BY WILLIAM CLOWES,
Northumberland-court.

1, *St. James's Street.*

# WILLIAM SAMS,

*HAS LATELY PUBLISHED THE FOLLOWING WORKS:*

A LETTER to the HOUSE OF COMMONS, on the Subject of the Litany, and the Allowance to the Queen. By the Author of the King's Letter to his People, 8vo. 2s.

THE CITY ADDRESS EXPOSED, in a Letter to the Right Honourable the Lord Mayor. By the same, 8vo. 2s.

OCCASIONAL REMARKS on Mr. TENNYSON'S *Observations on the Proceedings against the Queen.* By WESLEY DOYLE, ESQ., 8vo. 1s. 6d.

A FULL EXPLANATION of the Law respecting Prayers for the Queen and the Royal Family. By PROFESSOR CHRISTIAN.

TO-DAY, a POETICAL SATIRE. By ERNESTUS. Second Edition, 8vo.

A COMPLETE TREATISE on ROUGE et NOIR; in which is developed a Practical Method of successfully playing the Game. 2s. 6d.

THE VIEW and other POEMS, by CHANDOS LEIGH. fcap. 8vo. 5s.

ERATO'S LAYS, or LYRICAL POEMS, on Amatory, Satirical, and Incidental subjects, being the Ideas of a Fortnight. Post 8vo. 5s. bds.

OPOLEYTA, or a TALE of IND. A Poem in Four Cantos. By BERTIE AMBROSE, ESQ. Second Edition, 8vo. 6s.

JAMES THE THIRD, King of Scotland, a Tragedy, in Five Acts, 8vo. 3s. 6d.

CATHERINE de MEDICIS, a Tragedy. By the Author of James the Third, 8vo. 3s. 6d.

FASHIONABLE INTRIGUE, or the MATCH MADE UP, A Comedy, in five Acts. By the Same, 8vo.

TOO LATE FOR DINNER, a Farce, in Two Acts. By RICHARD JONES, Esq. of the Theatre Royal Covent Garden, 8vo. 2s.

THE YOUTHFUL DAYS of FREDERICK the GREAT, a Melo-drama in Two Acts, by WILLIAM ABBOTT, ESQ. of the Theatre Royal Covent Garden, 8vo. 2s.

A CATALOGUE of Two Hundred Popular Works for Instruction and Amusement, may be had of W. SAMS, GRATIS.

An ADDRESS to the IMPERIAL PARLIAMENT upon the PRACTICAL MEANS of gradually ABOLISHING the POOR LAWS, and Educating the POOR systematically; illustrated by an Account of the Colonies of Fredericksoord in Holland, and of the Common Mountain in the South of Ireland. By W. HERBERT SAUNDERS, ESQ.

# IN THE PRESS,

A LETTER on our AGRICULTURAL DISTRESSES, their Causes and Remedies; accompanied with Tables and Copper-Plate Charts, shewing and comparing the Prices of Wheat, Bread and Labour, from 1550 to 1821; addressed to the Lords and Commons. By WILLIAM PLAYFAIR. 5*s.*

*On the 31st of May next will be published,*

(TO BE CONTINUED MONTHLY,)

No. I. of BRITISH HONOUR and HUMANITY DIS-PLAYED, and RANK and PROPERTY DEFENDED, as being beneficial to all classes of Society; containing an account of those Noblemen and Gentlemen who are particularly attentive to the welfare and prosperity of their Tenants, Dependants, and the Poor. Edited by WILLIAM PLAYFAIR.

Printing for William Sams, 1, St. James's Street.

Not to have felt, with regard to myself, chagrin at this decision
of your Majesty, would have argued great insensibility to the obligations of decorum; not to have dropped a tear in the face of that
beloved child, *whose future sorrows were then but too easily to be foreseen*, would have marked me as unworthy of the name of mother ;
but, not to have submitted to it without repining would have indicated
a consciousness of demerit, or a want of those feelings which belong
to affronted and insulted female honour.

The " tranquil and comfortable society" tendered to me by your
Majesty, formed, in my mind, but a poor compensation for the grief
occasioned by considering the wound given to public morals in the
fatal example *produced by the indulgence of your Majesty's inclinations ;*
more especially when I contemplated the disappointment of the nation, who had so munificently provided for our union, who had fondly
cherished such pleasing hopes of happiness arising from that union,
and who had hailed it with such affectionate and rapturous joy.

But, alas! even tranquillity and comfort were too much for me to
enjoy. *From the very threshold of your Majesty's mansion* the mother
of your child was pursued by spies, conspirators, and traitors, employed, encouraged, and rewarded to lay snares for the feet; and to
plot against the reputation and life, of her whom your Majesty had
so recently and so solemnly vowed to honour, to love, and to cherish.

In withdrawing from the embraces of my parents, in giving my
hand to the son of George the Third and the heir-apparent to the
British throne, nothing less than a voice from Heaven would have
made me fear injustice or wrong of any kind. What, then, was my
astonishment, at finding that treasons against me had been carried on
and matured, perjuries against me had been methodized and embodied, a secret tribunal had been held, a trial of my actions had taken
place, and a decision had been made upon those actions, without
my having been informed of the nature of the charge, or of the names
of the witnesses! and what words can express the feelings excited
by the fact, that this proceeding was founded on a request made,
*and on evidence furnished, by order of the father of my child,* and my
natural as well as legal guardian and protector!

Notwithstanding, however, the unprecedented conduct of that tribunal—conduct which has since undergone, even in Parliament, se-

vere and unanswered animadversions, and *which has been also censured in minutes of the Privy Council*—notwithstanding the *secrecy* of the proceedings of this tribunal—notwithstanding the strong temptation to the giving of false evidence against me before it—notwithstanding that there was *no opportunity afforded me* of rebutting that evidence —notwithstanding all these circumstances, so decidedly favourable to my enemies—even this secret tribunal acquitted me of all CRIME, *and thereby pronounced my principal accusers to have been guilty of the grossest perjury.* But it was now (after the trial was over) discovered, that the nature of the tribunal was such as to render false swearing before it *not legally criminal!* And thus, *at the suggestion and request of your Majesty*, had been created, to take cognizance of and try my conduct, a tribunal competent to administer oaths, competent to examine witnesses on oath, competent to try, competent to acquit or condemn, and competent, moreover, *to screen those who had sworn falsely against me* from suffering the pains and penalties which the law awards to wilful and corrupt perjury. Great as my indignation naturally must have been at this shameful evasion of law and justice, that indignation was lost *in pity for him who could lower his princely plumes to the dust by giving his countenance and favour to the most conspicuous of those abandoned and notorious perjurers.*

Still there was one whose upright mind nothing could warp, in whose breast injustice never found a place, whose hand was always ready to raise the unfortunate, and to rescue the oppressed. While that good and gracious father and Sovereign remained in the exercise of his Royal functions, his unoffending daughter-in-law had nothing to fear. As long as the protecting hand of your late ever-beloved and ever-lamented father was held over me, I was safe. But the melancholy event which deprived the nation of the active exertions of its virtuous King, bereft me of friend and protector, and of all hope of future tranquillity and safety. To calumniate your innocent wife was now *the shortest road to Royal favour;* and to betray her was to lay *the sure foundation of boundless riches and titles of honour.* Before claims like these, talent, virtue, long services, your own personal friendships, your Royal engagements, promises, and pledges, written as well as verbal, melted into air. *Your Cabinet was founded on this basis.* You took to your councils men, of whose persons, as well as

whose principles, you had invariably expressed the strongest dislike.
The interest of the nation, and even your own feelings, in all other
respects, were sacrificed to the gratification of your desire to aggravate my sufferings, and ensure my humiliation. You took to your
councils and your bosom men whom you hated, whose abandonment
of, and whose readiness to sacrifice me were their only merits, and
whose power has been exercised in a manner, and has been attended
with consequences, worthy of its origin. From this unprincipled
and unnatural union have sprung the manifold evils which this nation
has now to endure, *and which present a mass of misery and of degradation, accompanied with acts of tyranny, and cruelty*, rather than
have seen which inflicted on his industrious, faithful, and brave people, your royal father would have perished at the head of that people.
When to calumniate, revile, and betray me, became the sure path to
honour and riches, it would have been strange indeed if calumniators, revilers, and traitors had not abounded. *Your Court became
much less a scene of polished manners and refined intercourse than of
low intrigue and scurrility.* Spies, Bacchanalian tale-bearers, and
foul conspirators, swarmed in those places which had before been
the resort of sobriety, virtue, and honour. To enumerate all the various privations and mortifications which I had to endure—all the insults that were wantonly heaped upon me, from the day of your elevation to the Regency to that of my departure for the Continent it
would be to describe every species of personal offence that can be
offered to, and every pain short of bodily violence that can be inflicted on, any human being. Bereft of parent, brother, and father-
in-law, and my husband for my deadliest foe; seeing those who
have promised me support bought by rewards to be amongst my enemies; restrained from accusing my foes in the face of the world, *out
of regard for the character of the father of my child*, and from a desire to prevent her happiness from being disturbed; shunned from
motives of selfishness by those who were my natural associates; living
in obscurity, while I ought to have been the centre of all that was
splendid; thus humbled; I had one consolation left—the love of my
dear and only child. To permit me to enjoy this was too great an
indulgence. To see my daughter; to fold her in my arms; to mingle
my tears with hers; to receive her cheering caresses, and to hear

from her lips assurances of never-ceasing love ;—thus to be comforted, consoled, upheld, and blessed, was too much to be allowed me. Even on the slave-mart the cries of "Oh! my mother, my mother! Oh! my child, my child!" have prevented a separation of the victims of avarice. *But your advisers, more inhuman than the slave dealers, remorselessly tore the mother from the child.* '

Thus bereft of the society of my child, or reduced to the necessity of imbittering her life by struggles to preserve that society, I resolved on *a temporary absence*, in the hope that time might restore me to her in happier days. Those days, alas! were never to come. To mothers—and those mothers who have been suddenly bereft of the best and most affectionate and only daughters—it belongs to estimate my sufferings and my wrongs. Such mothers will judge of my affliction upon hearing of the death of my child, and upon my calling to recollection the last look, the last words, and all the affecting circumstances of our separation. Such mothers will see the depth of my sorrows. Every being, with a heart of humanity in its bosom, will drop a tear in sympathy with me. And will not the world, then, learn with indignation, that this event, calculated to soften the hardest heart, was the signal for new conspiracies, and indefatigable efforts for the destruction of this afflicted mother? *Your Majesty had torn my child from me; you had deprived me of the power of being at hand to succour her ; you had taken from me the possibility of hearing of her last prayers for her mother; you saw me bereft; forlorn, and broken-hearted; and this was the moment you chose for redoubling your persecutions.*

Let the world pass its judgment on the constituting of a commission, in a foreign country, consisting of inquisitors, spies and informers, to discover, collect, and arrange matters of accusation against your wife, without any complaint having been communicated to her: let the world judge of the employment of ambassadors in such a business, and of the enlisting of foreign courts in the enterprise : but on the measures which have been adopted to give final effect to these preliminary proceedings it is for me to speak ; it is for me to remonstrate with your Majesty; it is for me to protest ; it is for me to apprize you of my determination.

I have always demanded a *fair trial*. This is what I now demand, and this is refused me. Instead of a fair trial, I am to be subjected *to a sentence by the Parliament*, passed in the shape of *a law*. Against this I protest, and upon the following grounds:

The injustice of refusing me a clear and distinct charge, of refusing me the names of the witnesses, of refusing me the names of the places where the alleged acts have been committed ; these are sufficiently flagrant and revolting; but it is against the *constitution of the Court itself* that I particularly object, and that I most solemnly protest.

Whatever may be the precedents as to Bills of Pains and Penalties, none of them, *except those relating to the Queen of Henry the Eighth*, can apply here; for here your Majesty is the *plaintiff*. Here it is intended by the Bill to do you what you deem *good*, and to do *me great harm*. You are, therefore, a party, and the only complaining party.

You have made your complaint to the House of Lords. You have conveyed to this House written documents sealed up. A secret committee of the House have examined these documents. They have reported that there are grounds of proceeding; and then the House, merely upon that report, have brought forward a Bill containing the most outrageous slanders on me, and sentencing me to divorce and degradation.

The injustice of putting forth this Bill to the world for six weeks before it is even proposed to afford me an opportunity of contradicting its allegations is too manifest not to have shocked the nation; and, indeed, the proceedings even thus far are such as *to convince every one that no justice is intended me*. But if none of these proceedings, if none of these clear indications of a determination to do me wrong had taken place, I should see, *in the constitution of the House of Lords itself*, a certainty that I could expect *no justice at its hands.—*

Your Majesty's Ministers have *advised* this prosecution; they are responsible for the advice they give; they are liable to *punishment* if they fail to make good their charges; and not only are they part of my *judges*, but it is they who have *brought in the Bill;* and it is too notorious that they have *always a majority* in the House ; so that, without any other, here is ample proof that the House will decide in favour of the Bill, and, of course, against me.

But further, there are reasons for your Ministers having a majority in this case, and which reasons do not apply to common cases. Your Majesty is *the plaintiff:* to you it belongs to appoint and to elevate peers. Many of the present Peers have been raised to that dignity by yourself, and almost the whole *can be,* at your will and pleasure, further elevated. The far greater part of the Peers hold, by them-selves and their families, offices, pensions, and other emoluments, solely at the will and pleasure of your Majesty, and these, of course your Majesty *can take away whenever you please.* There are more than *four-fifths* of the Peers in this situation, and there are many of them who might thus be deprived of the far better part of their in-comes.—

If, contrary to all expectation, there should be found, in some Peers, likely to amount to a majority, a disposition to reject the Bill, *some of these Peers may be ordered away to their ships, regiments, go-vernments, and other duties;* and, which is an equally alarming power, *new Peers may be created for the purpose,* and give their vote in the decision. That your Majesty's Ministers would advise these measures, if found necessary to render their prosecution successful, *there can be very little doubt ;* seeing that they have hitherto stopped at nothing, however unjust or odious.

To regard *such a body as a Court of Justice* would be to calum-niate that sacred name ; and for me to suppress an expression of my opinion on the subject would be tacitly to lend myself to my own destruction, as well as to an imposition upon the nation and the world.

*In the House of Commons I can discover no better grounds of security.* The power of your Majesty's Ministers is the same in both Houses; and your Majesty is well acquainted with the fact, that a majority of this House is composed of persons placed in it by the Peers and by your Majesty's Treasury.

It really gives me pain to state these things to your Majesty; and, if it gives your Majesty pain, I beg that it may be observed, and re-membered, that the statement has been forced from me. I must either protest against this mode of trial, or, by tacitly consenting to it, suffer my honour to be sacrificed. No innocence can secure the accused, if the Judges and Jurors be chosen by the accuser; and if I were tacitly to submit to a tribunal of this description, I should be instrumental to my own dishonour.

On these grounds I protest against this species of trial. I demand a trial in a Court where the Jurors are taken impartially *from amongst the people*, and where the proceedings are *open and fair*. Such a trial I court, and to no other will I willingly submit. If your Majesty perseveres in the present proceeding, I shall, even in the Houses of Parliament, face my accusers; *but I shall regard any decision they may make against me as not in the smallest degree reflecting on my honour;* and I will not, *except compelled by actual force*, submit to any sentence which shall not be pronounced by a *Court of Justice.*

I have now frankly laid before your Majesty a statement of my wrongs, *and a declaration of my views and intentions.* You have cast upon me every slur to which the female character is liable. Instead of loving, honouring, and cherishing me, agreeable to your solemn vow, you have pursued me with hatred and scorn, and with all the means of destruction. You wrested from me my child, and with her my only comfort and consolation. You sent me sorrowing through the world, and even in my sorrows pursued me with unrelenting persecution. *Having left me nothing but my innocence*, you would now, by a mockery of justice, deprive me even of the reputation of possessing that. The poisoned bowl and the poinard are means more manly than perjured witnesses and partial tribunals; and they are less cruel, inasmuch as life is less valuable than honour. If my life would have satisfied your Majesty, you should have had it on the sole condition of giving me a place in the same tomb with my child: but, since you would send me dishonoured to the grave, *I will resist the attempt with all the means that it shall please God to give me* .

          (Signed)                    CAROLINE, R.

*Brandenburgh-house, Aug.* 7, 1820.

---

\* The above letter from her Majesty, which is dated August 7th, was sent by the Queen's messenger early in the morning of the 8th to the Cottage at

# No. II.

*Letter of Lord Liverpool to the Princess of Wales, dated the 28th of July, 1814.*

" Lord Liverpool has had the honour to receive the Letter of her Royal Highness. Having communicated it to the Prince Regent, he has ordered him to inform her Royal Highness that he can have no objection to the intentions of her Royal Highness to effect the design which she announces to the Prince Regent, of returning to her native country, to visit her brother the Duke of Brunswick ; assuring her, that the Prince Regent will never throw any obstacle in the way of her present or future intentions as to the place where she may wish to reside.

" The Prince Regent leaves her Royal Highness at liberty to exercise her own discretion as to her abode in this country or on the continent, as it may be convenient to her.

" Lord Liverpool is also commanded, on the part of the Prince Regent, to inform her Royal Highness, that he will not throw any obstacles in the way of the arrangements of her Royal Highness, whatever they may be, respecting the House at Blackheath, which

---

Windsor, accompanied with a note to Sir Benjamin Bloomfield, *written by the Queen*, desiring Sir Benjamin to deliver it immediately to the King. Sir Benjamin Bloomfield being then absent, the letter was received by Sir William Keppel, who forwarded it immediately to Sir Benjamin Bloomfield, at Carlton-house, who returned it in the afternoon of the 8th to the Queen, informing her Majesty that he had received the King's commands, and general instructions, that any communications that might be made should pass through the channel of his Majesty's Government. The Queen immediately despatched a messenger with the letter to Lord Liverpool, desiring his Lordship to lay it before his Majesty. Lord Liverpool was at Combe-wood. He returned an answer that he would lose no time in laying it before the King. On the 11th, no reply having been received, *the Queen wrote again* to Lord Liverpool, requesting information whether any further communication would be made on the subject of the letter to his Majesty. Lord Liverpool wrote the same day from Combe-wood, that he had not received the King's commands to make any communication to her Majesty in consequence of her letter.—*Times* Newspaper.

belonged to the late Duchess of Brunswick, or the rest of the private property of her Royal Highness. But that, for reasons rather too long to explain, the Prince Regent will not permit the Princess Charlotte to be ranger of Greenwich Park, or to occupy any of the houses at Blackheath, which her Royal Highness has hitherto occupied.

" Lord Liverpool has also been enjoined, on the part of the Prince Regent, before he closes the letter which he has the honour to send to her Royal Highness, to tell her, in relation to the two articles which her Royal Highness has put in her letter concerning the rupture of the marriage of the Princess Charlotte with the hereditary Prince of Orange, as well as to the reason for which the allied Sovereigns did not, previously to their departure from England, pay their visit to her Royal Highness ; that, as to the first article, Lord Liverpool is commanded by the Prince Regent to inform her Royal Highness, that the Prince Regent is not persuaded that the private considerations of the circumstances in which the Princess is placed, can have been an obstacle to the marriage of the Princess Charlotte. As to the second article, Lord Liverpool is also enjoined, on the part of the Prince Regent, to signify to her Royal Highness, that the Prince Regent never opposed himself to the allied Sovereigns making a visit to her Royal Highness during their stay in London.

" Lord Liverpool has the honour to be, with all esteem and the highest consideration.

" P.S. The Prince Regent can make no difficulties on the subject of the directions which the Princess has the intention of giving as to the house at Blackheath ; neither will the Prince Regent oppose her Royal Highness's retaining the apartments in the palace of Kensington, in the same manner as she possessed them while in London, for the convenience of herself and suite."

THE END.

LONDON :
PRINTED BY WILLIAM CLOWES,
Northumberland-court.

# LETTER

#### TO

# THE KING.

THE

# REPLY

OF

# THE PEOPLE

TO THE

# LETTER

FROM

# THE KING.

London:

PRINTED FOR F. C. & J. RIVINGTON,

NO. 62, ST. PAUL'S CHURCH-YARD,

AND NO. 3, WATERLOO-PLACE, PALL-MALL;

AND TO BE HAD OF ALL BOOKSELLERS IN TOWN AND COUNTRY.

[*Price Two Shillings.*]

1821.

Printed by R. Gilbert, St. John's Square, London.

# A
# SECOND LETTER
##### FROM
# THE KING
## TO HIS PEOPLE.

*Carlton-Palace, May* 1821.

To all our loving Subjects and Countrymen,

WHEN I last addressed myself to my people, during that factitious irritation of the public mind, which has since been pacified by gradual reflection, I anticipated a procedure of weakness and of wickedness, which would rarely have been paralleled; nor do I find it needful, on my present consideration of past events, to qualify that prediction, however apparently reproachful and severe. So much has been essayed by factious malignity on the one hand, and hazarded by capricious petulance on the other, that violence, inconsistency, and dissension, have sensibly impressed the character of a party, which attempted, under the seducing banners of affected patriotism, to annihilate the moral principles of my realms, to degrade the solemnities of our religion, and to infuse into the bosom of our common country, the most unworthy and pernicious inferences of shallow and constructive casuistry. We have lived in times of the most important political events, both domestic and external. In a period, to

B

ourselves, so pre-eminently illustrated by the profound and energetic advocacy of conflicting principles, I have gravely attended to the anomalous
excrescences of the character of my nation ; I have
observed that questions of the highest moral or political importance, have uniformly raised a corre-
spondent zeal and sensibility in the generous spirit
of my people ; nor have I neglected to remark, that
after the dignified concession of *liberal* opponents,
there were always some unworthy murmurers below, who, having been useless, unnoticed, and un-
acknowledged in the real contest, would solicit notoriety by irregularities equally extravagant and
ignorant, contemplating a sequel of disturbance, so
congenial to the wishes of an abject spirit and limited capacity. I have remarked that in such aber-
rations of the public mind, the common sense peculiar to the lower order of my countrymen and people,
has gradually assumed its due precedence of excited
prejudice; that it has tranquilly approached the
source of its deception ; that it has canvassed and
detected the seducing fallacy ; that it has expiated
error by candid acknowledgment ; and that it
spurned the unmanly, and I will add, the un-British
insinuation (too anxiously employed by the insidious
and uncandid of all nations,) that honest recantation
and apostacy are the same. From such observations
of my countr men and subjects, I derived a conviction (even in the meridian fervour of their distem-
pered and abused sensibilities,) that time would
induce dispassionate consideration, and that reflection would reclaim those, whom the fantastic pre-

tensions of the factious had misled. My experience of the character of my subjects assured me of this result; and the king of a great nation may congratulate himself, that in such a calculation, he has found himself informed of the minds and bosoms of his people.

At such a season it cannot misbecome the monarch to address the subjects of his realm; the informality of such a condescension is readily explained by the novelty of the occasion; the Laws and all the Powers of the Constitution will protect the *King;* and surely while presumption and fatuity assail him as an *individual,* denied the choice of usual vindication, the high-minded men and females of his dominion will attend with impartiality, at least, to the arguments and reasons of the *man.* The feelings of our nature are the same, but *I* am denied the reparation which belongs to the meanest of my people; to offer insult to the monarch with security, is in the power of *all* my subjects, I am certain in the will of very *few:* to sustain it, is the hard condition of the King; and though thus placed by exaltation beyond the power of his own protection, he will, at all events, dispel the cloud of falsity and folly, which would veil the truth of past and present circumstances.

I feel with pleasure, that it is the essence of a people, so proverbially and virtually free as those of England, to adopt a vigorous opposition to every apparent encroachment on our constitutional immunities; and that one of the vulgar, though not useless, prejudices of the people, is that vigilant suspicion of

the powerful, which has always conclusively demonstrated, in its result, the virtue of the suspected
party, or the equable operation of our laws on the
delinquencies of the noble as well as of the mean.
Let not therefore prejudice impose on greatness one
further incumbrance than the weight of royalty, and
deny the King alone the impartiality of justice, that
birth-right co-extensive with his realms.

I can by no means more effectually exhibit to my
people the purpose of a faction, and the indiscretion
of the Queen, than by adverting to the Letter of
her Majesty, bearing date the 7th of August, 1820.
The ostentatious boldness of the assertions comprehended in that violent production, was an evidence
of desperation, which in the onset was publicly
mistaken (indeed it was intended so to be) as the
firm assurance of conscious purity. Few of my
subjects, who recur to the co-operating circumstances of that time, can fail to discover in each
insidious observation, a mockery of noble sentiment
and patriotic sympathy, directed at the agitated feeling of some portion of the people of the metropolis and
the suffering classes of the distant districts of the
kingdom. The freedom of the press had been endangered by treasonous and irreligious tracts, which
tended equally to subvert the altar and the throne.
The fallacious reasonings of impious men were
industriously scattered through the realm, and the
work of demoralization was profanely urged, as the
best preparatory measure, to ensure the dissolution
of civil order, and the introduction of an anarchy
destructive both of Church and State. The dignity

of the bench invaded; the sacredness of our religion ridiculed; the equal operations of the law
ascribed to the adjudication of dependent judges;
the implication of individuals of vulgar popularity
and incendiary principles; were either present to
the observation, or fresh on the remembrance, of the
public. Two men, ever wildly in quest of popular
clamour, and enamoured of illegal declamation,
affecting a spirit of independence, and evolving
sentiments of turbulent assurance, had made themselves, in the opinion of a misguided class, the objects of the public interest.

By the common artifice of palpable aggression,
at which no Government of strength or virtue could
connive, they affected to undergo a grievous martyrdom to conscience: and having duly calculated
that chastisement would wait on outrage, they
endeavoured to conciliate the voices of the disaffected, and to claim the suffrage of confiding folly,
which thought itself defended, at the very time that
it was manifested and cajoled. A band of dissolute
and idle men, the unfortunate disciples of a doctrine long disseminated by the captious discontent
of some Utopian theorists, had so far fostered the
pernicious tenets of their apostles, that the perpetration of a crime, almost unknown to England,
was digested, by which the ministers of my government were to have fallen by the hands of desperate
assassins. Need I expatiate on the expedients
which were requisite, at this alarming crisis, to arrest the progress of immorality, and disarm the evil
dispositions of those abandoned and deluded men,

who were addressing, without scheme or rational pretext, their public and their secret homilies, to every ignorant, desperate, unhappy, and credulous outcast of society? Need I labour to refute those trite and superficial prelections of false economy and radical amendment, which originated in perverse contradiction to practical benefit, and have now become the ridicule, the very laughing-stock, of almost all their earlier proselytes? To deter the preceptors of this methodized insanity from the propagation of *their* vicious theories, to repress the vehement excitement which the spell words of *radicalism, innovation,* and *reform* had created ; and to preserve from their contagious principles, the sane and salutary parts of my dominion, the prompt application of the powers of government was effectually and charitably adopted. Provisional acts of legislature, of consummate wisdom and indispensable expediency, adapted to the pressing exigency of the times, and frustrating, by their comprehensive and restrictive tendency, the evasive ambiguity of evil-doers, received from the supporters of all *other* innovation, a character of obloquy and hyperbolical denunciation. The *preservation* of the Constitution of the kingdom was denounced as a *violation* of the Constitution, and the reviling jargon of radical alarmists, was employed to stimulate the thoughtless and unwary to acts of outrage on their patient and resolute preservers. The vacillating conduct of the Queen at St. Omers ; the mysterious deportment of her Majesty's legal adviser; and, ultimately, the abrupt determination of her

Majesty to come to England, ensured the effectuation
of a preconcerted plan ; she arrived on the shores
of the kingdom, apparently deserted ; placed in a
condition imposing to the public mind : the effect
was obvious, and the evident unkindness of her reception was to attract interest and compassion to the
digested scenes of the ensuing tragi-comedy.

Ignorant as the people were of what had been
the usage of the Queen abroad, and what had been
her usage of the King, and of the honour of this
pre-eminent and glorious country, the hasty pre-
dilection of the people was one of those magnani-
mous demonstrations, which, however erroneous at
the time, exhibited, in all its force and bearing,
the chivalrous enthusiasm of a great and valiant
country. And happy, my countrymen and people, too happy, had your King been, could that
generous sentiment have been justifiably continued
to the Queen on the test of scrutiny ; by that
impartial public inquiry, to which the Ministers of
your Sovereign were, officially and dutifully, bounden
to cite the first illustrious, female personage of his
dominion !! I will not descend to notice the varied,
the incessant, the tumultuary methods used to pre-
possess the public sentiment, altogether uninformed,
in favour of the Queen ; to confer on me a myriad
of disgraceful calumnies essentially opposed to all
the peculiar moral feelings of our country, and to
effect a presumptuous anticipation of the finding of
the House of Lords ; machinations of the most illiberal and *ex-parte* character, generative , alike of
prejudice and misinformation ; in brief, a perfi-

dious tissue of enormous falsities and unimportant truths, from which uncandid sophisters might hope, with trivial facts to warrant monstrous falsehoods, and to establish specious premises for argumentative equivocation.

Having thus noticed the condition of the kingdom immediately antecedent to the arrival of the Queen in England, I shall proceed to lay before you an inquisitive analysis of the style and motives of the Letter of her Majesty. It may be in the remembrance of the people, that I communicated no instructions to the Earl of Liverpool, " *to make any communication to her Majesty in consequence of her Letter.*" To that Letter and its tenor, I by no means condescend, at present, TO REPLY : but, the dispassionate examination of its contents, may afford to the community at large, sufficient evidence of the intention and the hopes conceived by her Majesty, to effect, by the temporary embarrassments of my Government, an issue which it was utterly impossible to attain, except by the deliberation and decisive wisdom of my Parliament. For, even in those momentous times of popular vicissitude, which carry their alternate influence to a monarch's heart, I will rule by conscience, for the good and glory of the realm. I would still consult the reverence due to the example of my royal parents ; I will imitate, if I am unable to attain, the excellence of their remembered virtues ; duty, even at the sacrifice of popular affection, should govern me unshaken in the prosecution of my people's welfare ; and, though faction should achieve delusions painful

to the Monarch, the solemn funćtions of my royal
office would lead me to persist, and even rather
fall, with honour, from my station, than disgrace the
British throne by one unkingly compromise of
selfish fear.

I said that I would analyze the Letter of the
Queen. The evidence adduced before the House
of Lords is fresh in the remembrance of my people.
Let me, therefore, urge specifically on their notice,
the pompous inchoation of that specimen of chaste
effrontery. The King is charged with " *an unpar-
ralleled and unprovoked persecution, which, during a series
of years has been carried on against the Queen, under the
name and authority of his Majesty.*" This unhesitating calumny, so uniform with every other part of
that disingenuous and immodest document, is aptly
stated as the harbinger of her embodied injuries
The Queen proceeds: " It is not without a great
sacrifice of private feeling that I now, even in the
way of remonstrance, bring myself to address this
letter to your Majesty. But, bearing in mind that
royalty rests on the basis of public good; that to
this paramount consideration all others ought
to submit; and, *aware of the consequences that
may result from the present unconstitutional, illegal,
and hitherto unheard-of proceeding;* with a mind
thus impressed, I cannot refrain from laying my
grievous wrongs once more before your Majesty,
in the hope that the justice which your Majesty
may, by evil-minded counsellors, be still disposed
to refuse to the claims of a *dutiful, faithful, and
injured wife,* you may be induced to yield to con-

siderations connected with the honour and dignity of your crown, the *stability* of your throne, *the tranquillity of your dominions, the happiness and safety of your just and loyal people, whose generous hearts revolt at oppression and cruelty, and especially when perpetrated by a perversion and a mockery of the laws.*"

I might, in the first instance, assume the language of an illustrious and long-departed nobleman, and answer to the imputation of " *persecution under my royal authority and name,*" by saying, that the charge is too ridiculous to be refuted, and deserves only to be mentioned that it may be despised. On reference to recent facts, it hardly will be pleaded, by even the compassionate admirers of the Queen, that any considerable portion of private feeling was likely to be sacrificed by her Majesty, either in her address to me, or to ' *my* ' people. The uncontroverted moral axiom, which her Majesty admits in deference to our enlightened polity, but ill appears before the turbid and prophetic menaces of a conditional revolt ; before " *the consequences that may result from the present unconstitutional, illegal, and hitherto unheard-of proceedings,*" the " *considerations connected with the stability of my throne, and the tranquillity of my dominions ;*" and the " *oppression and cruelty perpetrated by a perversion and a mockery of the laws.*" England, Scotland, and Ireland, have heard or seen the solemn, the deliberate considerations of the aristocracy ; I therefore leave to them the painful commentary, which their King will not apply, to the inflated " claims of duty, faith, and injury."—But that the nation may duly estimate the latent objects in the contemplation of the Queen

and her pragmatic faction, I will call the steady observation of every separating and combining intellect
to the likely influence of their inflammatory innu-
endoes. I can with difficulty think that any party in
my realm could hope to awe, by such extended
threats, the *Monarch, or the servants of his Government ;* but I can readily suppose, that such allure-
ments were extended to the reposing class of baffled
*democrats,* whom exemplary penalties had recently
diverted from pernicious plans; and that they affected to evoke from the retirement of contrite depravity some few restless spirits of a questionable
penitence. That the Queen should have imputed
to the Lords an intended perpetration of oppressive cruelty, by the " perversion and mockery
of law," asserts an estimation of their House
which I shall not descend to controvert. Can
it be incumbent on the King to establish a defence for his Imperial Parliament, or Commons
House; or rather would it be compatible with decency to meet an accusation on the legislative body
of the Constitution, in refutation of such errant,
such captious impeachments ; of impeachments so
associated, and so preferred ? Having thus ex-
plored the leading paragraph of her Majesty's Letter,
I would ask the mass of all the people, who have
read or heard the evidence produced before the
House of Lords ; yes, even those whose sceptical
refinements would exonerate the Queen from the
specific guilt alleged against her ; What is the pur-
port, what the object, of that bold defiance and
casuistical lamentation pervading the inception of
her Letter to her husband ? I would adjure him by

his conscience, by his love of country, by his hope in God, and thus adjured myself, I could most solemnly declare, the object was vindictive, not conciliatory, subversive of, and not conducive to, the tranquillity and safety of my people.

The ensuing paragraph of the Letter of the Queen is of a more occult and enigmatical description. It would, however, very pointedly insinuate that the tenacious feminality of her Majesty forbears to bring to light the real causes of our domestic separation. That sentiments of delicacy should guide the conduct of the Queen, is doubtless creditable to her Majesty; but that concealment is desirable to me or to my deportment, on that unfortunate occasion, I distinctly and positively, to all my people, do deny. I solicit from the Queen no favours of suppression, and should conceive her Majesty the dupe of an unseasonable remission, if from delicacy to *my* demeanour, she neglected the paramount duty of establishing the propriety of her *own*. The figurative charge of " *driving a wife from beneath my roof with an infant in her arms*," is rather too imaginary to enter into the prosaic gravity of serious accusation, and will be scarcely entertained by those indulgent beings of condolence, whose affected sympathy has recently so much enlarged the teeming objects of her Majesty's complaints. That my separation from her Majesty " was a sentence pronounced on her without a cause assigned," might have been delicately requited on her part, by the inviolable, the honourable taciturnity which has governed me. I shall not indulge in any scrutiny of sentiment, however elegantly turned or pathetically associated ; but the disturbance of sanctified remembrances so dear to a paternal breast, might well, on such a point as this, be spared ; in that departed object of my own and of the nation's love, their hope and mine is lost for ever; it was the will of God, and I have bowed in resignation. If the memory of early virtue can atone for the desolation of the best of earthly hopes, such melancholy consolations are reserved for the internal communion of an afflicted spirit ; and, may it henceforth please Heaven, while the unhappy father is providing for the peace of his beloved people, that at least the recesses of affectionate retirement may not be profaned, by 'factious intercessions in the name of one so beloved while living, and now so revered in immortality !

The three succeeding paragraphs convey a body of invective, which, compounded of generalities, and derived from the incoherent and conflicting rumours to which loquacity, exaggeration and misconception give a being, are only to be met on contradictions equally diffuse and comprehensive. It would be needless to point out to a discerning people, that particularity of accusation is, to the accuser and the accused, the certain and most candid method of conviction or acquittal ; specific charges must be specifically met ; but imputations of so general and vague a nature as those collectively set forth against me by her Majesty, arise from the evident anxiety of a molested spirit, willing to embody accusations too insubstantial to be met, and too untrue to be refuted, and which the prejudice, or the prepos-

session, of an agitated public may possibly assume
as the mitigated statement of a person who would
hint her injuries, but not declare their name.

The seventh paragraph of the Letter I discuss, is
one of those surprising instances of froward pertinacy, which so perniciously revolts against discretion, and discovers the capricious vanity of an
assumed but an untenable position. My people
know the noble Lords who constituted in the year
1806, the Inquiry into the conduct of the, then,
Princess of Wales. Those names alone will vindicate the purity of that Inquiry, But can it be
possible to a personage of such illustrious descent,
of such exalted rank, and such immaculate pretensions as the Queen, to *triumph* in the issue of
that inquiry, and to dwell with an exulting smile
on the *qualified* result of its proceedings. What
lady in the realm would dare to glory in such
imperfect exculpations of suspected error, or vaunt
the issue of a scrutiny, which, however leniently
and delicately set, implies at least the dangerous
approaches of impurity. " This evasion of the law
and justice," such is the phrase her Majesty employs, might well have lowered the plumes of any
prince, to whom the hard alternative was left, of
vitally invading all the dearest interests of Britain,
or of bearing under mute conviction, the audacious
obloquy, with which presumption, shamelessness,
and base ingratitude requited his forbearance. Her
Majesty proceeds to eulogize my royal father, of
blessed and immortal memory. In such praises, I
and all my people heartily and fervently concur.

Nor could I, the successor to his vacant throne,
have more devoutly proved my reverence for the
best of kings, than by deferring to that wise selection of ministerial power, which had, under the principles of his irresoluble government, maintained the
glory of his kingdom against the world in arms, and
ultimately led the larger states of Europe to the demolition of that despotic tyranny, which had subdued and desolated the greater part of civilized
mankind. In the sacrifice of private friendship
to the paternal love and duty which I bear my people, have I not foregone the dearest happiness of
social life, denied to none but me? Could I have
been insensible, in the critical conjuncture of the
affairs of Europe, when, owing to the calamity of
my blessed father, I was called to the discharge of
his suspended functions, of the superior efficacy of
a practical administration to one of untried theory?
And how could I have compensated any national
calamity, which might have been produced by a capricious hazard of reputed but unascertained capacity? The character of my administration will
never justify the rash invective of her Majesty;
more than ever, at the present crisis, do, I see the
need of vigilant, determined, and experienced
statesmen. The generous spirit of my people can
uplift the powerful supremacy of Britain against the
leagued attempts of *foreign* enemies; but there are
latent foes *within*, who would disseminate despondency and discontent. The condition of the people must be gradually ameliorated; the establishment of universal satisfaction cannot be magically

attained, and during the imposing subtleties of the
misleading spirits of my kingdom, I feel assured
that I am best discharging the high duties of my
state, by employing the perceptive, energetic and
patriotic qualities, with which it has pleased the
Almighty, in these times of domestic trouble, to
endue the members of my administration. That her
Majesty should institute a comparison between myself and my revered progenitor, (omitting the inde-
licacy of its personality,) is, to say the least of
it, the consummation of disrespect. The Queen
has not neglected to avail herself of observations
incidental to that comparison, in uniformity with
those, which she has profusely dispersed throughout
her Letter, and which are exclusively directed at the
perturbation of the public mind; a disposition far from
dignity and grace, and disobedient to the precepts
which should emanate from, surely, any *ghostly guide*.

The paragraph succeeding is ushered in by libel-
ling, *en masse*, the nobles and component members
of my court. In the performance of this " female
and respectful office," her Majesty appears as indifferent to style as matter; or, perhaps, has studi-
ously adapted to the task the language which con-
formed more critically to its achievement. The
mortifications and privations of her Majesty, adverted
to herein, are, as usual, *generally* and not *specifically*
stated. Let the people refer to the Letter of Lord
Liverpool, bearing date the 28th of June, 1814 *.
The restriction imposed on the communion of the
Queen and Princess Charlotte, arose from the ap-

* Vide Appendix No. II.

parent propriety, which even ordinary parents must
discover in such control; but viewing the Princess
Charlotte as the heiress-apparent to the Crown, that
restriction seemed prescribed by reasons far more
cogent, than the need of domestic dispositions;
for reasons, which the King must conscientiously
have felt himself officially bounden to respect, in
honour and duty to that nation which, with the
permission of God, his daughter would have one
day ruled. To revive the discussion of that important point, the King would have to recall considerations of no peculiar satisfaction to the Queen;
the act was neither personal nor wanton, but purely
of a moral and political essence; the King cannot
abandon the incontrovertible authorities which acquiesced in its incumbent rectitude; and every retrospective consideration assures him of the indispensable necessity and justice of that provision.

Far be it from my hope to deny the Queen to
have possessed the natural affection of so dear and
close a tie; but let the people ask, when my beloved daughter was no more, should that calamity,
so mutual to the Queen and to myself, have shed a
gloom of chastening sorrow on our hearts and
minds; should that calamity have wooed us to the
solitude of pious resignation, and have bowed us
down in sorrow at so deep a visitation of afflicting
Providence? The Queen asserts, " this was the
moment chosen 'to redouble her persecutions."
When then, how circumstanced and how surrounded was the Queen, to be by any means, by

very stratagem itself, obnoxious to those persecutions?

The appointment of a Commission in a foreign country, the next in order of the points of grievance treated by the Queen, attempts to court the aid of one of those peculiar prejudices of the English people, arising more from name than evil virtuality of character. The object of inquiry was abroad; and if inquiry were deemed requisite, how were it possible to discharge, sincerely and effectually, for the purpose of elucidating doubt, the duties prescribed to that Commission, but by affording it the local opportunities of ocular knowledge, or immediate information? The odium of the names of *spy, inquisitor, and informer,* may, perhaps, remain; but innocence can never shrink from observation, question, or intelligence; would it not be preferable to any lady of tenacious purity, to be absolved by the inquisitive researches of such commissions, than to be aspersed by rumours in every European court; *if* innocent, the firm assertion of her innocence would instantly and justly have waited on its ascertainment; and have thereby baffled the malicious slanders of her false accusers. On the four succeeding paragraphs, the proceedings of the Lords sufficiently reflect.

That the Queen should have adopted so unjustifiable, so indiscreet, a bearing of contempt for the noble, the profound, the valiant aristocracy of my dominions, surpassed the estimation I myself had made of the erratic tendencies of her misguided

confidence. Whatever may be modern in that
august assembly, can adduce. the recent honour
of the Episcopacy, of the Jurisprudence, of the
Arms, or of the Civil Virtues of our Country; whatever is more ancient there, had sprung from
glories more remote, and is still actuated by the
emulation of ancestral fame and the continuance of
lineal honour. The science of the Law, Religion,
Virtue, Valour, all that is estimable both in Church
and State, had ennobled the members of the tribunal of the Queen; and, on a tribunal so composed, whose respective attributes were to protect
the accused,—to pardon the offender,—to judge in-
dulgently,—to feel for feminality an enthusiastic
chivalry,—how could the Queen have ventured to
impress a character of such contemptuous disre-
pute?

To those illiberal and sceptic cavillers, who ask
the demonstration of what, by human powers, is not
demonstrable, I feel that I address in vain such
observations. The truly virtuous will presume
in others the high-minded principles by which
themselves are swayed; it may belong to the
phlegmatic to misgive the generous propensities of
better natures; but can it for a moment bo supposed, by my unbiassed subjects, that in a court
of such a composition, so vigilantly scrutinised by
every party in the nation, the monarch or his ministers could dare to tamper for unholy purposes,
for the corruption of judicial virtue?

The remainder of the Letter of the Queen apparently designs the intimidation of my ministers, and

anticipates the stratagems by which the sentence
of the Lords would be secured. To those anti-
cipations the reply is brief, no "peers were ordered
to their ships, regiments, governments, or other
duties." Nor were "new peers created for the
purpose of giving their votes on the occasion." The
conclusion of the letter of the Queen, declares "I
*will resist the attempt with all the means that it shall
please God to give me."*

From this consecutive analysis of the Letter of
the Queen, it must appear to every candid mind
how much her Majesty was influenced by the
passive temperance attributed to her proceedings.
Beyond the positive assurance of her innocence,
and her protestation against the forms adopted in
the House of Lords, the introduction of extraneous
and inflammatory matter, promulged too at a time
of various co-operating causes of public ferment,
will demonstrate the ulterior objects of that ob-
lique appeal to popular enthusiasm. While this and
other specious pretexts were extended to the turbulent and discontented, the Government assumed,
in all its various departments, an attitude of most
preventive vigour; a measure of discreet anticipation,
which incurred alternately the reprobation and
irrision of the party of the Queen. The sequel has
at least evinced, that such a disposition *did* preserve
the peace, which the negligence of that arrangement might have possibly exposed to violation;
the hand of chastisement was thereby gratefully
relieved from its incumbent function; and the
fruitful cause of further turgid declamation being

totally removed, by provisions of attested prudence, it became a topic of affected triumph to the advocates of insecurity, that the powers of Government were uselessly arrayed to preserve subordination in the people. It would be a prostitution of the powers of reason, to meet by serious argument the multiform perplexities of hypothetical pretension, which still attempt to urge the preference of speculative possibilities to the real welfare so substantially secured by measures of precautionary foresight.

I have stated on a previous occasion, that I had hoped the absence of the Queen, of whose proceedings I was still informed, would have enabled me to confine her conduct within the pale of a domestic, personal calamity; to secure to myself and to the nation the advantage of tranquillity, the ample convenience of the Queen was regularly, I may add, munificently afforded; I rationally thought the Queen would see the obvious interest of her secession from the artful solicitations to political significance; and, that to have declined the opportunity of national disturbance, (which, as we have recently perceived, is at the influence of all notorious political offenders, however high or low), would indeed have manifested, on one occasion, that interest in the national benefit which her Majesty affects to feel so profoundly upon all. I entertained the more ardently this hope as I readily foresaw, that without benefit to the cause which had expressly brought her Majesty to my dominions, she would be assumed as an imposing instrument, in the hands

of a miscalculating party ; I foresaw with equal
ease, that though that party from political speculations would oppose by declamation the presumed
injustice offered to her Majesty, it would never
testify the cordial sincerity of its avowals by
having paid to her, as the first lady of the realm,
the deferential honours due to her from females
of its noble or its gentle families. I was well
aware both from personal and political knowledge
of many of the eminent and virtuous constituents
of the party opposed to my administration, that a
fastidious feeling of aristocracy, not inferior to the
sentiments attendant on my own exalted dignity,
would withhold from her Majesty the advantageous
countenance of that irreproachable and distinguished
reputation, by which alone the former rank of her
Majesty in the female precedence of the land,
could be restored. I was well aware that from
such scrupulous tenacity her Majesty was certain to
derive the tacit and condign humiliation of the very
party to which she directed her expectations of
unqualified support ; and, at the same time I apprehended that after so severe a frustration of her
hopes, an overruling sentiment of pity for *pretended zeal,* or the feelings of abandonment, would
ridiculously situate her Majesty within a group,
whose preposterous vanity exults at the hale association of a high-born lady. I predicted the attempts of that distinct and narrow-minded party, to
impart a political distemper to the mental constitution of the Queen, and for reasons probably
innate and inseparable from my high situation and

birth, I felt a mixture of regret and indignation that
the radical profession, the laughing-stock of England, should, by any means, have enlisted in its
ranks a female of the blood and house of Brunswick.

Having precisely prognosticated the only rank
which the Queen could possibly attain in the political condition of the country, I was naturally soli-
citous, as a man, that by her absence she should
thoroughly abstain from further experiments of impossible elevation ; that she should, at least, be
free from the absurd excesses of a party without a
head, an object, or a plan ; and that in the casual,
but still inevitable, errors of a confounding anarchy,
the name of royalty might not have been adduced in
palliation of its vulgar outrage. The insinuation of
such princely and such salutary hopes was followed,
need I now remark it? by conduct directly contradictory to those desires. The Queen has made
herself, on all occasions, the instrument of *one* party,
and on events of condescension will become so, if
occasion may require her, to *another.* If, therefore,
in the political controversies which arise between
the parties of the state, the incidental asperities of
opposition bear occasionally on the Queen, be it
not reproached to me or to my ministers that her
simplicity required advice, and that she entered un-
admonished on that hard-fought field. The *efforts*
of the party of her majesty have been displayed in
the most frugal dispositions of local and temporal
œconomy. In all those clamorous processions,
which vaunted the cordial participation of the *ladies*
of my kingdom, was it difficult to distinguish the

prevailing radicalism of their self-important congre-
gators? Was the object of those addresses simply
limited to the assurances of loyalty, and the conviction of the purity of the Queen, or did the various
banners of those holiday-parades set forth forgotten
grievance to the people? Time and place were
equally consulted for their appositeness to commotion. Constitutional apophthegms, expressed
with a sententious conciseness, and mutual to
the two high opposite parties of the Parliament
of my dominions, were craftily assumed on en-
signs, as if developing the exclusive principles of
those unwary revellers; wherever the imperfect
comprehension of some inept deviser had placed
some ambiguity of phrase or symbol on their up-
lifted trophies, the wandering imagination was at
liberty to interpret the confused idea into some
enormous injury of suffering virtue, to imply a grievance of intolerable oppression, or some inflated ex-
hortation to a violation of civil order.

I address myself to that part of my people whose
generous minds have been deluded, but which now
are undeceived; I appeal to those, who have returned from the extravagance of aberration, and
whose calm deliberations are divided between shame
and wonder at the imposing spell of such bombastic
mummery; not to that irreclaimable and hardened
class to whom the idle habits of precarious life have
rendered life indifferent, and reputation an incumbrance; for whom religion has no solace, and loyalty
no honour, and whom confusion blesses, since me-
ditation must accuse: I appeal to those men in the

middle and the humbler ranks of life, to whom domestic peace is dear; to whom industry is existence; who have the charities of life to cherish, and who would rear the offspring of their affection, through the honest paths of youth, to virtuous manhood; to those who love their King and Country, and adore their God.

I will recall my people to the character of those processions; I will unfold the motives of those weak and wicked men, from whom they took their origin, and display to the ingenuous minds of all my subjects the hidden hopes of their tumultuary confusion. Beneath the fair pretexts of liberty, it was the purpose of those evil agents to excite licentiousness; from bold discussion, treason; from harmless merriment, extravagant disorder. Excited by erroneous statements, deluded by bombastic declamation, and heedlessly allured by phrases of a national enchantment, a procession is undertaken and performed; the badges and devices of the fallacious cause beget extrinsic and provoke internal spirit; the most inapplicable yet powerful accession of loyal music elevates the spirit, and seems to consecrate the purpose of a mad enthusiasm: in the reciprocity of social glee, the pledge of friendship and fidelity is passed; the limit of propriety is broken, every sentiment exaggerated, and every bolder feeling fretted into action: thus stimulated, the procession has performed its object, and is dissolved: the *sequel* manifests the craft and cowardice of the projector; parties disperse, discuss, inveigh, project associations, and invade the law; while

the retiring knave who planned the mischief, pleads,
like Æsop's trumpeter, his innocence of blood-shed,
after having wound the trumpet that inspired the
carnage.

In this unexaggerated presentment of those
processions, which so disordered the affairs and
morals of the metropolis, there may be a homely in-
tuition of the monarch, surprising to the people.
But to me who am circumstantially coerced to
duties of perpetual elevation, it is one of the fondest
relaxations to descend, and ascertain the social virtues of the humblest of my people. Long may the
harmless enjoyments peculiar to my country continue to delight the leisure hour of industry, and
give the poor man ease!!—but far be from the honest
pleasures of that untroubled season the seducing
poisoner of homely peace and civil duty, who
would operate by visionary fears and hopes on virtuous contentment, and enlist unwilling dupes to
swell the foolery of mean importance!!

Having commented on the Letter and party situation of the Queen, I will proceed to animadvert on
some of the objections that have been specified to
the production of the facts which have transpired to
the nation, and on expedients which were offered
in substitution of the publicity which they acquired.

It has been said, that the disclosures necessarily made to establish the case against the Queen,
were infinitely more prejudicial to the public morals, and the dignity of the Royal Family, than a
tacit submission to the dishonourable reports of

Europe, and the connivance at "levities" committed in a foreign country. Not only does this
assumption carry with it an advocacy of the most
overstrained and jesuitical misprision, but at the
same time a somewhat summary and indelicate disposition of the feelings of the King. So capable
is selfish casuistry of attempting the support of argument on principles essentially at variance with
human nature, and with common sense! In respect to the suffering morals of the country, what
details have transpired on the trial of the Queen,
unknown to the ordinary investigations of our courts
on common prosecutions for criminal connexion?
Are the columns of any journal, which has in-
veighed against the public examination of the
Queen and her companions, expurgated of such
details, or does there ever happen a trial for adultery, however flagrant its attending circumstances,
which is shorn of any of the most impressive and
distinctive marks of its impurity? I am anxious to
be understood, that I by no means advocate the introduction of such details into the public journals, but
it is obviously requisite that I should shew, in times
of such illiberal distinction, that the promulgation of
the trial of the Queen was no enormous novelty;
and that a practice beyond the memory of any
living might have existed unreproved, had not the
carping spirit of invidious censure been tempted to
transform the following of common custom into a
dangerous innovation of immoral character. That
opposite dexterity of argument should have been
manifest on such a point, no question can be held,

in a country of such acute political disputation; it has formed on one hand the theme of exuberant dissertation, and the moral evils to be derived from it, have been treated in elaborate superlatives; but is it not to be admired, that the almost fretful vigilance of those protectors of the national morality should have never been elicited, until the common privilege of every subject of the realm appeared too precious an advantage for the *insulted honour of the crown?*

I next approach the supposition that the censure of the conduct of the Queen has tended to abate the general reverence for royalty and the national devotion to my family. The arguments, I should think, would here be found of inverted application. They apply in general to every family of decent reputation or of modest fame. And it will rest with present candour, and the impartial judgment of posterity, to say, whether the decisive amputation from my royal stock, of an infected branch, had not more attested and preserved the ancestral purity of the lineage of the House of Brunswick; than had I sought from falsity of honour to hide the blot of my pollution, by the concealment of a repugnant and insincere embrace. It has been additionally said, with an important air, that such disclosures would exhibit to the vulgar mind the purity of passion that pervades the royal and ignoble being; have the common people, in this age of sensible discussion and inquisitive research, remained yet ignorant of so physical a truth? But "*honour is the law of kings,*" it *should* be that of queens,

Its violation bears the penalty of national contempt.
The law must take its course.

It has been gravely stated, (but whether for the
purpose of argument or insult to myself, may well
be asked), that had her Majesty's obliquities abroad
been suffered to escape without a scrutiny at home,
oblivion might at length have cast its veil across
them; and thereby have secured the moral honour
of my country. How apt is prejudice with all its
nice contrivance to display the incongruities arising
from a forced accommodation! To what a violent
and contradictory plurality of sentiments is he reduced; who attempts to fix on others a conviction
not his own. But such is the character of those
implacable and witless prejudices. In the first
place, such a doctrine goes immediately to this, that
semblance, not reality, substantiates moral purity;
that character relies on kind anticipation of the future, and not on the impressive knowledge of the past.
In speculation it presumes that habitual passions,
of the grossest indocility, will shape themselves, immediately to staid and modest quietude; it justifies
the monarch, conscious of the Queen's unworthi-
ness, to place impurity collusively upon the throne,
and, by the debasement of his royal countenance,
betray the female honour of the realm to base associations; for himself, it braves the ignominious con-
tumely of his people and his conscience, and bids him
meanly brook the shame he should renounce. Such
is the doctrine framed to rear the moral honour of
the country! evasion and ineptitude, conceit, deception, treachery, and shame, to rule *expediently* the

conduct of the King, and prove him worthy of his
people's confidence and love.

To what endurance of contempt, to what irreparable acts of fraud, to what inexpiable weak-
nesses, it suits the partisans of folly and depravity
to recommend the King! How studious would they
be by hypocritical pretexts, to cloke the certain
shame which they project. How effective to the
hopes of discontent would be the situation of the
King, if royalty should stoop to compromise. How
eager would such seductive monitors not be, to
reach the hour of their apostacy; then how intense
would be the triumph of exulting treachery to find
its precepts had prevailed, and having speciously
beguiled the Monarch into labyrinths of darkness,
to have thrown malicious light upon his error, and
have cried—" Behold the King!!"

I am anxious by such elucidations of the objects
of a faction to exhibit to my people the shallow fallacy of their political professions, and to strip the
borrowed ornaments of patriotism from an association directed at the disturbance of my government,
and the indecent effrontery to my person. I address myself to my people in that spirit of liberality
and candour which should exist between the sovereign and the subject. I would ask, if, in the
choice of measures preservative of female purity, I
have espoused that which is more dignified and
certain; if I have adopted that which seems to
justify the explicit motive of a King? I am aware of
the relaxed condition of continental morals, and yet
may possibly concede that positive obliquity is sepa-

rable from indelicate appearance; but to ingraft the
wanton license of our foreign neighbours on the more
decent institutions of our insular propriety, would
leave but an imperceptible distinction between the
high-bred females of the land and those unhappy ministers to dissolute propensity, who disclaim the
chaste repression of severe and elegant reserve.
And wherefore, in a land asserting its ascendency
of female charms and virtue above the nations of
the universe, should I submit to the bare possibility of pernicious innovation, a stayed condition of
domestic excellence incapable of beneficial alteration? To all the advocates of such fantastic hazard
I would steadfastly oppose the power intrusted to
my hands; and hypocritical, indeed, would be the
vows of my devotion to the memory of my departed parents, if in opposition to the national conviction and my own, I placed on their vacated throne
a queen of even questionable virtue. With what
demeaned opinion of the kingdom's glory would
the nobility and gentry of my land abroad attend to
the invidious insolence of foreign flippancy; what
private feuds must have ensued between the animated British and the offending wits of other countries, if, having found a blot of such impurity in
our internal sufferance, they slurred with a contemptuous smile the female pride of the " unrivalled
nation."

From solicitations tending to impair the moral
maxims of my kingdom, another hope of more pro-
fane anxiety engrossed the zealous entertainment
of the same perplexing party. Aided by the spa-

cious opportunity of partial apothegms and garbled
doctrines taken from our holy law, the Queen's obsequious advocates embodied every insubstantial
argument that acquiesced with prejudice, and
seemed allowable by premises unfairly (need I say,
unblushingly?) assumed. Their pretensions placed
on the one hand the persuasive claims of charity
and the imperious obligations of forgiveness; on the
other categorical injunctions of religion were united
with sophisticated dogmas of a false morality.
Their object was professedly directed by the
humble spirit of the Christian law: yet under such
avowals, the explanation that her Majesty was
prayed for in the collective mention of the Royal
Family did not suffice, and the plausible humility,
originating that desire, concluded in the pompous
vanity of asking an express distinction. The subject underwent discussion; all that could be said in
dexterous confusion on the one side, was met by
separate analysis and explanation on the other.
Authorities incontrovertibly produced, to testify the
paramount and exclusive competency of the King
to direct and arrange occasional alterations in the
Liturgy, were met by oppositions of a nature too
informal and absurd to need a serious reprehension.
It was even hinted, that the competency of the
King should be submitted to the trial of a court of
common law; a wild anomaly in thought, so wil-
fully absurd, or so extremely ignorant, that it may
be indifferently assigned to impudence or to insanity.

On this, as on all other points connected with

her Majesty's pretensions, I had formed deliberately an irresoluble mind. To combat such insidious enterprise demands a vigilance and resolution which shall not be found deficient in the King. The religion of the land, the hope and solace of my people, shall receive the zealous aid of George the Fourth, as long as piety can claim one sanctuary in the realm; and whether our sacred institutions be menaced by the open insolence of impious atheists, or the more insidious introduction of plausible obscenities, the sovereign power shall be employed in its defence. With such determinations on my part, will my people be enabled to support that "only prerogative which we see to have been given always to all godly princes in Holy Scriptures by God himself; that is, that they should rule all estates and degrees committed to their charge by God, whether they be ecclesiastical or temporal, and restrain with the civil sword the stubborn and evil-doers*."

The last point to which I desire to draw the consideration of my people, is The Dutiful and Loyal Address and Petition of the Lord Mayor, Aldermen, and Commons of the City of London, presented to me on Saturday, the 9th day of December, 1820.

The reply returned to that Address embodied comprehensively the opinions, which such an effort *of loyalty and duty* was naturally calculated to produce. To have controverted at the time the various positions in that incendiary production, would have shorn the dignity of the crown, and

* Thirty-seventh Article of Religion.

D.

have borne the semblance of my suspicion of those
profound and loyal sentiments of my people, which
are to me, (as they must be to every sovereign of
a free and powerful people), the essential earnests
of the inseparable welfare of himself and of his sub
jects. I foresaw, too, that to have expatiated
more at large on the pernicious tendency of its
suggestions would have been an eager anticipation
of those results, to which the virtuous sense of the
community was certain to conduct it. I determined
on that occasion to afford an unrestrained procedure to the violence expressed in the address, and
to discover by a just persistence in the digested
measures of my government, the truth or affecta-
tion of the predicted consequence, of steady per
severance in the only policy conducive to the benefit
and honour of my dominions. The course, I deemed
it requisite to hold, occasioned none whatever of
those foreboded evils ; not even riot was begotten
by the coarse and angry terms which seemed so
appositely used to such a generation. But, even
had the public peace received a temporary shock,
the cause and object could in nowise have evaded my
distinction ; during the immediate influence of facts
misrepresented, no one would surely take precipitate
effects as the matured results of a prospective policy ; a more extended intellect would withhold its
judgment till observation had embraced a perfect
view, and comprehensively surveyed the gradual
progress of opinions. The burst of those indocile
soothsayers, who predicted anarchy and uproar, has
passed away and left behind it ease, tranquillity,

and peace; while their Address remains an earnest record of their impotence and hopes.

That I may in some measure display the evil tendencies of that Address, I will review concisely the objects it appears to meditate. It will be no doubt remarkable, that it derives, in the ·diversity of its complaints and in the incongruity of their association, its model from the Letter of the Queen. It seems, too, destined to co-operate with any of the languid feelings still remaining from the dissemination of that pompous missive. It was caused by no exclusive unity of accident, but suited its pretended fears and mawkish admonitions to the *time;* incorporating long-exhausted subjects of complaint, to which the parliamentary solicitude was then remediately applied; enlarging the distresses of the country; extenuating all the hopes and means and active measures for its gradual and sure relief; deducing the inevitable effects of war from the misstated prodigality of peace; ascribing causes to effects, effects to causes; constituting, in the aggre-·· gate, a common-place of overrated grievance and factitious misery and peril, accusatory of the King and of his Government, and disembogued at a conjuncture of mad excitement, to invigorate the short-lived violence of infuriated zealots, and abandoned mal-contents.

The graceful exordium of that *dutiful and loyal address,* affects a deep solicitude for the unprincipled injustice of my Government, of their oppression of the freedom and neglect of the prosperity of the nation, and for the dishonour and insecurity, which menace and surround the monarch's throne. On the subject of the war, and the observations of retrenchment, I regret that any body of my people should subject itself so openly to contradiction, which no feeling but politeness, could here forbid me to employ.

The ensuing paragraph presents a moody mixture of complaint against the *rigid application* of the law ; it at the same time states the acts of treason, which solicited the *prompt repression* of the law. On the very advocacy of a *lenient administration* of the standing law, the occasion of *expedient additions* to the legal powers is recorded. This surely was to recommend a kind indemnity for peril ; to abandon a defence when danger threatened. That sentiments of such distinct repugnance to the common understanding of mankind, should hold a place in any record of the wishes of a British people, might easily absolve me from inquiry into its ulterior views ; of such a senseless paradox it is enough to say, that either they who framed it must have calculated on the folly of him whom it addressed, or great must have been the folly of those by whom it was addressed to him. In the same style of ratiocinative accuracy, the *unwillingness* to remedy a state of commercial and agricultural distress, is equally ascribed to " *indifference, and the want of political skill.*"

Of the ensuing echo of the Letter of the Queen, in which indeed the unsupported dicta of the declamatory sophisms attendant on the subject are re-echoed, I have previously disposed in an

antecedent observation. The same ingenious and
respectful sentiment of duty having guided both
suggestions, they are equally deserving of a requital
of their reverent sincerity.

There is a malicious pleasure irrepressibly evinced
in violent assumptions of untruth, which gives de-
cisively a genuine character to the cause in which it
is excited. The liberal and open contest of brave
antagonists can have no shameful issue, and the
palm is often *yielded* as gracefully and honourably
as it is *won*. It is not so in those insidious ambus-
cades of mean and sweltering animosity ; the detected skulker may receive, but never can requite
forgiveness ; and the conscious meanness of himself
subsides into an impatient rancour of discomfited
malignity, indifferent to further shame, and still in
quest of further opportunities of evil. I have noticed former efforts of constructive error ; let me
notice this. It is stated, " a corrupt inducement was
offered to her Majesty to remain abroad in the state
of alleged criminality falsely ascribed to her." In
the first place, when was an inducement offered to
her Majesty " to stay abroad in a state of alleged
criminality ?" This was not so ; something is assumed,
and then associated ; it is not the association of the
King ; the interpolation is the City's ; and, considering
the literal propriety, so strictly advocated by some of
the advisers of the Address, it might have occurred to
their tenacious scrupulosity, that even for the rounding
of a period, meaning foreign to the King and Government, should not have been obtruded on his
sanction, at the wicked *hazard* of belief. The Ad-

dress secures the condemnation of its object in the
brief citation from the House of Commons. It was
the hope of Parliament to find the Queen above the
question of her guilt; the crown beyond the implication of impurity; the nation beyond the contagion
of immoral practice; but no—at the very first blush
of the business, the scrutiny was " *disappointing to
the hopes of Parliament, derogatory from the dignity of
the Crown, and injurious to the best interests of the Empire.*" Let then such an evidence, the optional
induction of the framers of that Address, dispose of
the invective raised on their pretended mis-concep-
tion. The defence of truth solicits not the aid of
stratagem; and accusations, justly founded, need
not sophistry to effect conviction. To fabricate new
points of imputation, where others have been
frail, is but to cover a disgraceful rout, by the effrontery of gross fool-hardiness; and scurrilous reproach is the last remaining pleasure of a party,
whose angry malice has survived its power to
wound.

Such, my people, is the essence of an Address
presented to your King; professing duty and humility, and personal affection. Under such a desig-
nation of its qualities, what candid person can forbear
to feel the mockery of forms, which *so* prescribe in
letter what the spirit *so* essentially evades. That
the King of England should affect indifference to the
pre-eminent, and virtuous, and valuable body of the
citizens of London, would be a supposition willingly
engendered by those seditious foes to harmony and
social union, who mistake their packed and petty

faction, for the wide, the loyal, the unbiassed
commonalty. That the King should look with
contempt on the successful treachery, by which
the tampering artifice of few, prevails above the
honest virtue of the many, is due to the excluded
candour and proverbial patriotism of those who *virtually do* compose the city; a portion of my people,
to which I turn with confidence and undiminished
love. Nor can I quit the subject of my present
strictures without expressions of regret, that in the
distant parts of my dominion, a supposition may
prevail, that the aggressive acts of a misled *epitome*
attest the feelings of that great and populous city,
in which merit, wealth, and liberality, are emulated
by encouragement, loyalty, and patriotism.

The circumstances attending the presentation of
that Address, did not affect to mitigate the coarseness
of its import; yet, but for the ensuing letter, which
appears to me too long for the subject it discussess,
I should have consigned to oblivion, a trespass of
uncouth intrusion, sufficiently excused by the ignorance that alone could have encouraged its presumption.

" *To the King's most Excellent Majesty.*

" Sire,

" There are occasions on which the exalted
situation of the Sovereign subjects him to the keenest
severity that personal feelings can endure. The
pre-eminent dignity which, in other cases, lifts him
beyond the ordinary vexations of his people, forbids

him, in such instances, to vindicate a personality,
except by the insufficient retaliation of his contempt. The very greatness of the King is the source
of his inability ; a helplessness commanding the respect of every cultivated, brave, and liberal gentleman. It belongs to the meanness of vulgarity and
ignorance to triumph by the seizure of opportunities,
which men of honour instinctively forbear to use.
That your Majesty may be convinced how sensibly
your subjects will participate in the indignation,
raised by any insult offered to your royal person,
under the wretched subterfuge of an official duty, I
have approached your Majesty with feelings of devotional respect, and have presumed to lay before
you the general opinion of your affectionate and
loyal people. No one can better appreciate than
your Majesty, the sobriety of judgment peculiar to
the empire, at the head of which it has pleased
God to place you. Permit me, then, to assure your
Majesty that, on no occasion was the reflecting
character of your people productive of a more una-
nimous disgust, than when it contemplated the perversion of political communication to the purposes
of gross discourtesy. Aware that your Majesty cannot descend to notice such encroachments on personal respect, but that the high observances of
kingly etiquette must elevate the observation of
your Majesty above insults, cognizable by the very
*highest subjects* of your realm, your people naturally feel the baseness of offences offered to you,
under that dastardly assurance of security. It is
grateful to a loyal subject, and a man of spirit, to

have heard a reprobation, co-extensive with the realm, of so abused a capability; nor can the per-, sons, by whose delegation the unmannered representative appeared before your Majesty, withhold the reproaches which are due to his invasion of decency and gentle breeding. Your Majesty will, I hope, believe, that ten men in your realms could not be found to imitate so shameless an example; and that, on this occasion, your Majesty may feel a greater share of pity than contempt for the offence; allow me, in behalf of that *untutored, self-taught* object, to present apologies, which may propitiate the tacit pardon of your Majesty.

"In the first place, Sire, allow me to remark, though self-taught men are always more remarkable for strength of mind than for refinement, taste, or chastity of feeling; the object to whom these observations are applied, is most unfortunately notorious for having *none* of these distinctive qualities. The fruits of education cannot be supplied on the unforeseen emergencies of life, which so conspicuously attest the disadvantages of its neglected cultivation; and how could such a man, perchance in early life a rational and modest being, have possibly anticipated situations, which were to place him as a vacant entity before the jeers and ridicule of his compatriots and fellow-citizens. Could I but engage the patient attention of your Majesty to learn the cause which, at a time of life by no means immature, advanced this object to a laughable degree of civic grandeur, your Majesty would readily suppose the vain pretensions nourished by such playful fantasies of fate. Afflicted with a talkative propensity, addressed with similar ineptitude to all things great and little, this superficial meddler indiscriminately contemplated commercial managements, the reform of prisons and of parliaments, the chastisement of easy virtue in the collective, and the palliation of public prostitution in an individual instance—Imagine, Sire, a man of the most stunted intellect, advanced by causes thus fortuitous to high official civic dignity, astounded like a second Sly, at his incredible condition. Imagine such a man assured that this was not a dream, and forming laudably a plan, by which to justify his elevation to a state of difficult responsibility. In quest of those internal aids, by which alone a public station can be rescued from contempt, suppose a creature so inane, in busy search for some capacity whereby to hit on the discharge of the most *easy* of his functions. Suppose that having chosen one of such direct facility, that genius must have laboured to depart from the exclusive unity of its discharge, and you will then observe the cause of vain congratulation to a little mind. Your Majesty has rarely, peradventure never, witnessed the amusing progress of so great a little man; hence, am I induced to enter on particularities, which may not be so competent to edify as to divert. Permit me, Sire, to draw your observation to his first official exploit; the achievement of ensuring nightly quietude in a specific ward, by the expensive method of numerical enlargements of the nightly watch. Observe the application of a mind so finely constituted for the task of almost imperceptible minutiæ. The magisterial genius took a literary turn, and having closeted itself within the still recesses of the Mansion-house, for purposes of weighty cogitation, it resolved; the justice-seat was taken with all the solemn gravity of settled and digested wisdom. The people waited with mute solicitude to learn the oracle of their exalted creature. The prefatory observations due to such a work of innovation on police, were heard with silent hopes and earnests of diffuse improvement. The magistrate pronounced, and the command was this, ' That every watchman wear a letter on his coat!!!' From this shrewd specimen of circumspection, which incurred some bright encomiums from the public prints, it may be easily inferred, how much the computation of the magistrate en-. larged his intellectual powers, then highly valued and extolled for their developement of legislative faculty. From these occasional encouragements, the flattered object felt, with laudable conviction, the possibilities of his improvement; and, having ventured on the area of the Common-hall, to catch the knackery of glib bombast from some of those prophetic babblers of the nation's grisly prospects, imbued too with their archetypal dignity and principles, he rose, as possibly your Majesty may know, to the uneasy place which he *proportionately* fills among the gentry of St. Stephen's; being now a pluralist of dignities, but no monopolist of hops, M.P. dubbed confidential lacquey to the Queen, and knight-errant of the holy order of St. Caroline.

" Having thus, Sire, accompanied to his parliamentary estate, the unlettered but fortunate successor of Bartolomeo Pergami, permit me to exhibit further grounds of intercession with your
Majesty, for the forgiveness of the senator, for that
intrusion, when recently he (what is aptly said of
vulgar men,) *forgot himself.*' When this important gentleman discovered that the meed of glory
in the Parliament did not exactly wait on those
displays so highly honoured in the Common-hall;
and, that among the gentlemen of dignity who
conscientiously dissent from the supporters of the
government of your Majesty, licentious insolence
was not the object or instrument of their endeavours, he was anxiously reduced to new contri-
vances, whereby to elevate the hue and cry, which
uniformly bay the heels of happy demagogues with
their inspiring discord. To one of the intuitive
perception and experience of your Majesty, I hardly
need pourtray the cross solicitude of trivial men, who
look with a dissatisfied conceit on all achievements
of importance, to which the obstructions of their
officious vanity are not allowed. Egotism, so often,
though not always, linked with ignorance, is one of
the unhappy qualities which operate with fatal
virulence on the object of my exculpation—not
that egotism, which will involuntarily dart a ray
from the irrepressible convictions of conscious
talent, but of a nature more capricious in proportion to its irrationality. The egotism of the man
for whom I plead, was fostered by the senseless
prodigality of vulgar praise, which seldom knows

the measure of desert; and which, if it be boundless
in original donation, is equally unceremonious and
ablative in reclaiming the superfluity it gave. The
better part of the mobility, if comparable parts
mobility can have, too soon discovered the impos-
ture of their exalted bugbear. They viewed with
sober sadness the ineptitude of such a creature, and
suspected (so they were informed,) that he had
caught a lazy sentiment from some translated
Lucan *. From the studied grace of the recumbency
with which he occupied his one-horse chaise, affecting Pompey, he questioned with a vacant stare the
dumb remembrance of the mob; but the responsive
acclamations were no more, and even as the hubbub
of his notoriety was on the wane, the opportune
dilemma of an " injured lady" allured the civic
Scaramouch beyond the sea, to play the leading
mime in chivalry burlesqued.

" After the few (I will not disrespectfully say)
hasty outlines which I have offered to your Majesty of the mental character of the person, whose
forgiveness I beseech, it will easily be conceived
by your Majesty, what manifold imaginations of
factitious greatness arose to the mind of that en-
thusiast, during his devoted errantry. He landed on
the shores of England under twofold influence; but

* ———————— Vergentibus armis
In senium ————————————
———————— famæque petitor
Multa dare in vulgus; totus popularibus auris
Impelli ————————————
———————— reparare novas Vires, multumque priori
Credere fortunæ stat ———————— umbra.
LUCAN, PHARSAL. l. 1.

whether, in remembrance of the feudal exploits of
Tom Thumb, he was pervaded by a knightly sentiment, or that the impressive recollection of the
school abridgment of his country's history, presented to him the comparative landing of King
Charles, King William, and himself, he bore the
chuckling look of self-sufficiency, and having
brought with him the means of popular excitement,
he was once more to be hailed or hooted (as the
term may suit) by that part of the rabble whose
wishes were congenial to his own. On the mis-
takes of etiquette arising from the vivacity of such
association, it may, perhaps, be hypercritical to
dwell. Decorum and distinction were overwhelmed
in the recommendatory principle of just equality,
and side by side, with the ' injured object' of his
*trip*, this champion of the lady entered London.
That from a homely denizen of much arithmetic
and little learning, of uncouth address and crude
deportment, an awkward exultation should have appeared in this noviciate, may be pardoned, when it
is supposed. I myself was witness to the scene.
That visage of absolute wisdom, of the affected
wisdom of Democritus, at times protruded through
the window, was on the wide-extended grin from
Deptford through the suburbs to the town. Had
Heraclitus viewed the cavalcade, he might have
shed his tears responsively to the derision of his
opponent sage. The partisans of ' Wisdom' flocked
from Bermondsey, Whitechapel, and St. George's
Fields, to testify the national opinion. The enlightened champion thanked the people, who sent
him back the votive wish of his longevity. Carts,

backs, and gigs attended on 'the rout; confusion,
drunkenness, and clamour solemnized the hour,
and radicals might look on it as the real zest of
civil privilege and reasonable freedom.  Your Majesty may well conceive, that to the spectators of
this mock-heroic, the *debutante* was calculated to
impose a certain portion of significance ; the clamour idly won on this occasion was cherished with
preposterous importance, and taken as the certain
harbinger of weightier and more intelligent ap-
proval.  A time had now arrived, when the discour-
teous subject of my observations was to take a part
of active operation, and to identify himself on all
occasions with his importation from abroad.  In all
the factious conjuration which ensued, the officious
presence of this unfortunate jack-pudding gave a
stamp of the ridiculous, truly fatal to the affected dignity of every pre-concerted pageantry.  One honour
more was yielded to the hopes of the aspiring zea-
lot, and in requital of his solemn mummery, a caricature of somewhat cruel sarcasm on the Athenian bird, depicted him as " Wisdom in the absolute."  I will not pause to mention when, on what
occasion, but in what a manner, the various calls of
purchased acclamation, brought the grateful citizen
to thank the mobs; indulgent to the errors of phi-
lology, those wary meetings gave the meed of
public approbation ; ' *The importance of the Cause*,'
' *A British Public*,' ' *The Evidence of the enlightened
Bodies of the People*,' commingled with the cant
and flummery of the Favell, Hunt, and Waithman
school, composed an apposite address of boister-

ous vapidity, which requited, at the periodical
huzza, the " *generous feeling of the People.*" While
this former mendicant of notoriety, assisted by
the airs of an apparent intimacy with superior rank,
received so full an influx of unenviable distinction,
it will not surprise your Majesty to learn that the
accession was too much for such especial imbe
cility to bear. Thus bewildered and intoxicated
with his glorious shame, the same officious super-
erogation still evinced the little wriggling, restless
love of being *mentioned, heard, or seen.* A misconception of the feeling of the people, yet, I fear,
a *knowledge* of the feeling of another party, be-
trayed this foolish truckler into the design of
raising his importance in the street and *balcony,*
by insolence of personality repugnant both to courage and decorum ; the opportunity appeared too
specious to be lost, and this important delegate addressing duty to another *quarter,* assumed the generous determination of insulting *you* in safety.

" Having thus far carried up my knowledge of the
man and his preferment, which is yet the object of
his own astonishment, I trust I have presented sufficient claims in his behalf, to the commiseration of
your Majesty ; and, although I apprehend that he
is too far lost in vanity to be reclaimed from folly,
yet we may be led to hope, he will afford less frequent and less flagrant exhibitions of fatuity. I
conclude by this assurance, that where your Majesty has *one* subject so seduced by mean allure-
ments, you have *thousands* who despise him ; and
that, if there be some few errant fools in Britain,

who exult in vulgar instances of disaffection, the
paramount good sense and principle of your dominions reposes its essential strength and glory in the
counteracting qualities of active loyalty and most
unqualified attachment.

A Subject."

I feel that my acknowledgments are due to the
generous intention of any of my subjects, who
would thus espouse, in my behalf, considerations
which my dignity forbids *me* to entertain. It is
grateful to me, even on a subject of this immeasur-
able lowness, to find that loyalty and spirit will in-
terpose themselves between the irreverence of rude
assurance and my personal toleration of its inde-
cency. Bounden, but still more willing, as I am, to
meet in open presence the manly expostulation of
my people, however contrariant to my own opinions, the essence of such remonstrances; it was
not without sensations of transitory indignation,
that I beheld an effort of unusual presumption, 'affecting the propriety with which a delegated trust
should be discharged. The facts assigned in the
Letter from a Subject are more than adequate to
gain the pardon of an individual compeer; addressed to *me*, they have extracted sentiments of
kinder will, perchance of greater aptitude, and,
with sincerity, I add to my forgiveness every gentle
feeling of commiseration.

My people, After a considerable lapse between
events which agitated a susceptible proportion

E

of the commonalty, I have addressed to you the
arguments and language which, I trust, become a
British King. I have spoken to you, not in the pompous tone of ostentatious vanity, of perplexing sophistry, nor of obsequious solicitation. Either method would have been unworthy of myself and
you. If I have employed the language of paternal
admonition, it was dictated by love. If I have entered on explanatory undertakings, it was not to
offer an apology. If I have uttered truths, which
in their application, may be keen and forcible, I
ascribe their utterance to justice, not to animosity.
Asperity, from *me*, has passed away ; and the con-
vulsions, which, in their origin, attracted my re-
proof to their suborners, have ultimately showered
on me all the mantling feelings of beatitude, that
can assure a Sovereign of the virtue and attachment
of his people. I will admit, or rather I am proud to
say, that I remarked with close and unremitting
watchfulness the restive progress of that irritated
sensibility so artfully, so shamefully, and so merci-
lessly galled ; I vigilantly waited on the possible
results of that infliction, patient without weariness,
and prepared without anticipation, to guide or to
restrain alarming symptoms of precipitancy. The
generous temper of the people was excited into
madness by external impulses, not self-delivered to
a rash depravity from operative vice within. The
lawless object of their foul betrayers was to stimulate temerity, discourage patience, incite repugnance, and annihilate subordination. The obvious
consequence of their contemplated success had been

the imperious, the indispensable necessity of more accessions to the hand of Government; a new occasion of declamatory lamentation, to the hypocritical perverters of temporary obligation into grievances of national disfranchisement.

The subsiding ferment of the public mind realized my expectation; it disappointed those flagitious plotters of disturbance, who retired in shame, vexation, and discomfiture; disclaimed, detected, and despised. What further objects occupied, or occupy, the minds of such insidious insult and inferior daring, were, or are occasionally, clamoured by the solitary voice of some subsidiary hireling. It was, and still may be, the lingering hope of insignificance; to catch importance from opposed authority; but to destroy the power of mischief in a mean cabal, it seems to me adviseable to give a scope, so ample to its weak endeavours, that vanity may lead it into little exhibitions on the wide arena; if I be just in my conclusions, contempt and ridicule will scoff its despicable antics to retirement; and as it has once excited apprehension in the land, let it now requite that apprehension by affording mirth.

At a period when fictitious rumours manifested an immediate influence, and my people generally were engaged in that comparative inquiry into past events, which promised peaceable conviction, I abstained from troubling their impartial scrutiny by any observations of a guiding or explanatory nature. From the hive of busy misinterpretation. I foresaw what misconstruction would have waited on the candour of the King; depriving, therefore, the perverting malice of such men of any chance of specious imputation, I delayed to exercise a fellowship of honest spirit, which sensibly allured me to communications of explicit candour and elucidation. It was for the ingenuous deliberation of my people to arrive at a conclusion; I predicted that conclusion, and it has arrived; to me the more honourable, as it was *unbiassed;* the more sincere, as prejudices existed to my disadvantage; the more complete, as they are utterly abjured. Had faction and conspiracy continued to affront and vex the Government, its course was fixed, not optional. The ultimate establishment of harmony afforded me the grateful opportunity, which I have now embraced, of pointing out by close analysis, the selfish objects of those dastardly and wicked men, who personally shrink from every penalty of violated law, that less suspicious votaries to discord may achieve their evil ends, and bear the certain weight of its adjudication.

I may hope with that profound solicitude for the prosperity and blessing of my people, which must embue the spirit of a British King, that the exposure of the subtle means and fruitless ends of factious anarchy, may henceforth prove a monumental beacon to the first perceptions of an errant will.

When I cast a retrospective glance on what is past, and see in the developement of the mysterious intricacies of a deadly will, such component and convulsive evils, so useless to the faction which engendered it, and so fatal to the community it menaced, I lay my hand upon my heart and thank Almighty God, that in consideration of the best of earthly governments, the redeeming power of virtue in this illustrious nation, so excels the possibility of wanton evil; and, I look on the frustrated efforts of iniquity, as an almost exclusive earnest of the love of God to the great and glorious people of my especial realm. When the agitation of the kingdom seemed to promise more to the abuse of popular credulity than effects have yielded, an ignoble rumour went abroad, that foreign force might be required to quell the stormy spirit of the Isle. Base and ungenerous idea!!! Preposterous impossibility!! Methinks the yet unsullied genius of the country had rather plunged in the oblivious depths, that plough their blue defiance round the land, than bow her helm and spear to uncongenial aid, demanding the repulsion of her patriotic shield; I should have thought that even faction had forborne to stigmatize the element of Nelson and of England, and to prostitute ideally to purposes of base enslavement the waves that had repelled it, and secured our freedom as a charter co-existent with the waters that surround us. A truce to such dishonest, such expatriating fabrications. I have met you recently, my people, on those occasions which are grateful to a Monarch; not with the attendant dignities and state incumbrances of my condition; on those felicitous occasions, the congratulations of my people have carried transport, almost insupportable, to my paternal heart; in those exulting moments I have felt the vivid reciprocity of that ennobled sentiment that binds the people to their king. In this unrivalled land, it bears the stamp of a divine endowment. God has linked with such indissoluble, such insepa- rable strength, the welfare of the people and the King of Britain, that they cannot be parted ; and, as it has pleased the great Disposer of events, to fix our union on the imperishable principles of in- stinctive compact, I will invigorate the bond by my example and fidelity, as long as it may please Al- mighty God to intrust to me the sceptre of my ancestors. With every devout wish for the people's health, both bodily and mental, the King resigns the pen. Farewell.

. That God may grant you all both national and individual happiness, is the fervent prayer of

THE KING.

# APPENDIX.

## No. I.

### *The Queen's Letter to the King.*

S I R,—After the unparalleled and unprovoked persecution which, during a series of years, has been carried on against me *under the name and authority of your Majesty*—and which persecution, instead of being mollified by time, time has rendered only more malignant and more unrelenting—it is not without a great sacrifice of private feeling that I now, even in the way of remonstrance, bring myself to address this letter to your Majesty. But, bearing in mind that royalty rests on the basis of public good ; that to this paramount consideration all others ought to submit ; and aware of the consequences that may result from the present unconstitutional, illegal, and hitherto unheard-of proceedings ;—with a mind thus impressed, I cannot refrain from laying my grievous wrongs once more before your Majesty, in the hope that the justice which your Majesty may, by evil-minded counsellors, be still disposed to refuse to the claims of a dutiful, faithful, and injured wife, you may be induced to yield *to considerations connected with the honour and dignity of your crown, the stability of your throne*, the tranquillity of your dominions, the happiness and safety of your just and loyal people, whose generous hearts revolt at oppression and cruelty, and *especially when perpetrated by a perversion and a mockery of the laws.*

A sense of what is due to my character and sex forbids me to refer minutely to the real causes of our domestic separation, or to the numerous unmerited insults offered me previously to that period ; but, leaving to your Majesty to reconcile with the marriage vow the act of driving, by such means, a wife from beneath your roof, *with an infant in her arms*, your Majesty will permit me to remind you, that that act was entirely your own ; that the separation, so far from being sought by me, was a sentence pronounced upon me, without any cause assigned, other than that of your own inclinations, which, as your Majesty was pleased to allege, were not under your control.

Not to have felt, with regard to myself, chagrin at this decision of your Majesty, would have argued great insensibility to the obligations of decorum; not to have dropped a tear in the face of that beloved child, *whose future sorrows were then but too easily to be foreseen,* would have marked me as unworthy of the name of mother; but, not to have submitted to it without repining would have indicated a consciousness of demerit, or a want of those feelings which belong to affronted and insulted female honour.

The " tranquil and comfortable society" tendered to me by your Majesty, formed, in my mind, but a poor compensation for the grief occasioned by considering the wound given to public morals in the fatal example *produced by the indulgence of your Majesty's inclinations;* more especially when I contemplated the disappointment of the nation, who had so munificently provided for our union, who had fondly cherished such pleasing hopes of happiness arising from that union, and who had hailed it with such affectionate and rapturous joy.

But, alas! even tranquillity and comfort were too much for me to enjoy. *From the very threshold of your Majesty's mansion* the mother of your child was pursued by spies, conspirators, and traitors, employed, encouraged, and rewarded to lay snares for the feet, and to plot against the reputation and life, of her whom your Majesty had so recently and so solemnly vowed to honour, to love, and to cherish.

In withdrawing from the embraces of my parents, in giving my hand to the son of George the Third and the heir-apparent to the British throne, nothing less than a voice from Heaven would have made me fear injustice or wrong of any kind. What, then, was my astonishment, at finding that treasons against me had been carried on and matured, perjuries against me had been methodized and embodied, a secret tribunal had been held, a trial of my actions had taken place, and a decision had been made upon those actions, without my having been informed of the nature of the charge, or of the names of the witnesses! and what words can express the feelings excited by the fact, that this proceeding was founded on a request made, *and on evidence furnished, by order of the father of my child,* and my natural as well as legal guardian and protector'!

Notwithstanding, however, the unprecedented conduct of that tribunal—conduct which has since undergone, even in Parliament, severe and unanswered animadversions, and *which has been also censured in minutes of the Privy Council*—notwithstanding the *secrecy* of the proceedings of this tribunal—notwithstanding the strong temptation to the giving of false evidence against me before it—notwithstanding that there was *no opportunity afforded me* of rebutting that evidence —notwithstanding all these circumstances, so decidedly favourable to my enemies—even this secret tribunal acquitted me of all CRIME, *and thereby pronounced my principal accusers to have been guilty of the grossest perjury*. But it was now (after the trial was over) discovered, that the nature of the tribunal was such as to render false swearing before it *not legally criminal!* And thus, *at the suggestion and request of your Majesty*, had been created, to take cognizance of and try my conduct, a tribunal competent to administer oaths, competent to examine witnesses on oath, competent to try, competent to acquit or condemn, and competent, moreover, *to screen those who had sworn falsely against me* from suffering the pains and penalties which the law awards to wilful and corrupt perjury. Great as my indignation naturally must have been at this shameful evasion of law and justice, that indignation was lost *in pity for him who could lower his princely plumes to the dust by giving his countenance and favour to the most conspicuous of those abandoned and notorious perjurers.*

Still there was one whose upright mind nothing could warp, in whose breast injustice never found a place, whose hand was always ready to raise the unfortunate, and to rescue the oppressed. While that good and gracious father and Sovereign remained in the exercise of his Royal functions, his unoffending daughter-in-law had nothing to fear. As long as the protecting hand of your late ever-beloved and ever-lamented father was held over me, I was safe. But the melancholy event which deprived the nation of the active exertions of its virtuous King, bereft me of friend and protector, and of all hope of future tranquillity and safety. To calumniate your innocent wife was now *the shortest road to Royal favour ;* and to betray her was to lay *the sure foundation of boundless riches and titles of honour.* Before claims like these, talent, virtue, long services, your own personal friendships, your Royal engagements, promises, and pledges, written as well as verbal, melted into air. *Your Cabinet was founded on this basis.* You took to your councils men, of whose persons, as well as whose principles, you had invariably expressed the strongest dislike. The interest of the nation, and even your own feelings, in all other respects, were sacrificed to the gratification of your desire to aggravate my sufferings, and ensure my humiliation. You took to your councils and your bosom men whom you hated, whose abandonment of, and whose readiness to sacrifice me were their only merits, and whose power has been exercised in a manner, and has been attended with consequences, worthy of its origin. From this unprincipled and unnatural union have sprung the manifold evils which this nation has now to endure, *and which present a mass of misery and of degradation, accompanied with acts of tyranny, and cruelty,* rather than have seen which inflicted on his industrious, faithful, and brave people, your royal father would have perished at the head of that people. When to calumniate, revile, and betray me, became the sure path to honour and riches, it would have been strange indeed if calumniators, revilers, and traitors had not abounded. *Your Court became much less a scene of polished manners and refined intercourse than of low intrigue and scurrility.* Spies, Bacchanalian tale-bearers, and foul conspirators, swarmed in those places which had before been the resort of sobriety, virtue, and honour. To enumerate all the various privations and mortifications which I had to endure—all the insults that were wantonly heaped upon me, from the day of your elevation to the Regency to that of my departure for the Continent it would be to describe every species of personal offence that can be offered to, and every pain short of bodily violence that can be inflicted on, any human being. Bereft of parent, brother, and father-in-law, and my husband for my deadliest foe; seeing those who have promised me support bought by rewards to be amongst my enemies; restrained from accusing my foes in the face of the world, *out of regard for the character of the father of my child,* and from a desire to prevent her happiness from being disturbed; shunned from motives of selfishness by those who were my natural associates; living in obscurity, while I ought to have been the centre of all that was splendid; thus humbled, I had one consolation left—the love of my dear and only child. To permit me to enjoy this was too great an indulgence. To see my daughter; to fold her in my arms; to mingle my tears with hers; to receive her cheering caresses, and to hear from her lips assurances of never-ceasing love ;—thus to be comforted, consoled, upheld, and blessed, was too much to be allowed me. Even on the slave-mart the cries of "Oh! my mother, my mother! Oh! my child, my child!" have prevented a separation of the victims of avarice. *But your advisers, more inhuman than the slave dealers, remorselessly tore the mother from the child.*'

Thus bereft of the society of my child, or reduced to the necessity of imbittering her life by struggles to preserve that society, I resolved on *a temporary absence*, in the hope that time might restore me to her in happier days. Those days, alas! were never to come. To mothers—and those mothers who have been suddenly bereft of the best and most affectionate and only daughters—it belongs to estimate my sufferings and my wrongs. Such mothers will judge of my affliction upon hearing of the death of my child, and upon my calling to recollection the last look, the last words, and all the affecting circumstances of our separation. Such mothers will see the depth of my sorrows. Every being, with a heart of humanity in its bosom, will drop a tear in sympathy with me. And will not the world, then, learn with indignation, that this event, calculated to soften the hardest heart, was the signal for new conspiracies, and indefatigable efforts for the destruction of this afflicted mother? *Your Majesty had torn my child from me;* you had deprived me of the power of being at hand to succour her; you had taken from me the possibility of hearing of her last prayers for her mother; *you saw me bereft; forlorn, and broken-hearted;* and this was the moment you chose for redoubling your persecutions.

Let the world pass its judgment on the constituting of a commission, in a foreign country, consisting of inquisitors, spies and informers, to discover, collect, and arrange matters of accusation against your wife, without any complaint having been communicated to her: let the world judge of the employment of ambassadors in such a business, and of the enlisting of foreign courts in the enterprise: but on the measures which have been adopted to give final effect to these preliminary proceedings it is for me to speak; it is for me to remonstrate with your Majesty; it is for me to protest; it is for me to apprize you of my determination.

I have always demanded a *fair trial*. This is what I now demand, and this is refused me. Instead of a fair trial, I am to be subjected *to a sentence by the Parliament*, passed in the shape of *a law*. Against this I protest, and upon the following grounds:

The injustice of refusing me a clear and distinct charge, of refusing me the names of the witnesses, of refusing me the names of the places where the alleged acts have been committed; these are sufficiently flagrant and revolting; but it is against the *constitution of the Court itself* that I particularly object, and that I most solemnly protest.

Whatever may be the precedents as to Bills of Pains and Penalties, none of them, *except those relating to the Queen of Henry the Eighth*, can apply here; for here your Majesty is the *plaintiff*. Here it is intended by the Bill to do you what you deem *good*, and to do *me great harm*. You are, therefore, a party, and the only complaining party.

You have made your complaint to the House of Lords. You have conveyed to this House written documents sealed up. A secret committee of the House have examined these documents. They have reported that there are grounds of proceeding; and then the House, merely upon that report, have brought forward a Bill containing the most outrageous slanders on me, and sentencing me to divorce and degradation.

The injustice of putting forth this Bill to the world for six weeks before it is even proposed to afford me an opportunity of contradicting its allegations is too manifest not to have shocked the nation; and, indeed, the proceedings even thus far are such as *to convince every one that no justice is intended me*. But if none of these proceedings, if none of these clear indications of a determination to do me wrong had taken place, I should see, *in the constitution of the House of Lords itself*, a certainty that I could expect *no justice at its hands.*—

Your Majesty's Ministers have *advised* this prosecution; they are responsible for the advice they give; they are liable to *punishment* if they fail to make good their charges; and not only are they part of my *judges*, but it is they who have *brought in the Bill;* and it is too noto-

rious that they have *always a majority* in the House ; so that, without
any other, here is ample proof that the House will decide in favour of
the Bill, and, of course, against me.

But further, there are reasons for your Ministers having a majority
in this case, and which reasons do not apply to common cases. Your
Majesty is *the plaintiff*: to you it belongs to appoint and to elevate
peers. Many of the present Peers have been raised to that dignity by
yourself, and almost the whole *can be*, at your will and pleasure,
further elevated. The far greater part of the Peers hold, by themselves and their families, offices, pensions, and other emoluments,
solely at the will and pleasure of your Majesty, and these, of
course your Majesty *can take away whenever you please*. There are
more than *four-fifths* of the Peers in this situation, and there are many
of them who might thus be deprived of the far better part of their incomes.—

If, contrary to all expectation, there should be found, in some
Peers, likely to amount to a majority, a disposition to reject the Bill,
*some of these Peers may be ordered away to their ships, regiments, go-
vernments, and other duties*; and, which is an equally alarming power,
*new Peers may be created for the purpose,* and give their vote in the
decision. That your Majesty's Ministers would advise these measures,
if found necessary to render their prosecution successful, *there can be
very little doubt ;* seeing that they have hitherto stopped at nothing,
however unjust or odious.

To regard *such a body as a Court of Justice* would be to calumniate that sacred name ; and for me to suppress an expression of my
opinion on the subject would be tacitly to lend myself to my own
destruction, as well as to an imposition upon the nation and the
world.

*In the House of Commons I can discover no better grounds of
security.* The power of your Majesty's Ministers is the same in both
Houses ; and your Majesty is well acquainted with the fact, that a
majority of this House is composed of persons placed in it by the Peers
and by your Majesty's Treasury.

It really gives me pain to state these things to your Majesty ; and,
if it gives your Majesty pain, I beg that it may be observed, and remembered, that the statement has been forced from me. I must either

protest against this mode of trial, or, by tacitly consenting to it, suffer my honour to be sacrificed. No innocence can secure the accused, if the Judges and Jurors be chosen by the accuser; and if I were tacitly to submit to a tribunal of this description, I should be instrumental to my own dishonour.

On these grounds I protest against this species of trial. I demand a trial in a Court where the Jurors are taken impartially *from amongst the people*, and where the proceedings *are open and fair*. Such a trial I court, and to no other will I willingly submit. If your Majesty persevere in the present proceeding, I shall, even in the Houses of Parliament, face my accusers; *but I shall regard any decision they may make against me as not in the smallest degree reflecting on my honour;* and I will not, *except compelled by actual force*, submit to any sentence which shall not be pronounced by a *Court of Justice.*

I have now frankly laid before your Majesty a statement of my wrongs, *and a declaration of my views and intentions.* You have cast upon me every slur to which the female character is liable. Instead of loving, honouring, and cherishing me, agreeable to your solemn vow, you have pursued me with hatred and scorn, and with all the means of destruction. You wrested from me my child, and with her my only comfort and consolation. You sent me sorrowing through the world, and even in my sorrows pursued me with unrelenting persecution. *Having left me nothing but my innocence*, you would now, by a mockery of justice, deprive me even of the reputation of possessing that. The poisoned bowl and the poinard are means more manly than perjured witnesses and partial tribunals; and they are less cruel, inasmuch as life is less valuable than honour. If my life would have satisfied your Majesty, you should have had it on the sole condition of giving me a place in the same tomb with my child: but, since you would send me dishonoured to the grave, *I will resist the attempt with all the means that it shall please God to give me *.*

(Signed)                                   CAROLINE, R.

*Brandenburgh-house, Aug.* 7, 1820.

---

* The above letter from her Majesty, which is dated August 7th, was sent by the Queen's messenger early in the morning of the 8th to the Cottage at

## No. II.

*Letter of Lord Liverpool to the Princess of Wales, dated the 28th of July, 1814.*

" Lord Liverpool has had the honour to receive the Letter of her Royal Highness. Having communicated it to the Prince Regent, he has ordered him to inform her Royal Highness that he can have no objection to the intentions of her Royal Highness to effect the design which she announces to the Prince Regent, of returning to her native country, to visit her brother the Duke of Brunswick; assuring her, that the Prince Regent will never throw any obstacle in the way of her present or future intentions as to the place where she may wish to reside.

" The Prince Regent leaves her Royal Highness at liberty to exercise her own discretion as to her abode in this country or on the continent, as it may be convenient to her.

" Lord Liverpool is also commanded, on the part of the Prince Regent, to inform her Royal Highness, that he will not throw any obstacles in the way of the arrangements of her Royal Highness, whatever they may be, respecting the House at Blackheath, which

---

Windsor, accompanied with a note to Sir Benjamin Bloomfield, *written by the Queen*, desiring Sir Benjamin to deliver it immediately to the King. Sir Benjamin Bloomfield being then absent, the letter was received by Sir William Keppel, who forwarded it immediately to Sir Benjamin Bloomfield, at Carlton-house, who returned it in the afternoon of the 8th to the Queen, informing her Majesty that he had received the King's commands, and general instructions, that any communications that might be made should pass through the channel of his Majesty's Government. The Queen immediately despatched a messenger with the letter to Lord Liverpool, desiring his Lordship to lay it before his Majesty. Lord Liverpool was at Combe-wood. He returned an answer that he would lose no time in laying it before the King. On the 11th, no reply having been received, *the Queen wrote again* to Lord Liverpool, requesting information whether any further communication would be made on the subject of the letter to his Majesty. Lord Liverpool wrote the same day from Combe-wood, that he had not received the King's commands to make any communication to her Majesty in consequence of her letter.—*Times* Newspaper.

belonged to the late Duchess of Brunswick, or the rest of the private property of her Royal Highness. But that, for reasons rather too long to explain, the Prince Regent will not permit the Princess Charlotte to be ranger of Greenwich Park, or to occupy any of the houses at Blackheath, which her Royal Highness has hitherto occupied.

" Lord Liverpool has also been enjoined, on the part of the Prince Regent, before he closes the letter which he has the honour to send to her Royal Highness, to tell her, in relation to the two articles which her Royal Highness has put in her letter concerning the rupture of the marriage of the Princess Charlotte with the hereditary Prince of Orange, as well as to the reason for which the allied Sovereigns did not, previously to their departure from England, pay their visit to her Royal Highness ; that, as to the first article, Lord Liverpool is commanded by the Prince Regent to inform herRoyal Highness, that the Prince Regent is not persuaded that the private considerations of the circumstances in which the Princess is placed, can have been an obstacle to the marriage of the Princess Charlotte. As to the second article, Lord Liverpool is also enjoined, on the part of the Prince Regent, to signify to her Royal Highness, that the Prince Regent never opposed himself to the allied Sovereigns making a visit to her Royal Highness during their stay in London.

" Lord Liverpool has the honour to be, with all esteem and the highest consideration.

" P.S. The Prince Regent can make no difficulties on the subject of the directions which the Princess has the intention of giving as to the house at Blackheath ; neither will the Prince Regent oppose her Royal Highness's retaining the apartments in the palace of Kensington, in the same manner as she possessed them while in London, for the convenience of herself and suite."

THE END.

LONDON :
PRINTED BY WILLIAM CLOWES,
Northumberland-court.

# LETTER

## TO

# THE KING.

# THE

# REPLY

OF

# THE PEOPLE

TO THE

# LETTER

FROM

# THE KING.

———

**London:**

PRINTED FOR F. C. & J. RIVINGTON,

NO. 62, ST. PAUL'S CHURCH-YARD,

AND NO. 3, WATERLOO-PLACE, PALL-MALL;

AND TO BE HAD OF ALL BOOKSELLERS IN TOWN AND COUNTRY.

*[Price Two Shillings.]*

———

1821.

testants also, *as the precise act of abjuring their religion* Hence several scores of Catholics have heretofore lost, not only their civil rights, but also their lives, for refusing to take it. Nor does the injunction of Queen Elizabeth, in the first year of her reign, which is referred to in the Bill, by any means remove the conscientious objection of sincere Catholics, as in that injunction she barely disclaims the actual exercise of the ministry, at the same time that in every act, whether legislative or regal, of her reign, she claimed the entire, supreme, spiritual jurisdiction, within her dominions, to the total exclusion of all such jurisdiction on the part of the Pope*. This is so clear and notorious, that we are convinced, in case our legislators should, in their wisdom and liberality, admit our people to the enjoyment of their civil franchises, notwithstanding their acknowledgment of the jurisdiction of their Church in faith and discipline, they will prefer the plain and explicit terms by which we abjure the Pope's authority in all civil and temporal cases, in the act passed for our relief in 1791, to the new-invented and forced construction of the act and oath of supremacy, by means of the above-mentioned injunction.

Again, though we ourselves, in the oath of 1791,

---

* "See the injunction in Bishop Sparrow's Collection, p. 83, also the whole Act of 1 Eliz. c. 1, to restore to the Crown the ancient jurisdiction over the estate ecclesiastical and spiritual, and to abolish all foreign powers repugnant to the same. See also Act 5 Eliz. c. 1. also Act 13 Eliz. c. 2. See also Archbishop Parker Homage to the Queen, in Collier's Eccl. Hist. vol. ii. Record. 81."

above cited, have abjured " the doctrine and position that Princes, excommunicated or deprived by
the Pope, or any authority of the See of Rome, may
be deposed or murdered by their subjects," &c. yet,
following the doctrine and example of our predecessors, who (chiefly on account of the extravagant and
false terms therein contained in King James's oath
of allegiance) refused the same, we declare that it
is utterly unlawful, and contrary to the doctrine of
our Church for a Catholic to condemn upon oath,
the *mere deposing doctrine*, as damnable and heretical *.

" With respect to the Bill of Pains and Penalties
against their Clergy, with which some modern Catholics are content to purchase civil advantages for
themselves, we declare,—1st, That we, the Clergy,
cannot conscientiously take the oath prepared for
us, in the terms in which it stands in the Bill: because, however remote we are from all traitorous
conspiracies against the establishments of our country, whether civil or ecclesiastical, yet we cannot
bind ourselves " never to have any correspondence
or communication with the Pope or the See of Rome,
or with any persons authorized by the Pope, &c.
(which words comprehend all the Catholic Clergy of
the United Kingdom,) tending directly or indirectly
to overthrow or disturb the Protestant Church:" in

---

* " See Supplementary Memoirs of the English Catholics,
lately published by Keating and Brown, Duke-street, Gros-
venor-square, in which the terms of their oath and the most
material incidents in the History of Catholics of late years are
clearly discussed."

as much as in our judgment, all our preaching, writing, and ministring, *tend indirectly to this effect.*

" 2dly, Though contrary to the fact, we were justly suspected, in our personal conduct and our professional ministry, to be disloyal and seditious ; and there were greater reason for Government interfering with our religious economy, than with that of the numberless sects protected by it, and especially with that of the Greek Schismatics, the German Moravians, and the Jews ; yet we know that we are not competent to concur in, or consent to the alterations in our Churches and Missions proposed in the present Penal Bill ; much less would it be lawful for the intended episcopal commissioner to take the oath prepared for him to take, this being *incompatible* with his existing oath and obligation.

" 3dly, As the revision by the commissioners and clerks of a new devised civil office, of all rescripts from the Holy See, implies in many cases *the breach of most sacred professional secrets on our parts,* and as such revision has been recently declared by that See to be a violation of her divinely constituted spiritual supremacy *, hence we declare, that we cannot concur in or consent to any such regulation. Nor would the difficulty be removed by referring the revision to the intended ecclesiastical commissioner, because, in the cases supposed, we are each of us

* " De Rescriptorum Revisione—ne tractatus institui potestnam cum libertatem Magisterii Ecclesiæ, divinitus concredit apprimè lædat, laïcæ potestati permittere aut tribuere nefas profecto esset." Card. Litta's Letter, by order of the Pope, to Bishop Poynter, &c. April 26, 1815. See Report from Committee of House of Commons, folio, p. 513."

as much bound to secrecy with respect to ecclesiastical as to lay persons.

"Such is our conscientious judgment, and that of
the divines and pastors of the Midland district, and
we have reason to believe of the Catholic divines
and pastors of England and Ireland in general on the
pending Bills: we therefore join our voices with
those of the Vicars Apostolic in 1817, in calling
upon the Catholics in general to employ whatever
constitutional and peaceable means or influence they
may possess, to prevent the enactment of the unlawful contents of them.

*Wolverhampton, March 15, 1821.*

"R. R. J. MILNER, Vic. Apost.
"Rev. WALTER BLOUNT, Arch Priest,
"Rev. WILLIAM BENSON, Secretary."

(M)

*(Texts and Comments from the Douay Bible.)*

MATT. vi. 24.

*No man can serve two masters. For either he will
hate the one, and love the other :- or he will sustain
the one and contemn the other. You cannot serve
God and mammon.*

Two religions, God and Baal, Christ and Calvin,
mass and communion, the Catholic Church and
heretical conventicles.

MATT. xxvii. 24.

*And Pilate seeing that he nothing prevailed, but
that rather a tumult was made ; taking water,*

77

*he washed his hands before the people, saying: I
am innocent of the blood of this just man, look you
to it.*

Though Pilate was much more innocent than the
Jews, and would have been free from the murder
of our Saviour, seeking all the means that he could
(without offending the people and the Emperor's
laws), to dismiss him : yet he is damned for being
the minister of the people's wicked will against his
own conscience. *Even as all officers are, and especially the judges and juries which execute laws of
temporal princes against Catholic men: for all such
are guilty of innocent blood, and are nothing excused
by that they execute other men's wills according to
the laws, which are unjust. For they should rather
suffer death themselves, than put an innocent man to
death.*

## MARK xii. 17.

*And Jesus answering, said to them: Render there-
fore to Cæsar the things which are Cæsar's ; and
to God, the things which are God's.*

These men were very circumspect and wary
to do all duties to Cæsar, but of their duty to
God they had no regard. So heretics, to flatter
temporal Princes, and by them to uphold their heresies, do not only inculcate men's duty to the Prince,
dissembling that which is due to God; but also
give to the Prince, more than due, and take from
God his right and duty. But Christ allowing Cæsar
his right, warneth them also of their duty towards

God. And that is what Catholics inculcate: obey
God, do as he commandeth; *serve Him first, and
then the Prince.*

## JOHN xi. 51.

*And this he spoke not of himself, but being the
High Priest of that year, he prophesied that
Jesus should die for the nation.*

How much more may we be assured, that Christ
will not leave Peter's seat, whose faith he promised should never fail, though the persons which
occupy the same, were as ill as the *blasphemous and
malicious* mouths of heretics do affirm.

## ACTS xxviii. 22.

*But we desire to hear of thee, what thou thinkest :
for as concerning this sect, we know that it is gain-
said every where.*

Whereas indeed the Protestants' doctrine is evidently convinced to be heretical, by the same arguments that Christ's religion is proved to be the only
true doctrine of salvation, and not an heresy. And
whosoever can deduce the christian faith from Adam
to this day, throughout all the fathers, patriarchs,
prophets, priests, apostles, and bishops, by descent
and succession of all laws and states of true worship-
pers and believers, (which is the only or special way
to prove that the christian faith is no heresy) he shall
by the same means, all at once, prove the Protestants' doctrine to be an heresy and a false sect.
That the Jews therefore and ill men in all places

contradicted the christian religion, calling it an heresy)
or a sect, as if it had a beginning of some certain)
sect master other than God himself, they were deceived: and the church of God nevertheless calling
the Protestants' doctrine heresy in the worst part that
can be, and in the worst sort that ever was, doth
right and most justly.

### GAL. i, 8.

*But though we, or an Angel from Heaven, preach a
Gospel to you besides that which we have preached
to you, let him be anathema.*

Lastly, St. Hierom useth this place, wherein
the Apostle giveth the curse or anathema to all false
teachers not once but twice, to prove *that the zeal
of all Catholic men ought to be so great towards all
Heretics and their doctrines, that they should give
them the anathema, though they were ever so dear
unto them.* In which case, saith this holy Doctor,
I would not spare *mine own parents.* Ad Pam-
mach, c. 3, cont. Jo. Hieros.

### 2 TIM. ii. 17.

*And their Speech spreadeth like a Cancer: of whom
are Hymeneus and Philetus.*

The speeches, preachings, and writings of Heretics are pestiferous, contagious, and creeping like
a cancer. *Therefore Christian men must never
hear their sermons nor read their books.* For such
men have a popular way of talk, whereby the un-
learned, and especially women laden with sin, are

easily beguiled. "Nothing is so easy (saith St. Hierom) as with voluble and rolling tongue to deceive the rude people; who admire whatsoever they understand not." (Ep. 2. ad Nepot. c. 10.)

## 2 Tim. iii. 9.

*But they shall proceed no further : for their folly shall be manifest to all men.*

All Heretics, in the beginning, seem to have some show of truth, God, for just punishment of men's sins permitting them for some time in some persons and places to prevail; but in a short time God detecteth them, and openeth the eyes of men to see their deceits; insomuch that after the first brunt they are maintained by force only, all wise men, in a manner seeing their falsehood, *though for fear of troubling the state of such common-wealths, where unluckily they have been received,* THEY CANNOT BE SO SUDDENLY EXTIRPATED.

## APOCALYPSE OF ST. JOHN xx. 12.

*And I saw the dead, great and small, standing in the presence of the throne, and the books were opened: and another book was opened, which is the book of life: and the dead were judged by those things which were written in the books, according to their works.*

This is the book of God's knowledge or predestination; in which that, which before was hid to the world, shall be opened, and in which the true record of every man's works shall be contained, and they have their judgment diversely according to their own works, and not according to faith only, or want of faith only. For all infidels (as *Turks, obstinate Jews,* and *Heretics*) *shall never come to that examination, being otherwise condemned.*

(N)

*Extract from a Circular Letter from Cardinal* FONTANA, *the Prefect of the Propaganda, to the Irish Prelates, on the Subject of the Bible Schools :—*

" My Lord,—The prediction of our Lord Jesus Christ, in the Parable of the Sower, ' that sowed good seed in his field ; but, while people slept, his Enemy came, and sowed Tares upon the Wheat,' Matt. xvi. 24, is, to the very great injury indeed of the Catholic Faith, seen verified in these our own days, particularly in Ireland.

" For, information has reached the ears of the Sacred Congregation, that ' Bible Schools,' supported by the funds of the Catholics, have been established in almost every part of Ireland, in which, under the pretence of Charity, the inexperienced of both sexes, but particularly Peasants and Paupers, are allured by the blandishments and even gifts of the Masters, and infected with the fatal poison of depraved Doctrines.

" It is further stated, that the Directors of these Schools, are, generally speaking, Methodists, who introduce Bibles, translated into English by ' the Bible Society,' and abounding in errors, with the sole view of seducing the youth, and entirely eradicating from their minds the Truths of the Orthodox Faith,

" Under these circumstances, your Lordship already perceives with what solicitude and attention
Pastors are bound to watch and carefully protect
their flock from ' the snares of Wolves who come in
the clothing of Sheep:' If the Pastors sleep, the
Enemy will quickly creep in by stealth, and sow the
tares—soon will the tares be seen growing among the
wheat and choak it.

" Every possible exertion must therefore be made
—to keep the youth away from these destructive
schools—to warn parents against suffering their children, on any account whatever, to be led into error.
But, for the purpose of escaping the ' snares' of the
adversaries, no plan seems more appropriate than
that of establishing schools, wherein salutary instructions may be imparted to the paupers, and
illiterate country persons

" In the name, then, of the mercy of our Lord
Jesus Christ, we exhort and beseech your Lordship
to guard your flock with diligence, and all due discretion, from those who are in the habit of thrusting
themselves insidiously into the fold of Christ, in order
thereby to lead the unwary sheep away; and mindful of the forewarning of Peter, the Apostle, given in
these words, viz. :—" there shall also be lying masters among you, who shall bring in seeds of perdition," 2 Peter ii. 1. do you labour with all your
might to keep the orthodox youth from being corrupted by them—an object which will, I hope, be
easily effected by the establishing of Catholic Schools
throughout your Diocese.

" And confidently trusting that in a matter of
such vast importance, your Lordship will, with un-

bounded zeal, endeavour to prevent the wheat from
being choaked by the tares, I pray the all good and
omnipotent God to guard and preserve you for
many years.

"Your Lordship's

"Most obedient humble servant,

"F. CARDINAL FONTANA, *Prefect*:

"C. M. PEDICINI, *Secretary*."

"Rome, Court of the Sacred Congregation for the
Propagation of the Faith, 18th Sept. 1819."

(o)

*Oath, as administered to His late Majesty, King
George the Third, of blessed memory, according to the
last settlement of its form by Parliament.*

The sermon being ended, the King uncovers his
head, and the Archbishop repairs to his Majesty,
and asks him, Sir, are you willing to take the oath
usually taken by your predecessors? The King
answers, I am willing.

Then the Archbishop ministers these questions, to
which the King answers as followeth:

*Abp.* Will you solemnly promise and swear to
govern the people of this kingdom of Great Britain,
and the dominions thereunto belonging, according
to the statutes in Parliament agreed on, and the
respective laws and customs of the same?

*King.* I solemnly promise to do so.

*Abp.* Will you, to your power, cause law and
justice, in mercy, to be executed in all your judgements?

*King.* I will.

*Abp.* Will you, to the utmost of your power, maintain the laws of God, the true profession of the Gospel, and the Protestant reformed Religion established by law? And will you maintain and preserve inviolably the settlement of the Church of England, and the doctrine, worship, discipline, and government thereof, as by law established, within the kingdoms of England and Ireland, the dominion of Wales and town of Berwick-upon-Tweed, and the territories thereunto belonging, before the union of the two kingdoms? And will you preserve unto the Bishops and Clergy of England, and to the Churches there committed to their charge, all such rights and privileges as by law do or shall appertain unto them or any of them?

*King.* All this I promise to do.

The King then goes to the altar, and laying his hand upon the Gospels, takes the oath following:—
The things which I have here before promised, I will perform and keep, so help me God. He then kisses the book and signs the oath.

THE END.

Printed by R. Gilbert, St. John's-square, London.

# JOURNAL

OF

## THE VISIT

OF

# HER MAJESTY THE QUEEN,

TO

TUNIS, GREECE, AND PALESTINE;

WRITTEN BY

## LOUISE DEMONT.

WITH OTHER CORRESPONDING PAPERS, COLLECTED IN
SWITZERLAND, AND TRANSLATED

BY

## EDGAR GARSTON.

———————

LONDON:

PRINTED FOR T. AND J. ALLMAN,
BOOKSELLERS TO HER MAJESTY,
PRINCES-STREET, HANOVER-SQUARE.
———
1821.

BARNARD AND FARLEY,
Skinner-Street, London.

# INTRODUCTION.

---

THE public curiosity has been considerably
excited, respecting a Journal* of the Visit of
her Majesty the Queen to Tunis, Greece, and
Palestine, written by Mademoiselle Demont,
in consequence of references made to its contents in a letter, addressed by her to her sister, which was produced, and read at the bar
of the House of Lords, during the late proceedings against her Majesty, and of her examination as to its contents, consequent upon
the production of the letter. It might therefore reasonably have been expected, that

---

* I believe that, though in the examination of Demont, the
Journal was only spoken of as a Journal generally, without
specification, it was a general impression that it related particularly to the ". long voyage," as it was termed, " par
distinction."

such a public feeling would have been grati_
fied, by the production of the Journal, either
by the lady herself, or some one of her friends,
unless there existed powerful motives for its
abstraction from public notice.

Into the existence or nature of these motives, I do not pretend to enter, but, as it appears certain, that by her or them the Journal
will not be brought forward, I have myself
determined upon giving to the public a copy
of it, which circumstances placed in my possession some time back.

After having acted as interpreter on the
behalf of her Majesty, at the bar of the House
of Lords, during the production of the evidence, or allegations against her, I had the
honour of being called upon to assist, on the
continent, in the preparation for the defence;
and for purposes connected with it, about the
middle of September last, visited the neighbourhood of the Lake of Geneva, in com-

pany with Mr. Tyson, law agent to her Majesty.

During our stay there, we directed some inquiries and researches to the existence of a Journal, as above stated, the result of which was, the ascertaining that the manuscript had been generally circulated throughout the Canton de Vaud, and that in some instances copies of it had been taken by those to whom it was lent. At Colombier, Demont's native village, we were further informed, that the original manuscript had been carried to England, either by Demont herself, or by an Englishman, who, since her departure, had been over at Colombier to take out some papers respecting her; but, that a copy of it was in the possession of Madame Gaulise, a lady, whose mansion is on an eminence close by the village. This information, combined with the circumstance that this lady is named in Demont's letter, (already alluded to, and a copy of which is annexed to these sheets) as

one who had viewed her Journal with peculiar interest, decided us to call at her residence, for the purpose of requesting her, if
the report of such a document being in her
possession were true, to give it up to us, for
the inspection or use of the advocates of her
Majesty.

We found that Madame Gaulise was from
home, but had an interview with Mons. Gaulise. He confirmed the correctness of the information which we had received, as to his
lady being possessed of a copy of the Journal; but met our request, by declining either
to give it up to us, or to afford us the means
of applying for it, with his sanction, to her;
under the plea of relationship to a noble
family, who might be unfavorable to her Majesty's cause, and of unwillingness to risk the
possibility of his name being introduced in
the business. Being, at that time, much in
haste, we passed on into Italy without having
obtained a copy. Shortly afterwards I re-

crossed the Alps, into the same part of Switzerland. When at Lausanne, I understood that Madame Gaulise was at her house, in that town. I immediately waited upon her, with the intention of making an application, similar to the one before made to Mons. Gaulise, and with yet more earnestness. My surprise was as great, as it was agreeable, when, after having announced my errand, in place of the objections and difficulties which I anticipated, I met an expression of regret, that my request had not been acceded to, on a former occasion. Madame Gaulise had brought the copy sought for, to Lausanne, hoping and expecting, she said, that as it was known that she possessed it, the refusal before given, would not prevent a second application. She accompanied the delivery of the papers, by an assurance, that the copy had been made by her daughter, from the original manuscript of Demont, at the time when it was most eagerly sought after and read, by those to whom Demont, her origin, and connexions, were known. It is from this copy, now in my possession, that the following translation is made.

After giving it up to me, Madame Gaulise expressed the utmost astonishment at the part which Demont had acted, she having always spoken of her Majesty with the highest respect, and in terms of unhesitating praise, whenever her name was mentioned during the visits, which, in consequence of her having held a place about her Majesty's person, and of the false colouring given by her to her return home, she was invited to make at her mansion. She was at a loss to account for it otherwise, than by ascribing it to the influence exerted over her by the Italian who conducted her to Milan*. These sentiments, I

* Her journey to Milan sunk her so much in the estimation of her friends, that it caused many to discontinue her acquaintance. The Demoiselles Jaqurod, whose names were mentioned in Martigny's testimony, were of this num-

already knew, were not confined to Madame Gaulise: they were as general as had been Demont's expression of her opinions, unreservedly and unequivocally avowed by her, to all those who received her after her return from the service of the Queen : these, equally with Madame Gaulise, had compared them with her after-declarations at the bar of the House of Lords. This feeling of astonishment at her conduct, and persuasion as to its immediate cause, were perhaps most strongly felt by those, who not only had heard her opinions verbally expressed, but had perused her Journal, and still remembered passages in it, more particularly one introduced with the description of her Majesty's entry into

---

ber, and gave her an intimation to that effect, through the medium of one who even then remained a friend to Demont. I mention their names with this circumstance, because they were much distressed at the idea of being connected, in the eyes of the world, with Mademoiselle Demont, in consequence of the testimony of Martigny.

b

Jerusalem, which, equally with her **verbal** expressions, and more gratuitously than they, belied her after declarations.

It may be proper here to remark, that in the letter of Demont, produced in the **House** of Lords, and already alluded to, she herself, mentioning her Journal, says, " *on se l'est pour ainsi arraché.*"

It is true, true in its fullest extent, that, **as** she writes in that letter, at the time the Journal was first circulated, it was read with the utmost avidity; not only by those who were actually acquainted with her, and her family, but both at Genoa and Lausanne, by those who were acquainted only with the circumstances of her life, and with her name and origin. The correctness of the allusion made to the Journal in that letter, will be recognised on a perusal of it—and if the perusal of her actions were as easy, it would be as easily known, that that letter, which she ex-

plained as a tissue of deception, was written
in full sincerity, for every sentiment which it
contains, relating to her benefactress, has its
prototype among those which she uttered,
without reservation, amidst her friends, where
deception, and " doubles entendres," would
be difficult and useless. Her conduct is so
revolting to the upright and manly feeling of
the true-hearted Vaudois, that they regard
her as a dishonour to their canton in the eyes
of the world. In truth, it appears that her
conduct must exclude her for ever from Colombier as a home, and from again associat-
ing with the friends of her early days.

I must here state, that at Morges, a
small town, distant about a league from Colombier, on the banks of the lake, I obtained
a copy of a Journal of the same voyage and
travels of her Majesty, on a more extended
scale, which was circulated by Demont after
her return to Colombier. This Journal cor-
responds for the most part minutely in the

facts, dates, and remarks, with the one now
given, with this difference, that the style of it
is superior, and the classical and geographical
notices so much more correct and extended,
that they must have been the result of subsequent labour and reflection on the part of
Demont. The arrangement is not that of a
Journal made " en route," and the descriptions of towns and their dependencies are
rather the fruit of reading, than of a day or
two's hurried visit. I have thought that extracts from this more elaborate performance
would not be inopportune, where they might
contribute to throw more light on the actions
of her Majesty, or on the sentiments of the
writer. It should be remarked that this was
not circulated till after Demont's return
home; the other was received at Colombier
before that time.

Respecting the faithfulness of the translation I need say nothing, as a comparison
with the Journal in its original language,

which will be its companion to the press, will speak for itself: respecting the style I merely have to observe, that the cause of, and apology for, its stiffness, rest alike in its faithfulness to the original.

My last remark is, that in offering this Journal to the public, I have conceived it to be no part of my duty, to deduce any arguments from its contents, or to make any observation upon its bearing or effect upon any of the questions agitated in the recent proceedings at the bar of the House of Lords. The intelligent and impartial reader will make his own reflections on these points.

EDGAR GARSTON.

*Surry Street, Strand,*
    *15th January,* 1821.

# LETTERS

---

*Letter from Louise Demont to her Sister Mariette,*
*dated Colombier, 8th Feb.* 1818.

" Dear and good Mariette,—Although you have not said
four words in your last letter, yet I love you too well not to
pardon you for it; and it is with real pleasure that I reply to
you. I hope, my dear sister, you are perfectly happy; but
I ought not to doubt it, so well as I know the extreme
goodness of her Royal Highness, and of all those with whom
you have any thing to do. Endeavour always to deserve such
kindness, by continuing the same way of life which has
procured it for you, that experience may not be useless to
you. Keep always before your eyes the trouble which
arises from rashness and inconsistency; you have lately
had sufficient proofs of that.

" You will no doubt be very desirous of knowing what is
my situation in our little country; I assure you, my dear, I
have been received in such a manner as you would have no
idea of. I have been every where sought after, and received
with the greatest cordiality at Lausanne, at Morges, and at

Cassonay. I passed a whole month at the last town, where every possible amusement was procured for me. You know how fond I was of sledge-riding; well, every day we made a party for it. At the beginning of the new year we had a delightful masked ball; last week two more, the best that have been seen in this town, and a number of other evening parties given by a friend of mine: in short, every day brought some new invitation. Conceive to yourself how, in the midst of all these numberless pleasures, I was sad and silent; every one quizzed me on my indifference: I, who used to be so gay before my departure. I was not insensible of my dulness, but, spite of all my endeavours, could not get the better of it.

" Can you not, my dear, divine the cause of all my sadness ? Alas! was it not the regret of having quitted her Royal Highness, and of knowing that she suspected my character, and taxed me with ingratitude? Oh, God! I would surrender half my life, could she but read my heart; she would then be convinced of the infinite respect, the unlimited attachment, and the perfect affection, I have always entertained for her august person.

" I should have wished, my dear Mariette, to have written to the Count, to thank him for the kindness he has shown me, but I was afraid to trouble him; tell him one line, if he would but have the goodness to write to me, would afford me a little tranquillity, since it would make me hope for pardon.

" I was afraid her Royal Highness would be displeased at the course I have taken in my journey. Judge, then, of my happiness when I learned that she was not at all angry at it; but, on the contrary, gave me leave to take it. In truth, this pretence has been very useful to me; for you are sufficiently acquainted with the world to suspect that I have been assailed with questions, particularly by great folks—for I am not vain enough to think that I have been sought after only on account of my beautiful eyes—and that a little curiosity has had no part in the desire to see me. Ah! why was not her Royal Highness at my side? She would then have found if I were ungrateful.

" How often, in a numerous circle, have I with enthusiasm enumerated her great qualities, her rare talents, her mildness, her patience, her charity; in short, all the perfections which she possesses in so eminent a degree! How often have I, seen my hearers affected, and heard them exclaim, that the world is unjust, to cause so much unhappiness to one who deserves it so little, and who is so worthy of being happy!

" You cannot think, Mariette, what a noise my little journal has made; it has been, if I may use the expression, snatched at. Every one has read it. —— begged me to let her carry it to Lausanne: all the English who were there wanted to see it immediately. I have been delighted at it, for you know I say in it a great deal of the best and most amiable Princess in the world; I relate in detail all the traits of sensibility and of generosity which she has shown; the manner in which she has been received, applauded, cherished, in all the places we have visited.

" You know that where the Princess is my subject I am not barren; consequently my journal is embellished with all the effusions of my heart, my greatest desire having always been that the Princess should appear to be what she really is, and that full justice should be rendered to her. I assure you, that although distant, it is not less my desire, and that I shall always endeavour with zeal that such may be the case, and as far as my poor capacity will allow. You may judge I shall not make a merit of this, since she will be ignorant of it, and even suspects me of ingratitude; but it will be only to content my heart, which would find a sweet satisfaction in this charming success.

" But I had almost forgotten to confide to you a thing which will surprise you as much as it has me. The 24th of last month I was taking some refreshment at my Aunt Clara's, when I was informed an unknown person desired to deliver me a letter, and that he would trust it to no one else. I went down stairs and desired him to come up into my room; judge of my astonishment when I broke the seal : a proposal was made to me to set off for London, under the pretence of being a governess. I was promised high protection, and a brilliant fortune in a short time. The letter was without signature, but, to assure me of the truth of it, I was informed I might draw on a banker for as much money as I wished. Can you conceive any thing so singular? Some lines escaped from the pen of the writer, discovered to me the cheat, and I did not hesitate to reply in such terms as must have convinced him I was not quite a dupe. Notwithstanding all my efforts, I could draw no eclaircissement from the bearer ; he acted with the greatest mystery.

" You see, my dear, with what promptitude the enemies of our generous benefactress always act. There must be spies constantly about her; for no sooner had I left Pesaro than it was known, with all its circumstances, in the capital

c

of Europe. They thought to find in me a person revengeful and ambitious : but, thank God, I am exempt from both those failings, and money acquired at the expense of repose and duty will never tempt me, though I should be at the last extremity. The Almighty abandons no one, much less those who act agreeably to him. A good reputation is better than a golden girdle.

" Since I have introduced the subject of money, my dear sister, I must give you some advice. Economize as much as possible, retrench every superfluity : did you but know the pain I feel in not having done so ! I do not think I ever was guilty of extravagance, but I have not deprived myself of many things which were almost useless. You know that every one here, as elsewhere, fancies the Princess of Wales throws her money out of the window, and supposes me possessed of a large fortune : from a species of self-love, and to prove still more her generosity, I do not try to undeceive any one; consequently, though I have great need of money, I don't dare to ask my guardian for any. I know how to be moderate, and am at no expence. I have often reflected, that if I had always acted in the same way, I should not be in the situation in which I am.

" Every one should economize as much as possible; one can gain by no other means. Profit by the lesson I have just given you; be assured that it will be salutary to you, for I speak from experience. M. ——— has not sent the packet; I wrote to him at Milan and at Paris. I expect his answer one of these days. If it should be lost, it will be very disagreeable, as the cloth cost a great deal. If I had known, it should not have been purchased, as my mother had a good spencer, and might very well have done without it. I regret the velvet very much, as I want it for my hat; besides, we did not get that either for nothing; and three louis are well worth lamenting, without reckoning the other baubles. Money will not come by whistling for it. A sous here and a sous there soon make a livre, and twenty-four livres make a Napoleon. You see I am become an adept in arithmetic. I will answer for it, however, that Mr. —— will make all good, if he has lost any thing. I shall show him no favour, and have written to him in such a manner as sufficiently shows I am not very well satisfied with his negligence.

" But, my dear Mariette, I perceive I have almost finished my letter without speaking a word of our dear parents. Our good mother is tolerably well, though her asthma, and complaint in her stomach, torment her sometimes, but nothing compared to what she has suffered this summer; my father . is very well; Henrietta is always charming. I give her every day lessons in writing and reading. She sews very well, and *repassie* as well; she has already worked several frills for me, and some gowns, with which I am very well satisfied. Her desire of travelling is the same; pray try to get her a situation; I am convinced she will give you no cause to regret it. She is much altered for the better; she is gay, and always in good humour, mild, obliging, in short, of a character to make herself beloved wherever she goes; for she has an excellent heart, and knows how to be contented in all situations. Margaret is entirely amiable, of a pretty figure, and so lively, that she makes one half dead with laughing. Louisa is very genteel. I assure you, dear Mariette, they are all changed very much for the better, and I am quite contented with them.

" I have been for this month past in my favourite chamber

c 2

at Colombier, where some repairs have been done; for example, a good chimney, and a small cabinet, wherein I sleep
I make little excursions often in our environs; and frequently
receive visits, which afford me amusement.

" I think I hear you say, ' Well, dear Louisa, what do you
mean to do? Won't you marry? What does —— do?' I
will tell you word for word.  I every day feel more and more
repugnance to marriage: ——— has done all in his power
to induce me to accept a heart, which, he says, he has preserved for me these seven years; what heroical constancy,
and little worthy of the age in which we live! I shall not,
however, be dazzled by it; and, although he be rich, charming, and amiable, I do not wish to retract the refusal I gave
him four years ago.

" If this amuse you, I will tell you of several other
lovers, not less desirable than he.  I am very foolish, perhaps, to refuse them; for they are infinitely better than I am—
perhaps I may one day repent it.  You know the proverb,
' He who will not,' &c.  But I cannot do otherwise.  Recent
events have created in me a sort of antipathy to men; I can
have no connexion, no communication with any of them.
I love and cherish sweet liberty alone, and wish to preserve
it as long as I can.

" Dear Mariette, I conjure you imitate my example, and
never think of marrying.  My mother and I forbid it, as long
as her Royal Highness shall wish to keep you in her service.
You can have no greater happiness.  It is impossible! Be-
ware of forming any attachment—you are too young—remain free.  Be assured you will be a thousand times more
happy.

" I do not recommend prudence to you, because I know you too well to distrust you; but, although it may be said of me that I would die rather than abandon it for an instant, and deviate from the strict path of virtue, the most precious good we possess, yet I have known some persons suspect my conduct. But I have God and my own conscience for witnesses. Are they not sufficient for my peace? no one can deprive one of that. No, I have nothing to reproach myself with on that head, and you know, therefore, I can give you such advice as you should follow, especially as it is also that of our mother.

" Dear sister, if you dare, place me at the feet of her Royal Highness, beseeching her to accept my humble respects: do not fail, I entreat you, when she speaks of me, to endeavour to convince her my repentance is still the same; that I conjure her to restore me to her favour. Tell me if her Royal Highness is still so enraged against me, and if there is not any appearance of a pardon; but tell me always the truth. Try also to persuade her Royal Highness that I am and always shall be so entirely devoted to her, that no sacrifice I could make for her would appear too great, and that she may even dispose of my life, which shall for ever be consecrated to her service. Tell the Baron also that I am very sensible of his remembrance, and beg him to accept the assurance of my perfect acknowledgment. Embrace for me the charming Victorine; repeat also my thanks to the Count, and assure him I shall never forget his kindness. Remember me to the Countess, Madame Livia, and Mr. William, begging them to receive the assurance of my sincere friendship.

" If I were to tell you all those who send you salutations,

I should want two more pages; for every one is interested for you, and they never cease to wish for your happiness. Believe, however, the most sincere wishes are made by us.

" You will tell Mr. Hieronymus that John is quite well, and that Mr. ———— is very well pleased with him in all respects. His board is not paid for; and tell Mr. Hierony-mus, on the receipt of this letter, I beg he will immediately send an order to ———— for six months' pay, and address it to me. He must not delay, for I have no money.

" You will not do wrong if you send at the same time the two Napoleons, to make up the twenty-five, if you can. It is I who send you the gown: instead of lace, you should trim it with muslin. Make my compliments to Mr. Hieronymus, and tell him the first time I write again I will give him more particulars respecting his son, because I hope to have more room. I wish very much to know how ink is made with that powder which he gave me, and what he has done with the two pictures I sent him at the Villa d'Este.

" Adieu, dear and good sister. We embrace you cordially. A reply at once if you please.

" LOUISA DEMONT."

" 8th February, 1818.

" A Mademoiselle Mademoiselle Mariette Bron, à Pesaro."

*Letter from Mademoiselle Demont to the Queen, dated Rimini, 16th November, 1817.*

" It is on my knees that I write to my generous benefac-tress, beseeching her to pardon my boldness, but I cannot resist my feelings. Besides, I am convinced that if her

Royal Highness knew the frightful state into which I am
plunged, she would not be offended at my temerity. My
spirits cannot support my misfortune; I am overwhelmed by
it, and I am more than persuaded I shall sink under it. I
feel a dreadful weakness: a mortal inquietude consumes me
internally, and I do not feel one moment of tranquillity. A
crowd of reflections, ' on the-past goodness of her Royal
Highness,' and ' on my apparent ingratitude,' overwhelm me.
May her Royal Highness deign to take pity on me; may she
deign to restore me her precious favour, which I have unhappily lost by the most deadly imprudence; may I receive that
soft assurance before I die of grief; she alone can restore
me to life.

" I dare again to conjure, to supplicate, the clemency and
compassion of her Royal Highness, that she will grant me
the extreme favour of destroying those two fatal letters; to
know that they are in the hands of her Royal Highness, and
that they will constantly bear testimony against my past conduct, kills me. The aversion which I have merited on the
part of her Royal Highness, instead of diminishing, would
be increased by reading them.

" I permit myself to assure her Royal Highness, that it is
only the granting of these two favours which can preserve
my life, and restore to me that repose which I have lost. My
fault, it is true, is very great and irreparable, but love is
blind. How many faults has he not caused even the greatest
men to commit! I dare flatter myself this is a strong reason
why her Royal Highness should condescend to grant me the
two favours which I take the liberty of asking of her.

" I allow myself to recommend to the favour and protec-

tion of her Royal Highness my sister Mariette, and also her
who is in Switzerland.  Her Royal Highness gave me to understand that, perhaps, she might be allowed to supply my
place.  The hope of this alleviated my distress.  It would
be an act of charity, for my sisters have only moderate fortunes, and in our small poor country they are not to be acquired.  I am certain her Royal Highness would have no
cause to repent her great goodness and extreme kindness towards a young girl who has always gained the esteem and
friendship of all to whom she has been personally known.

" I cannot sufficiently thank her Royal Highness and the
Baron for their kindness in sending Ferdinand to accompany
me; he has paid me all the attention and taken all the care
of me imaginable; I know not how to acknowledge so many
benefits; but I will endeavour by my future conduct to merit
them, and to regain the favourable opinion which her Royal
Highness entertained for me during the days of my good
fortune.

" It is with sentiments of the most entire submission, and
the most perfect devotion, that I have the honour to be,

" Her Royal Highness's most obedient Servant,

" LOUISA DEMONT."

*London, June 4, 1821.*

TO

# THE KING,

### HIS FAITHFUL SUBJECTS AND COUNTRYMEN RETURN THEIR MOST AFFECTIONATE GREETING.

SIRE,

.·WE are well informed, that upon the first announcement of " the Letter," which assumed your Royal Self as its penman, you felt indignant at a freedom so presumptuously, and so unexpectedly taken. The feeling was kingly; it was constitutional. But we also *know*, that when your Majesty had read the letter, accompanied as it was by a legal excuse, and personal apology (A), and had soon learnt how its electric effect operated throughout your kingdom, you assented to the obvious motives of its publication, you duly appreciated its good effects, you complimented the heart of the bold man who wrote it, and most graciously and condescend--ingly allowed a copy to be intermediately presented to you.

We do not infer from such permission the adoption of the letter in question; but we do consider it, to amount to a generous forgiveness of the use taken with your exclusive title; and to a tacit acknowledgement of the truths of the publication.

B

Your Majesty therefore now knows, that the Author was no courtier, no ministerial dependant; but a volunteer who at his own risque and single-handed, defended the honour of his King; and explained his conduct; when statesmen and courtiers shrunk from the responsibility.

But let us not be misunderstood; we mean not to reflect upon the House of Peers; for we fully accede to, and admire the constitutional caution with which all allusion to your Majesty, (as being individually interested) was avoided, during the course of the late unhappy investigation. Such forbearance, constituted that " absence of undue influence,". so essential to a right and impartial judgment; and that you were personally thrown into the back ground ; formed the beauty and the contrast of the whole judicial procenium. And when the passion of the moment, shall have subsided, future ages will mark the parliamentary proceedings (b); as a landsman on the summit of a rock, views a vessel buffeting a tempest; the skill and dexterity of whose management, are lost with the sense of immediate danger; but become evident when the storm is conquered, and the ship anchors in safety.

For the sake of perspicuity, we shall assume in our reply, that the letter *was written* by your Majesty; nor will such reply be less recommended to your gracious attention, because a coterie of your subjects, transmits it, on a day (4th June) sacred to the memory of your revered Parent; proud in the annals of undying history, and dear to the recollection of his surviving subjects, and to you more espo-

cially who amidst all circumstances, never ceased for a
moment to be the national model of filial duty.

The frankness with which the King addressed his
people, shall be our model ; and we will say in the
language of an unpublished drama, that,

    " The Monarch, who to his subjects' prayers
    " Turns a proud ear, oft from his truest friends
    " Refuses wholesome counsel————"

Thus far we premise.

Some of your Majesty's warmest adherents, have
greatly disapproved of that condescension, which,
overstepping the boundaries marked by the constitution, first induced you to address to your people
a public exposé in any other form than through
parliament, or by proclamation. Nothing indeed
could justify this aberration, but the peculiar circumstances of the case, so fairly stated by your
Majesty (c). For, that has happened which was
by them greatly apprehended.

A *second* letter upon the credit of the first, has
made its ridiculous and indecent appearance—justified by no overbearing circumstances, as in your
Majesty's first appeal, and which seems to be the mere
paper and print speculation, of a mercenary trades-
man, who being as he announces, bookseller to the Heir
presumptive, ought to have had prudence enough for
his own future interests, not to have made the royal
title common; by an unnecessary and unwarranted second assumption ; and it is to be hoped, that so low-
bred a violation of all decorum, and sound judgment, will not again occur,—for even the object of
scraping together a few pounds, by announcing fre-

quent editions of a few copies to each, will not be effected by such plagiarism *.

When your Majesty was pleased to acquit of disaffection to your person and government, the greater part of those of your misinformed subjects, who joined in the late madness; you spoke graciously and correctly; and when alluding to the discordance which marked its progress, you prophesied a return to public tranquillity; you displayed a confidence in the sound sense of your subjects, and a reliance upon their fidelity, in which you have not been deceived. The result of your conjectures has also been most correctly proved; the plain and intelligible narrative of circumstances and documents which you condescended to lay before the public, has righted popular opinion, and has truly superseded the tortured and distorted details which so lately pre-occupied too great a part of the nation (D). The letter itself has operated, as a public canvass, collecting into one focus, the votes and the attachment of your people.

And, Sire, we feel that this successful appeal ought to render the interests of us your subjects doubly dear to you; we feel also that a people who has thus responded from a state of commotion verging upon civil war, to one of almost undivided attachment to the Throne and the Altar, contains within itself the means of rendering your reign as glorious

* We are glad to learn upon inquiry, that the author of the first letter, is incapable of such conduct; could he, then indeed all his professions of loyalty would be vain, and he would lose the confidence of his countrymen.

as your regency. Its duration is in the hands of Providence.

The Queen has undergone every *moral* punishment adequate to her case. In the eye of the law she is acquitted, the withdrawing of the record established against her in the House of Peers, constitutes that acquittal. The sentence of public opinion, from which there is no appeal, has however passed against her. But the Queen is unfortunately still the wife of the Sovereign, though separated ; and as such, is entitled to every courtesy which can be granted to her, short of a public restoration to society. We view with abhorrence and detestation continued attacks upon her privacy ; they are not founded upon a regard either for public morals, or the regular march of government. The anonymous libellers, who indulge in them, know that should the Queen quit England, their occupation will be gone. They know that by goading her and her household with continued and fabricated slanders, they rouse her spirit, and retain her in the country. This is their selfish object, the whole tendency of their patriotism : and it is a gross insult to the nation to say that the wives and daughters of England require these continued irritations in order to check any renewed intercourse between them and unhappy royalty. These men, however, fancy themselves, and arrogate to themselves, the title of " your friends." Believe, Sire, that you have not among your subjects any more indiscreet or dangerous. Against your enemies you possess every capability of defence ; by such friends alone are you rendered vulnerable ; and we do not hesitate to assert that the conviction and subsequent punishment of Mr. Flindell, (much as we feel for him, and personally esteem him,) for a libel, pending the late investigation, is a sound and satisfactory proof of the impartial administration of the laws of the country,

Actuated by such feelings, we will pass over as briefly as possible the narrative of facts embodied in your letter; but we cannot refrain from pausing upon two points, on which, in our humble opinion, rests the body of your case. We select these, because they prove that case, without requiring any individual testimony; they speak for themselves; and our surprize is, that we have remained so long blind to circumstances, which being discovered, carry conviction to the plainest understanding.

The points to which we allude are, the precise birth of the late Princess Charlotte of Wales, and the absence on the part of the royal house of Brunswick, of all recrimination against yourself (E).

Your unhappy marriage took place on the 8th of April, 1795, and on the 7th of January following that period was completed, almost to the hour, which prescribes the birth of children. To medical men, and old nurses, more versed in the arcana of nature, we leave the solution of this remarkable and uncommon fact; but it certainly tends to corroborate the assertion you are pleased to make, that some previous wrong had been committed.

To the second point, we yield implicit assent—and we fearlessly ask our fellow countrymen, whether they can, or do believe, that there is one virtuous father, or mother, or brother, of any one

kings. It is very ancient, having been founded by
Etolus (one of the descendants of Noah), 320
years after the deluge. It possesses many antiquities worthy of remark ; among others, Dionysius's
ear; it is a grotto, hollowed in the rock in the form
of an ear, and was constructed by Dionysius, the
famous tyrant. The echo is surprising; a pistol
fired in it produces the effect of a cannon-shot;
and words uttered in a very low tone, are repeated
distinctly by the echo. It was here that the unfortunate victims of the tyrant's brutality were
confined! He had caused a small chamber to be
constructed above, in which all the complaints of
the prisoners below could be heard. He placed
a sentinel there, who, in the morning, related to
him what had been said against himself during
the night; and influenced by a fear, that the sol-
dier might disclose the secret of the small chamber,
he strangled him : every evening he caused a fresh
sentinel to be placed there, and every morning he
was, himself, his assassin. It was the same tyrant
who would not suffer himself to be shaved, from a
fear that the operator might cut his throat with the
razor: he compelled his daughters to take off his
beard for him; but, afterwards, suspecting even

press, in tl    termii    d impartial manner,
which it bec(    ge :o    and great King to entertain from a    ık ıd fr    ›eople.

Before we enter upon m    : minute particulars, it
may not be unnecessary to    lace before your Majesty, the features of the late reign ; for it was by
tracing back to their source, your domestic mise-
ries, that all the subsequent proceedings appeared
justified.

His late Majesty ascended the Throne during the
German war ; the issue of that war established
this principle, "That the British nation would
never engage heartily in any conflict, whose object
was the upholding of any continental measures not
immediately connected with her own interests." The
English nation did not, and does not, consider the
union of the Crowns of Hanover and Great Britain
imperative upon the latter, to support the former;
and upon the termination of the German war no
Minister would ever after propose such offensive or
defensive alliance. The English nation will never
fight from etiquette, in honour of a foreign ap-
pendage.

The period from 1763 to 1775, was one of fever-
ish peace ; the power of the Crown was attacked in
every possible way ; the changes of its administra-
tions rendered those attacks more effective, but, several fundamental and excellent principles were established in favour of the people. At the same time
the great question of American independence split
the nation into violent parties, and served to introduce another principle ; namely, " that    ːnt states,
when they have nursed up their col    ıto a ma-

turity of power, must not expect to hold them in
allegiance—like marriageable children they *will* run
alone." ' .

The American war (continued from 1775 to
1783,) was not ended without various cabinet
changes, and great diplomatic difficulties. It was,
throughout, a conflict in the heart of your good
Father, in defence of a right of possession as King,
and against the introduction of republicanism, as
influential upon his kingdom of Great Britain. It
ended, however, in establishing the axiom already
named, and at this period

" Chatham's great son, seized England's destiny."

From 1784 to 1792, the period of peace was
clouded by the first serious indisposition of your
revered Father,' but during it, many most important
improvements, upon which now rests the Commercial superiority of our Country, took place; more
particularly the perfection and general introduction
of the Steam Engine; and the rapid epistolary communication established throughout the kingdom—
but it was a period marked by the active and incessant discussion of republican doctrines; doctrines
which produced a sanguinary revolution in France ;
the abuses of whose government, the imperfection of
whose legislative institutions, and the derangement
of whose finances, afforded not the same power of
self preservation by which your revered Father's
firm principles, aided by Pitt's vigour, saved this
country—The character of this interval was " precaution against threatened danger."

The first French war from 1793 to 1801, (when

middle of the forehead) wrought the instruments of hell. Catania is very clean; the streets, for the most part, are straight, and the houses well built, and new. About it are scattered masses of fire-stone, in size equal to cottages, and in colour like coal, which have fallen from Mount Etna. For-merly there was a port, which the lava has now choked up. The ruins of the old port, where Ulysses anchored his vessels, on his way to the destruction of Troy, are still to be seen.

On the 25th February we left Catania, and arrived in the evening at Augusta, a small town, with nothing remarkable except the harbour, which is safe and good. On the 26th March, the small vessel, called the Royal Charlotte, belonging to her Royal Highness, arrived. We embarked the 1st April, and steered for Girgenti, a town of great antiquity; but which we were unable to visit, on account of the shallowness of the harbour. The island of Sicily is the largest in the Mediterranean, and very fertile; the land yielding every sort of produce spontaneously: the seeds are put into the earth, and left without any culture until the harvest. We saw the corn springing amidst stones

for the last bloody battle of Waterloo, the Continent
would have had to contend a second time, for her
political and independent existence.

This period of twenty four years, interrupted by
two short and deceitful intervals of peace, is thus
characterized by an anonymous writer under the
signature of " Paul Silent." We present them to your
Royal attention, and if the picture is indeed true,
who is there that may not glory in the pre-eminence
of his envied country!

" How varied! how momentous! how unparalleled have been the occurrences of the last twenty-
four years.—We have been enabled to pass through
its eventful and finally brilliant period, by a strict
adherence to sound national principles.—We have
humbled the proud; supported the weak; encouraged and invigorated the doubtful; nor have these
results been the efforts of casual policy, but the consequences of consistent perseverance, unshaken by
difficulty, unawed by opposition,"

" Within this period we have beheld a nation betray her ancient dynasty; surrendering her republican enthusiasm into the hands of a military adventurer; that adventurer carrying conquest to its
utmost limit, and seducing the people to become the
ready tool of the warrior. We have beheld that
fickle nation who had annihilated all hereditary and
legitimate rank, again embody it in the higher style
of Emperor, surrounded by a newly created military
nobility. We have lived to see such power, so
created, subverted by conquest, and that mighty arm
which had subjected Europe, become nerveless;
leaving the giant fabric of its creation, to crumble

like the Heathen image, -into its own component
parts. The march of the firebrand was the progress
of demoralization, and yet the wonderful career was
ended by the restoration, to his ancient throne, of the
descendant of the murdered prince."

" During the contest, every principle whether as
existing between nations, between the governing and
the governed, or betwixt man and man in all his
social relations, has been put to the test, been tried,
substituted and restored. The peasant's cottage has
not been less violated by the spirit of these times,
than the palace has been insulted and disgraced.

" At length, every principle for which England had
contended, was consummated on the plain of Waterloo; the blood of which established our military
superiority. The amor patriæ was the feeling of
every individual who fought under the great captain of the age.

"During this conflict, tremendous and overwhelming to others; England, (whose rampart is the sea,)
stood proudly erect, firm, defying and undaunted;
her people preferring the most arduous exertions,
and personal sacrifices, to the smallest aberration
from political integrity' or national faith. Nay
more—amidst the chaos of contention, Christianity,
the arts and sciences, liberty, valour, and progressive wealth, had never ceased to flourish. The ad-
mirable pattern of religious and domestic life set
before the nation, by their late Majesties; the independence of the judges; the value of personal
character; the perfection of machinery; the establishment of mail coaches; the abolition of the slave
trade; sovereign princes embracing our protection;

shores of Africa! We did not, however, get into
the roads of Tunis till night. "Happy is he
who gets into port after a storm."

On the 4th of April we disembarked at the Goletta. (Note a.) After passing the Mole, there is
a small lake, between the Goletta and Tunis, twelve
miles in length, from which the town presents a
delightful view. At Tunis it is customary to walk
out on the roofs of the houses, and there are ter-
races, upon which it is practicable to make a tour
of the town; but the streets are very dirty and
narrow. Women, of a certain rank, never step beyond their own doors: when their husbands go out,
they lock them up, like slaves, and carry the key
in their pocket. Occasionally, but very rarely, a
few women of the lower class are met with; they
wear ample cloaks upon their shoulders, and two
handkerchiefs over the face, disposed in such a
manner, that merely the point of the nose, and the
eyes partially, can be discovered: they have the
feet always naked, wearing only an undersole of
wood; very wide trowsers are worn by some, pet-
ticoats by others. If a husband meet his wife in
the street, he cannot accost her, under pain of

ink manufactures, fr ı ı it is almost impossible for any but the m lɩ ıed, or the most labo-
riously critical, to make     an useful or authentic
selection.  A decennial lite: ary *auto da fè* would
make a wonderful; lditiɩ  of sound sense to the
caputs of us your rea    ı l-writing-mad subjects.

  But, Sire, during t   ın   al between the American War and the French Revolution, the greatest
injury was done, to the fu   mental points of religion and good government.  It was an age of phi-
losophical literature, in which the wildest, the most extravagant and most absurd theories were certain of
creating the greatest attention ; and during the first
French War, the fruits of these theories were anxiously expected ; but thank God ! a sense of national
danger, which generally acts as a bond of union,
blighted the hopes of the Jacobins, Liberals, and
Republicans.

  A second change, (and it was a great change),
took place at the period of 1797, when Mr. Pitt
discovered with a prophetic eye, that upon public
faith and individual credit, he could raise a substitute for a metallic circulation.  By advising the
Bank of England first to suspend their payments in
specie, and from time to time legalizing the act, Mr.
Pitt, who acted in this instance upon a correct
knowledge of the temper of his countrymen, taught
those countrymen to depend upon their own re-
sources.  His language amounted to this—" The
war drains us of gold to support our own troops, and
to make good engagements to our allies.  Gold in
itself is that commodity the value of which being generally understood, is received in payment of, and

have constantly in their hands a chaplet of seeds,
and count them, saying over every seed, " God is
God, and Mahomet is his prophet." They pray
every two hours, and never without washing their
hands, feet, and ears. Their mosques are very lofty,
and without bells; at an appointed hour, a man,
whose duty it is, stands in a box, over the centre
of the mosque, and cries out that it is the hour of
prayer. The women never go to the mosque, or
church, but pray at home. They have no chairs in
their houses, and remain all the day stretched out on
the floor, with long pipes in their mouths, drinking
incessantly thick coffee, without sugar; which is,
in truth, the most horrible composition that can be
swallowed. The Turks eat with their fingers, and
neither the great nor the vulgar are possessed of
knives and forks. Before each repast, they wash
their feet and hands, and after it repeat the same
ablution.

On the 12th her Royal Highness went to pay
a visit to the Bey (c.), at his country residence. All the Turkish officers accompanied her,
and on the road went through a very pretty ma-
noeuvre to entertain her. They galloped forward

publicanism and liberalism, and all those schisms
and isms for which the age is so notorious.

The press then, still in continued and increased activity, poured forth its lucubrations, but very violent
effusions no longer suited general readers. The
government under which humble merit grew rich,
became to be better appreciated, and the introduction of a paper currency, at a moment when the
metallic circulating medium was at its last dregs,
operated the most extraordinary change upon the
political feelings of this country. At least so it appears to us, and we submit our opinion with due
deference to your known discrimination.

The present state of the press, is that of an over-
charged and too extended a trade, in which every
public occurrence is weighed in the balance of profit
and loss. Formerly public opinion took its tone
from the press; now, the press panders to a vitiated
public taste, which its own licentiousness has mate-
rially created. Your Majesty may smile at our
assertion, when we state (and the assertion is true,)
that such is the degraded taste of a portion of the
reading population, that a murder, or other miserable occurrence, is one of the most lucky hits for the
Sunday newspapers which can possibly happen.
" Be sure and make a good leading article of the
*murder*," would the venal proprietor of a Sunday
paper say to his editor.

In this principle of venality is to be traced the
conduct of the " Old Times" throughout the late
popular commotion. The occasion was too good a
hit not to be turned to account; and the Jesuistry of

that faithless journal can only be accounted for upon the principle, that right or wrong, no matter how or by what means, whether to the destruction of the throne, or the subversion of the altar, whether at the expence of every feeling dear to honourable minds; that truthless print determined to advocate the cause of the Queen, because it was the side which would certainly " pay its two lady proprietors best." In our humble opinion, the press, so far from being free, is bound by the most galling fetters of factious insolence, partiality, palpable falsehood, and personal invective.

If the public were as well acquainted with the press as we are, they would despise, as we do, its artifices and mercenary conduct, and it will ever be so conducted whilst it is in the hands of proprietors, not themselves possessing the necessary qualifications for being their own *responsible editors.* Much as we may differ in political sentiment from Hunt, Thelwall, Wooler, Hone, and men of similar opinions, yet we will do them the justice of saying that their conduct is infinitely more manly than that of the generality of what are termed ministerial papers. These men give their sentiments to the world, and are ready to suffer for it, but the daring openness of their attacks renders those attacks harmless and remediable. In manliness of conduct, the opposition papers have, generally speaking, a superiority above their contemporaries; and in a great degree it is owing to this shew of responsibility that a preference is given to their reading, even by persons differing from them in opinion.

C

Either the neglect of prosecutions on the part of your law officers, or an ultra zeal in favour of the constitution, has given rise to a political combination, which, without professing to do so, appears to take upon itself the duties of the Attorney-General, and to combine with those duties an extended correspondence, and the encouragement of writers of their way of thinking. The society takes upon itself the title of " THE CONSTITUTIONAL ASSOCIATION," and is immediately aimed at the press.

The well-intended motives for this association, we candidly confess, drew us at first into an approbation of it ; but when we reflect that your Majesty is not the king of any one particular sect or party, but the sovereign of a whole and undivided, although a party-distinguished people ; we feel that you, Sire, cannot approve a system of combined attack made by one part of the thinking community upon the other. The principle therefore is, in itself, *ab initio* erroneous. We confess to have brought ourselves to think so with reluctance, but your Majesty can comprehend that a change of opinion, proceeding from conviction of its necessity, is not fickleness. Pounced upon by the Whigs in early life, but now opposed by them in matters of government, your Majesty is by far a better judge of political party than any one of your subjects ; your government being selected, after a change of opinion, arising from experience and conviction.

Either " the Constitutional Association" is, or is not in aid of, or to the supersedence of the political exercise of the functions of the Attorney-General ;

either it is or is not a gratuitous assumption, on their part, of an irksome duty, which the crown imposes upon itself by becoming a public prosecutor.

When the Attorney-General exercises his high constitutional power of *ex-officio* information, he passes over the previous protection which the accused receives from the first opinion of a grand jury, and this very omission of a protective step renders the performance of his duty at all times painful and invidious. It is the extreme jealousy with which such extra jurisdiction is viewed by the people, which renders the proceeding seldom resorted to, but in important cases. And it is this wholesome fear of the people which induces the Attorney-General to confine his duty to such cases, as in their verdicts, would be probably followed by the acquiescence of the kingdom in their propriety.

The first objection therefore to the mode in which " the Constitutional Association" proceeds, is, " that there appears to be no prevention to the members of the grand jury, (not liable to challenge) sitting to decide upon an indictment, instituted by the very political society of which themselves might be members." It is true that such members might retire on the presentment of such indictments, but a possible case might arise, when, from such honourable delicacy, the jury might be reduced below an adequate efficiency. The initiatory proceedings of justice may thus become clogged, or be rendered difficult.

" The next interference which such association creates with the regular march of the courts of law, is, "the additional cause it creates for the challenge of jurymen, and the irritation occasioned by such challenge." The jurymen who are members, will upon challenge, become disqualified for their duty; those who are not members will consider this act of special challenge, as an act of imputation, and may proceed to a consideration of their verdict, under circumstances, by possibility, creative of prejudice. This may or may not be an extreme view of the case; but however remote, it ought not to exist.

As we consider, Sire, that the causes for prosecution which would be selected by this Association, would only be such, as aimed by libel, whether of caricature or in writings, to subvert the Constitution in Church and State, and to bring into contempt the person or persons connected with the executive of such constitution; no counter society could be set up against it. That insinuation therefore of Mr. Brougham's is puerile and visionary, because the objects and motives of the Association are laudable, excellent, and praiseworthy; and therefore its antagonist would be exactly the reverse—and this its opponents know; and had not the office of Attorney-General been in existence, we should then have viewed this society (conscientiously founded, as we believe it to be, upon a pure attachment to the kingdom;) as one of essential value and general importance.

Neither do the funds, which have been subscribed towards the objects of this Association, render it dangerous, because in cases of indictment by the Attorney-General, the power of the crown and the purse of the people, are both engaged against the individuals so indicted; and compared with these, the capability of the Association is puny and weak. Indeed, if it could by possibility be shewn, that indictment by the Association is less hard upon individuals than an ex-officio proceeding, then some good tempered excuse ought be framed for its existence,—for that is no bad design which aims to supersede the odium of crown prosecutions; and whose object is, to protect the Constitution against sedition and disloyalty, from motives of attachment to, and personal admiration of, such Constitution.

But, the very nature of the power of ex-officio information is, in political matters, one of exigence, or of last resort. To bring, therefore, a similar power into more frequent operation, (which we submit, Sire, would be the effect of a private combination,) would keep a constant irritation alive in your kingdom;—this is unadvisable, inexpedient, and may be dangerous,—it would establish a *raw* on the body of the community, always in a state of blister.

We could point out to your Majesty a hundred, nay, a thousand libels, as well against your person and government, as against the principal executives of the administration, which daily pervaded the Old Times and its imitators upon a late occasion; but who is there who would be so indiscreet and vindictive as to advise prosecutions *now?* And it is the major acquiescence of the country in the propriety of such ex-officio indictments, which have of late years taken place; and the general character of forbearance which marks the conduct of that responsible law-officer, the Attorney-General, which command respect for an office not the best liked among

our various institutions, and gives a character of great
political toleration to the government of the country;
of this character it may be deprived by the com-
panionship or rivalship of a subscription association.

The means of superior information, which ought
to be, if it is not possessed by the Home Department, enable the responsible head of that secretary-
ship to direct public prosecutions with a more discreet selection.   It is not the mere publication of a
libellous or blasphemous work which creates the
sole mischief, such a work may be printed and still
not find its way into circulation.   Prosecutions may
in some cases tend to diffuse the poison; and therefore too frequent prosecutions increase the evil,
which they are intended to check.   Many obnoxious
works would of themselves die away, for want of
that degree of excitation which is frequently given to
them by prosecution.   Considering, therefore, these
nice points as not likely to direct the judgment of
a private association, we make it an additional objection.

There is scarcely an axiom of religion, of government, or of policy, which has not within these latter
years, been freely, perhaps too freely canvassed by
the press; and thousands of thousands have bled in
the attempt to carry their most pernicious doctrines
into effect; yet England exists, prouder, safer, and
greater in spite of these attempts; and we conceive
that if there was a moment, when any ultra-associa-
tion was unnecessary, it is at this present public calm:
for though the circulation of the Bible, without com-
ment, may perpetuate and increase dissent from the

5

Established Church, yet it must certainly tend at least to check blasphemy, and in a great measure obstruct sedition ; and it would be a most lamentable discovery to make, should it be found, that with extending education, dangerous principles were co-equal and co-existent. If such is not the case, (and we cannot but think the pains of so many active public characters are not thrown away ;) then is there a power already in operation, which will of itself progressively decrease, and render useless the operations of such an association. Besides, the six acts which passed a very short period previous to your Majesty's accession, have had great effect in promoting the tranquillity of the country, as connected with the press.

As to the objections made against " the Constitutional Association" upon the grounds of its inherent illegality ; such grounds being referential to the 39 Geo. III. cap. 79. none can be so absurd or utterly dissimilar,—that act is against secret societies ; not against anonymous subscribers who may contribute towards the support of public institutions. In the concealment of the name of a contributor, no improper secrecy takes place. " Let not thy right hand know what thy left doeth," is a scriptural axiom : but the secrecy meant by law, is *the secrecy of design.* Now, the objects of the Constitutional Association are plain, comprehensible, and decided. They are, " to repress by every legal means in their power, disloyalty and sedition." These are no secret objects, they are as open as the noon-day. But not so were the secret societies, aimed at by the Statute alluded to. Of these however public the subscription, or the names of the members; the object was so base, and so traitorous, as not to be entrusted indiscriminately to its association. Such members indeed might *believe*, that when they aided with their purse or their influence they gave effect and vigour to some *secret* proceedings, which were to produce the object of their revolutionary inclinations; but the mode of proceeding being in itself illegal and traitorous, could not bear the light. The Statute therefore of 39 Geo. III. cap. 79. aims not at the *secrecy of contribution*, but at the *concealed purpose* to which such contribution was to be applied.

There is, however, Sire, a very strong objection to any association being formed for the prosecution of political offences, namely, that bad as are the effects of such offences upon the community, they are still " matters of opinion, which can be counteracted by the press itself." We consider that Dr. Watson's Apology for the Bible, did more towards discountenancing the infidel writings of Tom Paine, than years of prosecution would have done. The Society for Promoting Christian Knowledge, does not proceed by indictments against blasphemers and Atheists; no! its efforts are all argumentative, they answer the dogmas, and confute by reasoning, the sophistries of the day.

A comparison has been drawn between this association and the Society for the Suppression of Vice; but the difference between the two is obvious. An obscene print, or snuff box, a book which denies Christianity, or the breach of the Sabbath, are declared offences at common law; they require proof only of the fact to become cognizable to punishment.

But, in political cases, the fact of publication being proved, still leaves the libel as matter of opinion, and, that such opinion may vary, is evident in the result of Hone's trial, and that of a country bookseller: the one was acquitted in London, and the other found guilty in the country, *upon the same publication, and similar prosecution.*

The answer of the one society in reference to the objects of the other, thought by many to be similar, is, "*they* look at *political* offences, *we* at breaches of decorum; denials of Christianity; and the profanation of the Sabbath." Yet an honourable Baronet has declared in the House of Commons, that he was induced to become a member, because he was told that its object *was not political.*

Your Majesty may possibly discover from these pro and con arguments, that good as are the motives of such an association, yet the attempt to carry them into effect, deranges the usual course of the laws; it supersedes or divides the duty and office of the Attorney-General; it interferes with the particular department of the Home Secretary of State, whose office is co-existent with the Constitution, which an ephemeral society cannot be; it confuses or may confuse the discharge of the duties of grand juries; it provokes an unnecessary challange to the special or common juryman—but, should such association abandon its system of prosecution, and upon proper occasions call on the Attorney-General to do his duty, or point out to him cases deserving public indictment; if with such vigilance they promoted at the same time, the efforts of conscientious and consistent writers, by aiding the first introduction of their works into circulation, they might possibly accomplish all their good and well-intentioned designs, in as certain and in a much more unexceptionable manner. At all events they aim only at legal decisions.

We have, Sire, unavoidably been carried into minute observations on this newly-sprung society; certainly connected with the press greatly;—and of the general state and character of the periodical Journals, we may now venture to submit to your Majesty, "That it is in a high degree venal, and irresponsible, and does not possess that union of proprietorship and adequate talent, centered in individuals, so necessary to elicit truth;" that " the close union of such property and such talent in the same individuals, would rectify the licentiousness of the press;" for if there is any one occupation, which, as connected with the general welfare of the kingdom, and the happiness of individuals, should be conducted with all possible absence of mercenary motive; it is the periodical press;—and men of the first talent and influence in the kingdom, should not stand idly by, and leave so important a duty as the guidance of public opinion, in the hands of interested tradesmen. The trading quality of the periodical press occasioned the late attempt which scarcely stopped short at revolution. The generosity of the transaction was in favour of an accused Queen; generosity has a very bewitching sound in the ears of your subjects; and the speculation answered to the utmost extent of the wishes of the two Lady proprietors of the Old Times. "*The Queen shall be innocent; it will pay us best as tradesmen; and,*

*right or wrong, black or white, we will defend her
through thick and thin;"* discovers the talisman of
the whole transaction.

Your Majesty is pleased to allude to the effects
which the press produces on the mind of a Sovereign, and more particularly on your own (1). As
we are no proprietors of Newspapers, and are
wholly unconnected with the periodical journals,
and dare to act and think for ourselves, your Majesty may possibly now receive courteously from us,
if not able, at least impartial opinions, upon the
character of your administration, and the state of
your kingdom, in some of its important branches.

First, then, Sire, what is the character of your
Cabinet?

The great feature of your administration is, its
lengthened duration; for though five nominal
changes have occurred, of which one of them was
a feeble attempt at a coalition of discordant parties,
and another a short trial of the capabilities of whig-
gism, yet, from 1784 to the present day, (a period
of thirty-seven years,) has the policy of " Chatham's
great son," guided, animated, and directed, the measures of government. Such a lengthened duration
must at least have given a systematic character to
the present executive. The Cabinet has also this
peculiarity; it is formed by you in opposition to
those attachments which you are known to have entertained at an earlier period of your life; and the
reasons alleged by you, Sire, for such choice, do
honour to you as a son and a Sovereign; and have
gained, as they deserve, our confidence (k).

Whether, therefore, the individuals themselves

were more experienced than their opponents, or inferior to them, in political acumen, at all events they were selected, *not upon the principle of favoritism,* which has guided heretofore the formation of many Cabinets.

Again. The great officers of the Crown are as individuals distinguished by a high character of private worth; their subordinate coadjutors are not deficient in such excellence, and certainly all form together an almost unexceptionable body of intellectual diplomacy. To their personal merits, their keenest opponents bow. But the Cabinet possesses one unfortunate fault, which it cannot remedy. It *betrays its age;* all its members are courteous, systematic, correct and punctual; but two only are vigorous: Of these, the one with the gravity of a mentor, preserves the spirit and the wit of youth; the other is, and ever was, bold, undaunted and decisive. Both are no half-measure politicians, or expediency-mongers in cases of threatening danger. There is also a schism in your Majesty's Council, which may eventually endanger the kingdom, and work the downfall of the present Constitution: but of it generally we acknowledge, that though it is the best Cabinet in Europe for carrying public measures into practical effect; yet its age, its age, Sire, renders it unwilling to originate new ones: it is also *almost too amiable* towards its political antagonists.

Of those antagonists it may be said, that such as are in the House of Lords seem tired of controversy; and appear to acquiesce in silence to the measures of administration: though that such opposition can become formidable on great occasions, is evident

from the superior talent, eloquence, and legal acumen so eminently displayed during the late trial.

Of the opposition in the Commons' House of
Parliament it may be said, that the collisions of
those rival statesmen Pitt and Fox, have left little of
novel principle to be discussed in matters of government or of policy. The present discussions are
either confined to the introduction of fine drawn
theories in the place of practical results, or the petty
details of official disbursements. If, however, no
very commanding talent is displayed by the opposition, there is enough of that puzzling acumen to
keep the ministry on the alert, and the clerks in
office with their eyes wide awake. Harassed by
such minute enquiries, the ministry has with difficulty prevented the public service from being impaired by too rigid an economy: for the principle
of economy does not *wholly consist*, in diminishing
every expence not immediately productive of results ;
but also in preventing the increased cost, at which,
in the event of a war, the revival of suppressed
establishments would occasion. There is a sort of
economy which in the end might be found the very
height of extravagance; but keeping in view this
latter object, *it is due to the people of England, who
now provide for an enormous burthen of public
debt, that not an unnecessary shilling should be ex-
pended.*

The difference of measures between the government and the opposition appears to us to be—that the
one looks to futurity; the other would legislate from
day to day, and depend upon their luck. The one
perpetuates establishments which may hereafter be

useful; the other would avoid their expence, in the hope of not wanting them. But peace is at best but the nurse of war. Which policy is wisest, and more conformable to historic experience?

But, Sire, the great danger which threatens the country, arises from its finances; we do not mean from the weight of taxation more than from the necessity of a new and more vigorous, and at the same time a more economical mode of finance: and it is here that your cabinet wants vigour, and betrays no genius. Never was the loss of the great Pitt's influence more felt than at the conclusion of the war, when the discussion of continuing or abandoning the property tax took place. The Chancellor of the Exchequer appeared neither to have had influence or eloquence sufficient to keep together that phalanx which had supported the war. No sooner was it ended, than an impatience of taxation (by the bye a very unlucky expression, though a most pertinent one) shewed itself; and by the artful management of the men of property, petitions upon petitions were procured against the tax from the very classes of the community *whose interest it was to perpetuate it.*

It was said at the time, that the tax upon property was thrown out by the voice of the people, acting through their representatives; if so, we ought never again to be told, that the nation is not represented, or that its representatives sit in mockery of the rights of the people. We contend in its fullest sense for the important benefit of petition to parliament, on all public measures which are in their nature fit subjects for such addresses; but where the right is exercised

as an occasion of insult, then it is violated ; and we
also think that it well becomes every one who
signs a petition to either House of Parliament, to
put to his own honest heart a few previous questions; possibly such as these:—"Am I interested
in this measure? Am I acting upon my own free
judgment, or am I biassed by the opinions of others?
Am I actuated by a sincere and honest intention
towards the general welfare of my country?. Am I
not the passive instrument of a party? Do I rather
wish to gain to myself some private advantage, than
to make a little sacrifice to the public welfare?"
If the petitioners against the property tax had asked
themselves these questions, they had not fallen into
a measure which was calculated to benefit the rich,
and perpetuate the burthens of the intermediate
classes of the community.

As a convincing proof of this, the following official declarations are evidence :

*Extract from the Speech of the Chancellor of the
Exchequer.*

(Old Times, 6th March, 1816.)

" By the abstract of the population returns, it
appeared that 1,131,000 families were employed in
trade and in handicraft occupations. Of these only
266,000 had made returns under the property tax
act; and consequently, three out of four of the
families so employed had not only never paid, but
had never been called upon to pay. Of these
266,000 no less than *one hundred and nine thousand
families were exempted,* having returned that their

Incomes were less than 50*l.* per annum; and the number which really contributed to the tax was therefore reduced to 157,000, or for the sake of round numbers to 160,000. Of these families 121,000 had made returns of incomes to a less amount than 150*l.*, and were consequently entitled to an abatement; and only 41,000 had paid for incomes above 150*l.*—32,000 returned a less sum than 1000*l.* per annum, and 3692 above that sum."

*Extract from the Speech of the Chancellor of the Exchequer.*

(Old Times, 8th March, 1816.)

" Having now given a statement of the number of the poorer classes of tradesmen who were exempted, he would now state a similar return which had been made with regard to the farming interest. The total amount of the families assessed under the tenant's tax was 589,000. Of these families 324,500 paid under the reduced scale, having an income of less than 150*l.* The persons paying at the rate of 200*l.* a year, being the full rate, were 42,000 only."

After these statements we would ask, how many of the 109,000 poorer families pay assessed taxes? and of the agricultural class, how many of the 432,500 pay now a greater sum in assessed taxes than they would by a reduced property tax?

Why, the petitions against the income tax were signed by twice the number of persons *more than had ever paid it !*

women. The port is six miles distant from the old
town, agreeably with the system anciently pursued
by the Greeks, through motives of policy, of con-
structing their ports at a distance from their cities.
On the 29th we set sail, and the following day the
wind became so violent, that we were obliged to
come to an anchor off Cape Colonne. On a
mountain above the road are the ruins of an ancient temple of Minerva Poliades, built of splendid
white marble : there still remain fifteen columns,
which we visited.

The first of June, the wind being again favorable, we set sail, and on the 3d reached the isle of
Tenedos, opposite to the plains of Troy. It was
thither that the Greeks retired, whilst the wooden
horse, with ten thousand men enclosed in it, was
introduced within the walls, for the purpose of destroying this great and beautiful city, after it had
withstood a siege of ten years. There is no longer
a stone to be seen of its once proud edifices, and
its site is an unbroken plain, planted with olive
trees. We twice passed the Scamander, which
formerly crossed the city. At a trifling distance is
New Troy, built by Alexander the Great. The

F

the least violation of the faith pledged to them by government, would render loans at any future period uncertain, difficult, and precarious. But, Sire, this thraldom will be increased by delay; and now is the time to originate such a measure, when it might possibly be supported by the agricultural and internal commercial interests. The measure is a vigorous one, but is necessary, and better done now than at the approach of a war.

We are well aware that in the cant language of the day, a flourishing exchequer would be thought too great a temptation to the extravagance of ministers, and increase the influence of the Crown. But, Sire, late events have shewn us that those bugbears do not carry in them half the danger, or half the reality which they did in former times.

A flourishing exchequer at this moment would tend more to the preservation and duration of peace, than any other national demonstration. It is only in our debt that we are considered vulnerable by foreign nations; and the diminution of the credit of Great Britain, or any serious derangement of her finances, would be the signal for attack. Any surplus, therefore, which might arise by a new system of taxation, would arise from the payments of those who now pay nothing, and by whose non-payment a greater weight is thrown upon particular interests. Any surplus which might thus arise, would be strictly confined by the House of Commons, either to the sinking fund, or in an adequate abandonment of smaller branches of the revenue; and the same jealousy of new charges or expenditure should be as strictly exhibited as it is now.

7

But, Sire, we would in the amount of this property tax, also include the provision for the poor
rates, which, as at present provided for, gnaw the
very vitals of the land. Vain, Sire, is the attempt,
session after session, to prop up a system radically
bad—by select vestry bills, and new vagrancy acts.
The very execution of the acts relating to the poor,
costs annually (as we understand) about 60,000*l.*

Now, Sire, let us suppose every act of parliament
regulating the poor (one only excepted) repealed; it
will create a freedom from all that confusion with
which half-witted lawyers and system-mongers surround it. The act upon which we propose to build
the system, is the 43 *Eliz. cap.* 2. passed in the year
1601. The preamble of that act contains the whole
essence of regulation as to the poor. It provides
*work* for the unemployed, *competent payment* to the
lame, impotent, old, blind, and such other among
them, being poor, and *not able to work;* and also
*the means of apprenticing* children to work.

Work, Sire, when the party is not incapable, is
the basis of the act of Elizabeth; and by whom are
the funds to be provided, and upon whom levied?
" Weekly, or otherwise by taxation of every inhabitant, parson, vicar, and other; and of every occu-
pier of lands, houses, tithes impropriate, propriations
of tithes, coal mines, or saleable underwoods in the
said parish, &c."

There being at the time of the passing of this act
no such a hydra as a national debt, and the above
description of liable payers comprehending all the
existing descriptions of property extant; we do not
think it would be too bold a supposition to throw

out, "that had there been a national debt in the days of Elizabeth, it would have been comprehended as a fund applicable, among other properties, to the relief of the poor:" And it is, upon this argument, we submit, that the poor-rates may be, with justice, raised upon a general property-tax, *including the funds*.

Your Majesty will, at once, perceive the operation of our arguments, by a statement of very little intricacy.

| | £. | s. | d. |
|---|---|---|---|
| Amount of assessed taxes, ending 5th January, 1821 ............. | 6,309,680 | 13 | 2¼ |
| Annual poor-rates (about)............. | 6,000,000 | 0 | 0 |
| | £12,309,680 | 13 | 2¼ |

We suggest to abolish the assessed taxes, and the present mode of raising the poor-rates, which operate too exclusively upon agriculture, and replace them with a ten per cent. property tax.

The income of the kingdom (arising from real property) is estimated at two hundred millions, but suppose it taken only at one hundred and fifty millions, the produce will be fifteen millions; or a surplus of nearly two millions and a half, of ways and means; which, added to the surplus of the ways and means already existing, (which will not be affected by this change to *a vigorous* system of finance;) create an efficient sinking fund of four millions; and the new system will operate to the relief of thousands and tens of thousands of little farmers, artificers, and shopkeepers, now paying away their earnings in poor-rate assessments, and assessed taxes.

The machinery by which the poor-rates are to be raised, and distributed, is not intricate; but we have not space now to enter fully into its discovery, or applicability; we, the few individuals who now respectfully approach you by letter, on the part and on behalf of the people, beg leave to invite the attention of public characters to such a proposition; and profess ourselves ready to lend any and every aid in our humble power to promote a better arrangement of the poor rates, and administration of the poor laws.

But, Sire, before we quit the subject of *vigorous finance*, we cannot but draw your attention to the transfer which has taken place in the property of the country, occasioned by a long continuance of war, and the great increase of the public debt. That debt some propose to annihilate in part, or degree, as the means of avoiding national bankruptcy. To us the accumulation of the national debt suggests this proposition—" To render part of it permanent and un-redeemable, by converting the value of the tythes of the kingdom, by instalment purchases, into perpetual and unfluctuating stock," and this not by any compulsory measure, but by agreement between the parties, in which they may avail themselves of the facilities of an act of parliament. But as this measure may at first alarm the Church, of which we are zealous though unimportant members, we beg to state to your Majesty, as head of that Church, that even the future discussion of such a measure, must proceed upon certain clear and unequivocal principles.

1. A fair and *bonâ fide* valuation of the tythe.

2. A solemn national guarantee to the Church, of

the inviolability of their property, invested in lieu of tythes.

3. A provision for the fluctuation of their income, rising and falling by the value of corn in which the tythe is to be estimated; so that the Church shall preserve an income, at all times, referential to the value of landed property.

4. That the act of parliament shall be an available, and not a compulsory act.

By these two measures, "the supply of the poor-rates from the general property of the kingdom," and "the purchase into stock, of the tythes of the kingdom by the land-owners;" agriculture would revive, and yet corn be cheap; at present, with less means, agriculture supplies three parts of the taxation of the kingdom, being a third more than equitably belongs to it.

The financial state of the country points out another principle, namely, "That the funds, possessing in themselves an instant capability of transfer; by which any fund owner may, at his pleasure, dissolve his contract with the government, which borrows on behalf of the nation, the time *is now come* when such funds may be considered, to all intents and purposes, as available and permanent property, and not of that kind temporarily lent, and which may be wanted for other purposes. Transfer is equal to repayment. The funds, generally, is that portion of the wealth of the nation which can be spared from its active commercial capital; consequently the due payment of the interest is of more essential moment, than any redemption of its principal sum." Indeed the setting loose, by redemption (were it possible) of the capital debt of the nation, would raise the price of land to double its value, and consequently enhance every article of subsistence in adequate proportion.

Thus much for the finance of the country, in the due appreciation of which no measure is so likely to instruct the humbler classes of us your Majesty's subjects, as the various saving-banks which are now so beneficially established throughout your kingdom of England. A general report of whose collective proceedings, annually laid before parliament, would afford a most important clue to the state of industrious labour; and the happiness of the individuals belonging to it.

We should exhaust your royal patience, were we to enter upon every subject open to discussion, which the various interests and feelings of the community present continually in restless change; as fully as we have, this topic of vigorous finance. We need only enumerate some.

Whether secondary punishments will prevent crime more effectually than the fear of death; whether prisons may or may not be robbed of their terrors by the introduction of too philanthropic a feeling; or, as Sir William Curtis tritely observes, whether they are to be furnished with sofas and Turkey carpets: whether the perfection of the Bank Note will not turn the attention of foreigners to the forging of notes of a larger amount: whether a paper of one peculiar colour, which shall not be allowed to be made, stained, or colored, by any paper maker in England, except those fabricating it for the Bank of England, or be imported, would not present as complete a check to forgery, as expensive machinery can supply; whether education will or will not improve the morals of the lower classes of the community, whilst blasphemous and seditious cheap publications remain so greatly in circulation: whether the Bible should or should not be circulated with notes: whether the Society for Promoting Christian Knowledge, or the Bible Society, be the best of two religious institutions: whether civil and religious liberty be a good substitute for defined doctrines, and obedience to government, or vague and unsatisfactory terms: whether public institutions do not, in many instances, destroy private benevolence; or whether we are more charitable one to another privately and individually, because the nation is publicly so: whether our laws are, or are not becoming obscure by their multiplicity: whether many private bills do or do not enforce a taxation much more oppressive than the taxation of the State: whether the daily publication of the debates of both houses of parliament has or has not of late years exhibited all the arcana of government; shewing us all how we are governed; effecting a *personal* reform among its members; and establishing a check against corrupt measures, through the immediate influence of public opinion: whether we are improved in our generation in wisdom and happiness; or, as the French say, have a shadow only of morality, and a shadow of liberty: whether England will recover from the pressure of an enormous debt, or sink gradually into national bankruptcy: whether gold or silver, or both should be the standard of relative value: whether trade should be un-

customed, or manufactures unbountied : whether
trading monopolies should or should not exist,—are
some of the many important topics which continually
call forth the faculties and the labours of the greatest and best men among us ; and, Sire, although we
are continually boasting of the duration and wisdom
of our institutions, it would seem as if, at the same
time, all our efforts were directed to trifle with or
destroy them. Our ancestors *did* great things; we
talk greatly about little matters ; yet, notwithstanding all this talking and writing, we have not *as yet*
essentially undermined those great fundamental
truths upon which our Constitution in Church and
State is seated ; and, indeed, it is only among a free
and intelligent people that such vital collisions of
varying opinion could exist, without producing dis-
organization or treason.

But, Sire, in a former part of our Letter we frankly stated that a schism did exist in your Cabinet,
which may eventually endanger the kingdom and
work the downfall of the present constitution. Your
Majesty will instantly recognize that our allusion is
to Catholic Emancipation, or as we should say, "the
undermining of Protestant ascendancy." But in calling
it *a schism* in the Cabinet, we are far from condemn-
ing the consideration of this most important question,
as carried on without combination in the ministry, as
improper: on the contrary, as you are, Sire, King
as well of your Catholic as Protestant subjects, so
your Council ought to comprehend those who are
versed in the interests and policy of both persua-
sions. Our regret is, that there is occasion for
schism.

...Those who now take upon themselves to reply to your Majesty's Letter, are decided members of the Established Church; they cannot therefore but rejoice that the late attempt failed. Introduced as was the discussion under Tom Paine's doctrine of the rights of man in a state of nature, unconnected with the performance of duties, or undistinguished by gradations of qualification; yet it was subsequently argued with great acumen, and a calmness of temper which did honour to both parties in the debate. We rejoice also, that the Heir Apparent to the throne, that the constitutional ruler of your Majesty's conscience, (the Lord High Chancellor) and that your Majesty's Prime Minister all united to oppose the demands of the Catholics. We argue from it (perhaps wrongfully and presumptuously) that your Majesty had also decided *to abide by the pure faith of your royal forefathers.*

But, should the qu t      even present itself to your Majesty, in the         a bill to be sanctioned by your royal signatu     see no alternative, too        rejection,    t  il       To this alternative ur protestant          never can, and never ll expose you     C      int we should tremble  our   r  c       r a moment entertain t     t  t f       disparity of age, and in the c       tu     e Crown of England should ever   nd   n       head of the Duke of Sussex    t  Si    re       that the union of protestant      c can       To the latter, we of t  f  faith,    no  ice, no uncharitableness,    u  ris  n f       e ground our objection to t    n, first, upon fear for our own safety, and

43

secondly upon the want of proof on the part of the
Catholic, that his faith, or his doctrines are so
changed or so altered, as safely to amalgamate with
the tolerating spirit of the Church of England. In the
discussion of this measure in both Houses of Parliament, much stress was laid upon the liberalism
and enlarged views of the Catholics, and their
participation in the enlightened spirit of the age.
But not one proof, not one witness, not one avowal
by petition of such fact; not one acknowledgement
of a change of faith, or of feeling toward a differing
establishment was exhibited, but on the contrary,
as the following paper will testify *, as well as the
resolutions of many of the Roman Catholic Clergy
in Ireland †.

It should also, Sire, be remembered that this
question was one, in which silence ought not to imply consent; the tables Sire, of both Houses of Parliament *ought to have groaned under the weight of
petitions; disclaiming on the part of your Catholic
subjects, all those obnoxious tenets which create the
barrier between them and Heretics.* Had this been
done, some basis for believing that the Catholic
temper was changed, would have existed ‡.

* Theological Judgmei : of the Catholic Divines. (1.)
† Against this Theolo      Jud      t, it has been argued
that Dr. Milner is a zealc        so,    nay turn out, that Dr.
Milner adheres to his reli; i      f,    ilst the Catholics as a
body, are gliding into pro
‡ A more minute exam              petitions as were presented, might tend to d   o    , t   those protestants who
petitioned in favour of th   (    iolic   ethren, were politically
adverse to your governm   ; a   hoped by such junction to
gain stren   to such op   ion.

It was also an occasion, in which, in our humble opinion, previous to any parliamentary discussion, a convocation of the two Churches ought to have been held, to have attempered if possible their differences; and to have agreed upon some suitable oath ; for we cannot but consider an oath, a religious, rather than a political act.   Upon such a proposition, what would have been expected from the Roman Catholic Clergy?   Does your Majesty think they would have obeyed any mandate from *you* to attend such convocation, without leave from their Pope? and if not without such leave, is there not then a power existing, paramount to your own, and that too within your own dominions?   We shall be told, that this is spiritual power—so much the worse ;—which is of greatest influence in the regulation of Kingdoms? spiritual or temporal power.   We say that even in our own tolerant Church, spiritual power by which we mean the influence of Religion, is greater than any mandate issued in opposition to it, by any temporal authority exercised by your Majesty. We acknowledge you Sire, as Head of our Protestant Church, but could we for one moment dwell upon a case, in which your Majesty should attempt the destruction of that Church; we should fly to her protection in defiance of your temporal authority.   But your Majesty reigns over us by the happy and felicitous union of spiritual and temporal power, which forms the rock on which your throne is embedded.   This union of Church and State, is the pith, the heart-core of the Constitution.

Much has been said, or presumed upon the change of feeling in the Catholic towards their Protestant

fellow-subjects. When and how is this proved?
We do not find it in the document already subjoined; we do not find it in the notes of the Douay
Bible, circulated throughout Ireland, by episcopal
sanction. In the notes of that Bible, your Majesty
is by inference denounced as a heretic, and of course
subject to anathema; and the same horrid curse is
poured out, as violently, and as fanatically against
all your Protestant subjects, as it ever was under the
bigoted Mary (M).

 But, Sire, from the very circulation of this Bible
with notes, the alarm of the Catholic Clergy is evident. The Bible was published in 1816, and three
years after, a further evidence of the alarm of the See
of Rome for the conversion of its flock was afforded,
by a rescript from the seat of his Holiness the Pope,
of which we subjoin an extract (N).

These, Sire, the protest and explanation of Dr.
Milner, the Notes of the Douay Bible, and this rescript from papal Rome, are *stubborn facts*, and
oppose themselves to all the assertions so loudly and
clamourously made, that the Catholic Religion is
become one of a milky liberalism. Upon the good
conduct of the Catholics, as subjects, we have only
a few remarks to present. The Catholics of England are very few in proportion to the population,
are estimable members of society, possess the unmo-
lested exercise of their religion, are secured in their
property, and can at any time lay their grievances
before Parliament. Does that Government which
thus protects them, and that Church which thus
tolerates them, deserve otherwise from them than a
grateful return of temporal obedience? Does that

Government or that Church, do more than circum
scribe them from *originating* the laws, of which when
passed they enjoy the protection equally as much
as your Protestant subjects? That Government and
that Church speak not to them legally and spiri
tually in stronger language than this. "We are
ready to receive you into close and intimate connec
tion, upon terms prescribed by the laws, whilst
those laws are unrepealed, and you conscientiously
adhere to your self-willed separation, we secure to
you the full exercise of your religion, the protection
of your persons, and the enjoyment of your pro
perty. The tests by which the Government in
Church and State is identified and preserved, are
not to you laws of exclusion, so much as they pro
pose to you terms of admission. We are ready to
receive you, but do not punish your contumacy." lo
To the Irish Catholics the same conciliatory lan
guage is held, accompanied by a nearer step toward
political power. There, as your Majesty knows,
Catholics are admitted to the functions of the magis
tracy, and freeholders and copyholders are all al
lowed to vote at elections. This variation or dif
ference in the rights of the Catholics of your two
kingdoms, is founded on the different ratios of popu
lation, and the approach to the political pale as
close as Protestant generosity can wisely admit.
It must be evident to all that Protestantism
in your kingdom of England has become preponde
rating, by *conversions from Catholicism;* possibly the
remaining *Catholics* might be admitted as an iso
lated body within the Parliament; for they would
have no more weight in either House, than what

they derive from the possession of property already.
But, since the Union with Ireland, their exclusive
admission is impossible, because it would be unjust.
Ireland has not yet possessed those religious lights,
(we speak as Protestants,) which have shone so re-
splendently on your kingdoms of England and Scotland. The Union has, however, produced a greater
interchange of society, a greater community of interests. We have already shewn that a fear of
conversion, arising from the circulation of the English Bible, and from a system of education, is displayed by the acts of the propaganda at Rome. If,
therefore, these causes which create this fear, continue in activity, why may we not hope that the
seeds, which have in England produced the Protestant flower, may not hereafter bring forth a sister
blossom in Ireland? That therefore, which is now
demanded as an inherent right of nature, (Tom
Paine's doctrine!) will hereafter become a legal right,
by the voluntary renouncement of those doctrines
or dogmas, which alone create the impediment to its
possession.

If the state of Catholic Europe is taken into consideration, and also the active exertions of Protestant missionaries, as also the translation of the Bible
into all known languages, we may infer that Catholicism has to struggle with an active opponent, an
opponent which already supplies the place, in numerous instances, of its missions. As your kingdoms
of England and Scotland have surrendered their
bigotry to the truths of the Bible, what unfair or
improbable inference do we draw from these premises, when we predict that the time may come when

Ireland will follow the example? The grounds off which Catholic emancipation (as it is falsely called, I is now demanded, are political; we wish them to rest upon less objectionable motives; nor do we wish to see it wrested from your Majesty upon the plea of Irish loyalty. Such language would imply, that the Irish would have deserted their King in the late war, but that they fought under his victorious banners, looking forward to Catholic emancipation as a boon and as a reward. Such an argument degrades the disinterested loyalty of your Irish subjects, and has been used by most injudicious advocates.

Sire, the Irish in your army never dreamt of Catholic emancipation, they never knew its meaning or its import; they knew only one duty, which was to beat your enemies whenever or wherever they were marched against them.

Happy will the day be, when Catholicism and Protestantism may meet in the same judicial chamber; but till such union can be undeniably proved to be a band of strength, and not the rope of sand, your Majesty will observe the oath, which you are about to take before God and in the sight of all your people;—your coronation oath (o). We should be inclined to think that whenever a King of England places the Catholic Church by the side of the Protestant, that should such King at the time have been crowned, the act would require a repetition of the ceremony: so truly do we think Protestant ascendancy to be the true intent and meaning and object of that oath.

The arguments, as to the favourable change of

6

the Catholics as a body, must have been derived
from specimens of the higher and middling classes
of that community; for, alas! can we look for it
among the four millions of the labouring Irish? and
indeed have not increased disorders of the most horrid and barbarous description broken out at the
very heel of the rejection of the late bill? such disorders requiring several districts to be proclaimed
as in a state of extraordinary disturbance, demanding ultra-legal measures of restraint?

We therefore, your Majesty's Protestant subjects,
look forward to the time when, by the dispersion of
the Bible, and the increased progress of a faith
grounded upon the actual examination of its truths,
the Catholics shall render themselves eligible to
every office of the state without distinction, since
by doing so they will cease to be Catholics. In the
mean time we shall continue to live in harmony and
peace, opposing them only in defence of those tests
which identify the Constitution, and without which
the Constitution loses its distinctive character.

We here submit to your Royal consideration, one
final question—" If Catholicism is now exposed to
the active efforts of conversion founded on a knowledge of the Bible, ought such efforts to be counteracted by giving to it in its decline additional
encouragement? ought it not to be allowed to come
gradually and willingly within the pale of Protestantism?"

We now approach towards the close of our reply,
a reply in which we cannot expect to carry the opinions of all our fellow subjects; but of this we may
hope, that it will be the adopted language of a vast

E

and overwhelming majority of your people. From
the facts and the arguments we have adduced, it
will be seen that in offering to your Majesty the
homage of our willing and our affectionate allegiance, we have good and substantial and indisputable
grounds for so doing. The act of our homage
arises from the conviction of our understandings;
not from mean flattery.

Our's is no paper constitution of modern fabric;
it was given to us by a King, preserved from pollution by the nobility; defended by the lives of our
forefathers; cemented and perfected by the wisdom
and experience of great, good, and eminent men, with
whom it has pleased Providence from time to time
to bless your envied and enviable nation. A constitution, so admirably constructed, so broad and
deep in its base, and so comprehensive in its applicability, that the dangers which have surrounded it,
have served to prove its adamantine foundation,
length of years has tended to embellish with suitable
improvements. Even those who seem to oppose it, or
seek its destruction, are forced to affect a love and
a veneration for it, as a mask to their secret intentions.

If among ourselves, a variety of opinions are
afloat, they serve more as the amusements of the understanding, than as proofs of political decay. The
inquisitive spirit of the people pries into every thing;
but that is doubly strong and doubly valuable, which
survives the test of innovation, or the satiety of
caprice.

To the superiority of the House of Peers during
the late reign, and at this moment, beyond any pe-

riod of former history, all your subjects implicitly
bow; its superiority consists in close attention to public business, in increased political knowledge, in
great personal attainments, in practical experience,
in superior power of debate, in legal acumen, and in
independence of the lower House.

To the corruption against the House of Commons, we may oppose that of more ancient parliaments. We ask those of our fellow subjects to
point out to us any which have been less contami-
nated with undue or selfish influence. Failing to do
this, or to establish the proof of such gross corruption, we have a right to say, that reform has already
taken place. Nor must the contest for office be
mistaken for the efforts of patriotism. In these latter years, with every word uttered in parliament,
and the conduct of every individual member open to
severe scrutiny, so few have been the causes of personal exception, that we have a right to say of the
members of the House of Commons, individually,
no matter of what party or bias, that they are all
men of unimpeached character. The question of
reform then narrows itself into two issues—Which
is best? to have various modes of returning representatives to parliament, so that men of ability, of
peculiar attainment, and practical knowledge, can
be *certainly admitted?* or that the mode shall be
similar in all cases; and so multitudinous in its
practice, as to render the return of each member a
matter of faction, fickleness, or chance? Which
promises the best result to the national honour and
prosperity, the progress of public business, and the
perpetuity of the Constitution, exposed as the House

of Commons is to daily public examination during
its sessions? We cannot see how a member may retain his seat in the face of any known violation of
the laws of his country, or of personal honour. Has
not therefore the publicity now given to parliamentary
proceedings effected imperceptibly a reform, of which
most of us have been unconscious? We think it has—
nor according to the genius of the Constitution, or the
practice of it, is there one of us, however humble in
society, but who may approach either House of
Parliament, with a suitable and respectful petition.
Every one, whether a voter at an election or not, is
therefore virtually represented, since his petition
becomes matter of consideration. This will be
granted by all but those who consider, *concession* to
the prayer of any petition, however interested, or
however obnoxious, the touchstone of representa-
tion.

Upon a review of the several circumstances, admis-
sions, matters, and facts, which we have thus
frankly laid before your Majesty, for and on behalf
of the vast majority of your people, the following
may be the summary.

That the reign of your late revered Father and
King was a constant alternation of war, and of agitated peace; in the midst of which, notwithstanding,
no kingdom ever made such rapid strides in virtue,
in arts, and in arms. And more particularly in the
latter part of it, during which, Sire, you, as Regent,
directed the authority of your most excellent and
blessed parent.

That the close of the late war, was marked by
a most extraordinary circumstance, viz. "That after

the creation of an immense national debt; and after twenty-four years of almost uninterrupted contest;" such was the wealth of the nation, and its means of resource, that "one British mercantile House contracted to guarantee and pay to the belligerents, on behalf of the conquered, the price of the peace."

That the charges of corruption, and violations of our envied Constitution, are not substantiated by the conduct, the suspicion, or the conviction of our official public characters.

That at no period of our history was the moral character of your kingdom ever so pure as at the present moment.

That at no period of her greatness did the honour of your Kingdom stand in higher estimation, among her cotemporaries and rivals, than at the present moment.

That at no period of her political animosities was the party opposed to the government, ever left so completely without argument or ground of accusation.

That at no period of her domestic agitations have so many vital and important discussions been entertained with such calmness and dispassionate enquiry.

That never was the soundness of the constitution, the pure administration of justice, and the attachment of your subjects ever more conspicuous than at the present moment, which so shortly precedes the national ceremony of your coronation. For, has not the constitution rebounded from an attempt made upon its existence? Do not the prisons at this moment contain the convicted of *both* political opinions?

and has ever King been more affectionately wel
comed into public than has been your Majesty?

For these reasons, Sire, we now, unsolicited an
unadvised, and on behalf of several of our fello
subjects, venture to suggest to your good heart, th
remission of all political sentences, as an act of grac
to your Coronation.   Your enemies are prostrate
your friends are roused, vigilant, powerful, and tru
The late treasonable attempts have shewn us th
danger of supineness, and have united us as one mai

And now, Sire, we take our leave, and to th
altar, which you are about to approach in the fac
of us your people, do our hearts accompany yo
Never was a crown placed upon England's king s
full of maturity of glory:—but there is a crown (
far greater glory—May your earthly one be but th
type of a more heavenly diadem!   And may Go
Almighty, guide, protect, and preserve our King! f
the welfare and happiness of

HIS PEOPLE.

*Explanatory Extracts from " The Letter,"*
*and other Notes.*

---

## (A)

### APOLOGY.

SHOULD the readers of the preceding Letter, have entertained doubts of its authenticity, the Author and Publisher beg leave to satisfy those doubts, by stating, " That it is one of those literary fictions, which can only be justified by a good cause." Indeed they feel so high a degree of veneration for the sacred name of " The King," which (speaking constitutionally), " Never dies;" and so anxious a desire, that nothing directly or indirectly should appear to trifle with its use; that previous to their determination to publish, they submitted the following Question to the opinion of a most eminent Counsel; which question at once proclaimed the author's motive, and the answer subjoined, contains (we trust) our justification.

### THE QUESTION SUBMITTED.

Suppose A. writes a letter entitled " A Letter from the King," and having written and published such letter, states, in a Postscript annexed, that such title was adopted to excite curiosity, and extend its political utility; and that such Letter was neither directly or indirectly written by the King;

will such acknoyledgι κϑ ιιυ assumption of
the King's name, out ιy and every statute of
*premunire ?*

## OPINION.

 J n ly ιι , that such acknowledg-
ι ιt is ll .e the Letter out of the
 of *ni.* Tl · term and the offence
 re, ɔ y sɔunds ; but I decidedly
tl k, that t Letter pr ed, written in the tone
 s it ι ι is ed, will not render the
·i b to *ιlty whatever.*

*Te e, December 4th,* 1820.

Thus far as to the legality ɔf the act; but should
our most gracious Sovereign, chance to see a Publication thus imputed to him ; we beg leave most respectfully to deprecate any sentiment of personal
dissatisfaction, which he may feel at our bold assumption ; assuring The King, that he does not possess among his people, a more disinterestedly loyal
subject, than the Author of this Letter.

### (B)

A Bill of Pains and Peι lties was brought in by
the Earl of Liverpool, : long and elaborate arguments upon the pr ι and applicability of the
proceeding, had taken p in the House of Peers.
The case presented an ɔmaly, for no statute existed, applicable to cl : of adultery committed
by a Queen of Eng ɩ *foreigner.*
This nice distinction k from within

the pale of high treason, for inasmuch as the principal was not amenable to the laws of the country, consequently, the *particeps criminis* could not be judicially recognized by the statutes of treason. Every preliminary of this great measure was discussed to the very letter, with a degree of eloquence and profound learning which reflected unfading lustre upon the House of Peers, and on the individual noblemen, who led both sides of the debates. The question appeared new, and every aspect of its bearing was most minutely and rigidly examined; great debate more particularly took place on the question of allowing to the illustrious accused a list of witnesses, as in cases of high treason; when it was at length decided to open the case, produce the evidence, and allow the Queen an interval, (such as her counsel should deem requisite) to prepare her defence. Thus her Majesty was not only supplied eventually with a list of witnesses; but had the further guide of their sworn testimony. The Attorney-General, (Sir R. Gifford) opened the case according to his instructions, and by command of the House, with little preliminary remark, and certainly without inflation. Her Majesty's cause was less upheld by the evidence of the witnesses against her, (of whom the popular feeling pronounced a pre-judgment of perjury) than by a deficiency of refutation on her own part. The Queen was most ably, most zealously, and most eloquently defended by Messrs. Brougham, Denman, Lushington, and others; and the House bore the license of their harangues with a noble equanimity of patience. After hearing both the charge and the defence, which occupied forty-five days, the House of Lords adjourned two days before it met to debate the principle of the bill; which discussion occupied four days. The second reading was carried by a majority of 28, the numbers being *for it* 123, *against it* 95. During the progress of the measure, several protests were entered on the Journals of the House, in one of which, the Lord Chancellor and the Prime Minister were directly opposed to each other; a brother of the King absented himself wholly from the investigation; a cousin of the King voted against the measure in all its stages; both the Ministry and the Opposition were divided amongst themselves, and intermingled their votes; the preamble of the bill underwent but little alteration in the committee; and in the clause for pronouncing a divorce as part of the pains and penalties, all the Cabinet Ministers, (nine) voted against it. The divorce clause was, however, carried by a majority of 67, there being contents 129, non-contents 62. Most of the peers who had till this moment contended against the principle of the bill in all its stages, argued (with much plausible appearance of reason) that since the Queen was virtually pronounced guilty of an adulterous intercourse, by the votes of the second reading, *divorce became the natural consequence, as part of the sentence of the bill;* they therefore voted for it. The third reading of the bill was carried on the 10th November, by the small majority of nine; the numbers being for it 108, against it 99.

Lord Liverpool, (who had brought in the bill, as an individual peer, and not as a member of the administration,) immediately moved, that " the bill

be read that day six months," alleging the smallness of the majority, as the motive.

### (c)

Although it is presumed that I become acquainted with political occurrences and opinions, solely
through the channel of my official advisers, and can
only constitutionally address my people through the
regular organ of parliament, or of my council; yet,
at this momentous crisis, pregnant with evil to our
common country, and to me so interesting as a man
and a husband, but above all, as the inheritor of
my Royal Father's crown; the form and mode of
this communication may stand shielded and excused,
in the generally anomalous character of the circumstances to which I shall hereafter advert: nor, on
so singular an occasion, do I think it derogatory to
the dignity of my exalted station, to attempt the dispersion of a mist, in which too many of my subjects
have wandered, led on by a generous delusion.

### (D)

I will not accuse, I do not accuse, of disaffection
either to my person or government, *all* who are
advocates for the cause of the Queen; for in that
cause, I perceive plainly a variety of motives in
activity; in the combination of those motives, differing widely from each other, the immediate danger appears to consist: but it is also, from their discordance, that future tranquillity may be expected.
I am persuaded that, could my subjects be brought
to consider calmly and dispassionately the probabi-

lity of my being an injured and calumniated Prince, they would abstain from further insult to the crown inherited from GEORGE THE THIRD. I am also persuaded, that public opinion, (although forced into extremes by the goadings of a portion of the daily press, alike unrestrained by truth, and as devoid of principle, as lost to the common civilities of society,) would soon right itself; when a plain and simple narrative, such as any man of reasonable mind might comprehend, should supersede the distorted and tortured facts which have lately pre-occupied too great a part of the nation.

## (E)

" *But the morning which dawned on the consummation of this ill-fated marriage, witnessed its virtual dissolution.*

" Our daughter, the lamented Princess Charlotte, the child of a fond and admiring nation, was born precisely at the moment prescribed by nature.

" Of the cause which led to this immediate separation, which, however, for a time was most carefully concealed ; and concealed, I trust, from no ungenerous feeling on my part, it does not belong to me to detail the explanation.

" But who beside ourselves was interested in it? Surely the family of the illustrious female in question! Did they complain? Did they remonstrate? Did they demand a restitution of conjugal rights between us? Did they interfere to conciliate, to palliate, to explain? *Never!!* By their silence then, was I justified in requiring at a proper moment, a more openly avowed separation.

" *The first wrong was done to me.*

" But, although the match was forced, and I was left (unlike my subjects) to no voluntary choice, I had still a right to expect in a Princess of exalted ancestry, and one previously allied to me by relationship, a female of chaste person and uncontaminated taste."

(F)

" ' *It was always competent for the Princess of Wales to demand from me, if she felt herself so justified, the restitution of her conjugal rights.*' That a female of her lofty daring should not have taken such a step, admits a very strong argument in favour of the retiring husband; at all events, it allows of the inference, that there was a domestic and personal cause for separation, to which the parties mutually consented."

(G)

" I have thus brought down the material circumstances of my *expedient* marriage, to the period of the departure of her Royal Highness for the Continent: the transactions in themselves, however unfortunate, are plain and simple, easily understood and as capable of explanation, when viewed without, a selfish tendency to party or faction. The incidents may be thus briefly stated :—

" 1. Our private separation.

" 2. Our public separation.

" 3. The interval between our public and the enquiry of 1806.

" 4. The complaint of the Princess in 1813, as
to the restricted intercourse between herself and
daughter.

" 5. The retirement of the Princess to the Continent.

" *The first point,* (the reason of our private separation) it does not become me to explain; her
Royal Highness might, if she had so pleased, have
claimed in the proper Court, the restitution of her
conjugal rights. Such a proceeding would have
produced an explanation.

" *As to the second point*—We separated upon
terms mutually understood, and to which the Princess added herself a peremptory condition; those
terms have by me been inviolably preserved; as a
husband, I enabled my wife to maintain the dignity of
her rank and station as Princess of Wales; I visited
her separation with no pecuniary privations, but, on
the contrary, paid for her, debts exceeding her means
of expenditure, to the amount of forty-nine thousand pounds; the Government of the country, at
the same time, liquidating a further sum of thirty-
one thousand pounds.

" *As to the third point*—The preceding remarks,
in part apply. On the subject of the actual enquiry,
I may be allowed to say, that the Prince of Wales
is born with certain rights previously created, as a
line of duty to be by him fulfilled. The preservation of the chastity of his wife, with a view to the
purity of the succession, is one of those duties.
When, therefore, in consequence of rumours, too
loud and too deep to remain unheard, I demanded

an enquiry, as part of the duty of my high birth and
national rank, I submitted the case to the responsible Ministers of the Crown; I acquiesced in the
sentence passed upon the termination of the enquiry,
and bowed to the decision which had been pronounced by the warm and zealous friend of the
Princess, who was judge upon the occasion.

"*As to the fourth point*—I endeavoured, by
every means in my power, to prevent our disputes
from taking a political turn, embarrassing to the
Government of the country; and I most particularly aimed at preserving, in the mind of the Princess Charlotte, a neutrality on the delicate occasion;
the restriction imposed on the intercourse between
the Princess and her daughter was connected with
the system of her education, which, by law, rested
with the Sovereign. When, at a subsequent period,
in 1813, the Princess of Wales addressed to me as
Regent, a letter alluding to such restriction, and also
to the proceedings of 1806, almost grown out of recollection; I submitted such letter to noblemen,
differing in political opinion from those who had on
the former occasion made a report on the conduct
of the Princess; the result of this re-enquiry produced no change, no imputation on the former statements and evidence, and I still continued to consider
the whole affair as *one of domestic inconvenience*,
inasmuch as the succession to the Throne was pronounced *not to be endangered*.

"*As to the fifth point*—Upon the retirement of
her Royal Highness to the Continent I continued to
the Princess her residence in a royal palace, leaving
it as a domicile open to her return; and I declare,

upon my honour as a Prince, that I never, on any
previous occasion, interposed the slightest obstacle
in the way of her Royal Highness's comfort, tranquillity, and domestic arrangement. The affairs of
Princes cannot be conducted in the same obscure
and unostentatious mode as those of private individuals; to snatch a few moments of private life is,
in a Prince, to enjoy real happiness. All the difficulties which have occurred in the case in question
have been produced and created, they were not of
natural origin, but have been foisted on the original
evil by factious persons, seeking to advance their
own political purposes. Had not the Princess
placed herself avowedly in such hands, many of the
mortifications of her situation had been avoided;
they would, indeed, have had no existence. Finally, I declare again, upon my honour, that my
conduct aimed to keep the whole unhappy affair
within the character of a domestic and purely personal misfortune; and it is only by the attempts
made by faction, to give to it a political complexion,
that the attention of the people has been fixed upon
it as a national grievance."

(II)

" This liberty of the press, in itself a great abstract good, capable alike of being converted into a
bane or antidote; and, by discreet and conscientious
management, capable also of promoting and effecting
immortal benefits to mankind, or inflicting upon them
irremediable ills, keeps up at least a constant communication between us; depriving the courtier of
the power of concealing from his Sovereign public

opinion, and placing him within the effect of inquiry. With such a constant possibility of explanation, a Monarch may be misguided, but cannot be misinformed; he may adopt decisive rules of government, but cannot remain ignorant of their effects."

### (I)

" The liberty of the Press does not permit to your King, the possibility of remaining ignorant of passing events, or unaffected by the public agitation: at one and the same time it conveys to me sentiments of satisfaction or grounds of complaint, the promised support of the constitutional, and the threats of the disaffected. My own conduct, the measures of my executive, the state of my kingdom, and the condition of my subjects, are placed before me in as many various, confused, and contradictory positions, as the greater or lesser degree of information, the rivalship of party, the animosity of prejudice, or the insidiousness of faction alternately suggest. In this chaos of contrariety, to me the first great difficulty is, to discover the truth; the next, so to manage the discovery, as to produce from it some sound and dispassionate course of action."

### (K)

" I have previously remarked, that from the period of my becoming Regent, the differences between the Princess and myself had assumed a political character, and been treated by many as a party question.

F

" The companions of my youth, and the distinguished characters with whom in my earlier years I had intimately associated, had created in the public mind a widely-extended, and readily believed opinion that when the sceptre of my Father should descend to me, I should, from among those associates, have chosen the members of my administration.

" During the discussion of the terms of the Regency I was careful to avoid giving any pledge. of the line of policy I might find it expedient to adopt. A short previous Administration, composed of those political friends by whom it was conjectured my councils would have been directed, had enabled me to form some opinion of their executive talents; and *notwithstanding*, an overture was made by me to them, to propose an Administration. But when I found the conditions required would have reduced me to a mere political automaton, of which they were to possess the key: that not content with forming the Administration, they required also that I should be surrounded in my household by their adherents, and left to no choice in the appointment of my own attendants; when with this, I compared the candour and the unequivocal absence of all personal feeling with which the bill creating the Regency was carried by the then Ministry; and, above all, the frank, loyal, and respectful regret which was shewn to the calamity of my revered parent; and the so immediate provision made for the resumption by him of the regal dignity, that should it have pleased Providence so to have restored my royal Father, he would have awakened as if from a dream, and have found himself unreminded of his affliction; when to this I

4

added the important consideration, that the flame of
freedom was beginning to glimmer in Spain; that
the then Administration were prepared to take advantage of every circumstance favourable to the
destruction of the Military Tyrant of Europe; and
when all these various considerations were upheld
by the weight of personal character which was contained in the then Administration; I felt sufficiently
justified in not suffering former prepossessions to
stand for one moment in the way of newly-created
duties. I felt that an existing experienced executive,
was, at such a time, safer than a theoretical Cabinet.
I had also a doubt in my own mind, whether, during
my Sovereign's life, I ought, as Regent, to adopt the
principles of those who had been violently opposed
to my Royal Father's measures, or pursue a line of
policy unchanged, and such as my King would have
continued, had he remained the active head of the
Empire. This was a feeling of the heart; it was
mine."

( L )

*The Theological Judgment of the Catholic Divines
of the Midland District on the two Bills pending
in Parliament.*

"However desirous we are that our laity should get
free from the civil disqualifications under which
they labour, yet we are well assured that they cannot conscientiously purchase this boon by taking the
oath of supremacy; the taking of which has always
hitherto been considered by all Catholics, and Pro-

testants also, *as the precise act of abjuring their religion* Hence several scores of Catholics have heretofore lost, not only their civil rights, but also their lives, for refusing to take it. Nor does the injunction of Queen Elizabeth, in the first year of her reign, which is referred to in the Bill, by any means remove the conscientious objection of sincere Catholics, as in that injunction she barely disclaims the actual exercise of the ministry, at the same time that in every act, whether legislative or regal, of her reign, she claimed the entire, supreme, spiritual jurisdiction, within her dominions, to the total exclusion of all such jurisdiction on the part of the Pope *. This is so clear and notorious, that we are convinced, in case our legislators should, in their wisdom and liberality, admit our people to the enjoyment of their civil franchises, notwithstanding their acknowledgment of the jurisdiction of their Church in faith and discipline, they will prefer the plain and explicit terms by which we abjure the Pope's authority in all civil and temporal cases, in the act passed for our relief in 1791, to the new-invented and forced construction of the act and oath of supremacy, by means of the above-mentioned injunction.

Again, though we ourselves, in the oath of 1791,

---

* "See the injunction in Bishop Sparrow's Collection, p. 88, also the whole Act of 1 Eliz. c. 1, to restore to the Crown the ancient jurisdiction over the estate ecclesiastical and spiritual, and to abolish all foreign powers repugnant to the same. See also Act 5 Eliz. c. 1. also Act 13 Eliz. c. 2. See also Archbishop Parker Homage to the Queen, in Collier's Eccl. Hist. vol. ii. Record. 81."

above cited, have abjured " the doctrine and position that Princes, excommunicated or deprived by
the Pope, or any authority of the See of Rome, may
be deposed or murdered by their subjects," &c. yet,
following the doctrine and example of our predecessors, who (chiefly on account of the extravagant and
false terms therein contained in King James's oath
of allegiance) refused the same, we declare that it
is utterly unlawful, and contrary to the doctrine of
our Church for a Catholic to condemn upon oath,
the *mere deposing doctrine,* as damnable and heretical *.

" With respect to the Bill of Pains and Penalties
against their Clergy, with which ' some modern Catholics are content to purchase civil advantages for
themselves, we declare,—1st, That we, the Clergy,
cannot conscientiously take the oath prepared for
us, in the terms in which it stands in the Bill: because, however remote we are from all traitorous
conspiracies against the establishments of our country, whether civil or ecclesiastical, yet we cannot
bind ourselves " never to have any correspondence
or communication with the Pope or the See of Rome,
or with any persons authorized by the Pope, &c.
(which words comprehend all the Catholic Clergy of
the United Kingdom,) tending directly or indirectly
to overthrow or disturb the Protestant Church :" in

---

* " See Supplementary Memoirs of the English Catholics,
lately published by Keating and Brown, Duke-street, Gros-
venor-square, in which the terms of their oath and the most
material incidents in the History of Catholics of late years are
clearly discussed."

as much as in our judgment, all our preaching, writing, and ministring, *tend indirectly to this effect.*

" 2dly, Though contrary to the fact, we were justly suspected, in our personal conduct and our professional ministry, to be disloyal and seditious; and there were greater reason for Government interfering with our religious economy, than with that of the numberless sects protected by it, and especially with that of the Greek Schismatics, the German Moravians, and the Jews; yet we know that we are not competent to concur in, or consent to the alterations in our Churches and Missions proposed in the present Penal Bill; much less would it be lawful for the intended episcopal commissioner to take the oath prepared for him to take, this being *incompatible* with his existing oath and obligation.

" 3dly, As the revision by the commissioners and clerks of a new devised civil office, of all rescripts from the Holy See, implies in many cases *the breach of most sacred professional secrets on our parts,* and as such revision has been recently declared by that See to be a violation of her divinely constituted spiritual supremacy *, hence we declare, that we cannot concur in or consent to any such regulation. Nor would the difficulty be removed by referring the revision to the intended ecclesiastical commissioner, because, in the cases supposed, we are each of us

* " De Rescriptorum Revisione—ne tractatus institui potestnam cum libertatem Magisterii Ecclesiæ, divinitus concredit apprime lædat, laicæ potestati permittere aut tribuere nefas profecto esset." Card. Litta's Letter, by order of the Pope, to Bishop Poynter, &c. April 26, 1815. See Report of Committee of House of Commons, folio, p. 513."

as much bound to secresy with respect to ecclesiastical as to lay persons.

" Such is our conscientious judgment, and that of the divines and pastors of the Midland district, and we have reason to believe of the Catholic divines and pastors of England and Ireland in general on the pending Bills: we therefore join our voices with those of the Vicars Apostolic in 1817, in calling upon the Catholics in general to employ whatever constitutional and peaceable means or influence they may possess, to prevent the enactment of the unlawful contents of them.

*Wolverhampton, March* 13, 1821.

> " R. R. J. MILNER, Vic. Apost.
> " Rev. WALTER BLOUNT, Arch Priest,
> " Rev. WILLIAM BENSON, Secretary."

(M)

*(Texts and Comments from the Douay Bible.)*

### MATT. vi. 24.

*No man can serve two masters. For either he will hate the one, and love the other : or he will sustain the one and contemn the other. You cannot serve God and mammon.*

Two religions, God and Baal, Christ and Calvin, mass and communion, the Catholic Church and heretical conventicles.

### MATT. xxvii. 24.

*And Pilate seeing that he nothing prevailed, but that rather a tumult was made ; taking water, he washed his hands before the people, saying: I am innocent of the blood of this just man, look you to it.*

Though Pilate was much more innocent than the Jews, and would have been free from the murder of our Saviour, seeking all the means that he could (without offending the people and the Emperor's laws), to dismiss him: yet he is damned for being the minister of the people's wicked will against his own conscience. *Even as all officers are, and especially the judges and juries which execute laws of temporal princes against Catholic men: for all such are guilty of innocent blood, and are nothing excused by that they execute other men's wills according to the laws, which are unjust. For they should rather suffer death themselves, than put an innocent man to death.*

### MARK xii. 17.

*And Jesus answering, said to them: Render therefore to Cæsar the things which are Cæsar's; and to God, the things which are God's.*

These men were very circumspect and wary to do all duties to Cæsar, but of their duty to God they had no regard. So heretics, to flatter temporal Princes, and by them to uphold their heresies, do not only inculcate men's duty to the Prince, dissembling that which is due to God; but also give to the Prince, more than due; and take from God his right and duty. But Christ allowing Cæsar his right, warneth them also of their duty towards

God. And that is what Catholics inculcate : obey
God, do as he commandeth ; *serve Him first, and
then the Prince.*

### John xi. 51.

*And this he spoke not of himself, but being the
High Priest of that year, he prophesied that
Jesus should die for the nation.*

How much more may we be assured, that Christ
will not leave Peter's seat, whose faith he promised should never fail, though the persons which
occupy the same, were as ill as the *blasphemous and
malicious* mouths of heretics do affirm.

### Acts xxviii. 22.

*But we desire to hear of thee, what thou thinkest :
for as concerning this sect, we know that it is gain-
said every where.*

Whereas indeed the Protestants' doctrine is evidently convinced to be heretical, by the same arguments that Christ's religion is proved to be the only
true doctrine of salvation, and not an heresy.  And
whosoever can deduce the christian faith from Adam
to this day, throughout all the fathers, patriarchs,
prophets, priests, apostles, and bishops, by descent
and succession of all laws and states of true worship-
pers and believers, (which is the only or special way
to prove that the christian faith is no heresy) he shall
by the same means, all at once, prove the Protestants' doctrine to be an heresy and a false sect.
That the Jews therefore and ill men in all places

contradicted the christian religion, calling it an heresy)
or a sect, as if it had a beginning of some certain
sect master other than God himself, they were deceived: and the church of God nevertheless calling
the Protestants' doctrine heresy *in the worst part that
can be, and in the worst sort that ever was,* doth
right and most justly.

### GAL. i, 8.

*But though we, or an Angel from Heaven, preach a
Gospel to you besides that which we have preached
to you, let him be anathema.*

Lastly, St. Hierom useth this place, wherein
the Apostle giveth the curse or anathema to all false
teachers not once but twice, to prove *that the zeal
of all Catholic men ought to be so great towards all
Heretics and their doctrines, that they should give
them the anathema, though they were ever so dear
unto them.* In which case, saith this holy Doctor,
I would not spare *mine own parents.* Ad Pam-
mach, c. 3. cont. Jo. Hieros.

### 2 TIM. ii. 17.

*And their Speech spreadeth like a Cancer: of whom
are Hymeneus and Philetus.*

The speeches, preachings, and writings of Heretics are pestiferous, contagious, and creeping like
a cancer. *Therefore Christian men must never
hear their sermons nor read their books.* For such
men have a popular way of talk, whereby the un-
learned, and especially women laden with sin, are

easily beguiled. "Nothing is so easy; (saith St.
Hierom) as with voluble and rolling tongue to deceive the rude people, who admire whatsoever they
understand not." (Ep. 2. ad Nepot. c. 10.)

## 2 Tim. iii. 9.

*But they shall proceed no further : for their folly
shall be manifest to all men.*

All Heretics, in the beginning, seem to have
some show of truth; God, for just punishment of
men's sins permitting them for some time in some
persons and places to prevail : but in a short time
God detecteth them, and openeth the eyes of men
to see their deceits : insomuch that after the first
brunt they are maintained by force only, all wise
men, in a manner seeing their falsehood, *though for
fear of troubling the state of such common-wealths,
where unluckily they have been received,* THEY CAN-
NOT BE SO SUDDENLY EXTIRPATED.

## Apocalypse of St. John xx. 12.

*And I saw the dead, great and small, standing in
the presence of the throne, and the books were
opened: and another book was opened, which is
the book of life : and the dead were judged by
those things which were written in the books, according to their works.*

This is the book of God's knowledge or predestination, in which that, which before was hid
to the world, shall be opened, and in which the true
record of every man's works shall be contained, and

they have their judgment diversely according to their own works, and not according to faith only, or want of faith only. For all infidels (as *Turks, obstinate Jews,* and *Heretics*) *shall never come to that examination, being otherwise condemned.*

(N)

*Extract from a Circular Letter from Cardinal* FONTANA, *the Prefect of the Propaganda, to the Irish Prelates, on the Subject of the Bible Schools:—*

"My Lord,—The prediction of our Lord Jesus Christ, in the Parable of the Sower, 'that sowed good seed in his field; but, while people slept, his Enemy came, and sowed Tares upon the Wheat,' Matt. xvi. 24, is, to the very great injury indeed of the Catholic Faith, seen verified in these our own days, particularly in Ireland.

"For, information has reached the ears of the Sacred Congregation, that 'Bible Schools,' supported by the funds of the Catholics, have been established in almost every part of Ireland, in which, under the pretence of Charity, the inexperienced of both sexes, but particularly Peasants and Paupers, are allured by the blandishments and even gifts of the Masters, and infected with the fatal poison of depraved Doctrines.

"It is further stated, that the Directors of these Schools, are, generally speaking, Methodists, who introduce Bibles, translated into English by 'the Bible Society,' and abounding in errors, with the sole view of seducing the youth, and entirely eradicating from their minds the Truths of the Orthodox Religion

" Under these circumstances, your Lordship already perceives with what solicitude and attention Pastors are bound to watch and carefully protect their flock from ' the snares of Wolves who come in the clothing of Sheep.' If the Pastors sleep, the Enemy will quickly creep in by stealth, and sow the tares—soon will the tares be seen growing among the wheat and choak it.

" Every possible exertion must therefore be made —to keep the youth away from these destructive schools—to warn parents against suffering their children, on any account whatever, to be led into error. But, for the purpose of escaping the ' snares' of the adversaries, no plan seems more appropriate than that of establishing schools, wherein salutary instructions may be imparted to the paupers, and illiterate country persons      *      *      *      *

" In the name, then, of the mercy of our Lord Jesus Christ, we exhort and beseech your Lordship to guard your flock with diligence, and all due discretion, from those who are in the habit of thrusting themselves insidiously into the fold of Christ, in order thereby to lead the unwary sheep away; and mindful of the forewarning of Peter, the Apostle, given in these words, viz. :—" there shall also be lying masters among you, who shall bring in seeds of perdition," 2 Peter ii. 1. do you labour with all your might to keep the orthodox youth from being corrupted by them—an object which will, I hope, be easily effected by the establishing of Catholic Schools throughout your Diocese.

" And confidently trusting that in a matter of such vast importance, your Lordship will, with unbounded zeal, endeavour to prevent the wheat from being choaked by the tares, I pray the all good and omnipotent God to guard and preserve you and many years.

" Your Lordship's

" Most obedient humble servant,

" F. CARDINAL FONTANA, *Prefect*.

" C. M. PEDICINI, *Secretary*."

" Rome, Court of the Sacred Congregation for the Propagation of the Faith, 18th Sept. 1819."

## (o)

*Oath, as administered to His late Majesty King George the Third, of blessed memory, according to the last settlement of its form by Parliament.*

The sermon being ended, the King uncovers his head, and the Archbishop repairs to his Majesty, and asks him, Sir, are you willing to take the oath usually taken by your predecessors? The King answers, I am willing.

Then the Archbishop ministers these questions, to which the King answers as followeth:

*Abp.* Will you solemnly promise and swear to govern the people of this kingdom of Great Britain, and the dominions thereunto belonging, according to the statutes in Parliament agreed on, and the respective laws and customs of the same?

*King.* I solemnly promise to do so.

*Abp.* Will you, to your power, cause law and justice, in mercy, to be executed in all your judgements?

*King.* I will.

*Abp.* Will you, to the utmost of your power, maintain the laws of God, the true profession of the Gospel, and the Protestant reformed Religion established by law? And will you maintain and preserve inviolably the settlement of the Church of England, and the doctrine, worship, discipline, and government thereof, as by law established, within the kingdoms of England and Ireland, the dominion of Wales and town of Berwick-upon-Tweed, and the territories thereunto belonging, before the union of the two kingdoms? And will you preserve unto the Bishops and Clergy of England, and to the Churches there committed to their charge, all such rights and privileges as by law do or shall appertain unto them or any of them?

*King.* All this I promise to do.

The King then goes to the altar, and laying his hand upon the Gospels, takes the oath following:— The things which I have here before promised, I will perform and keep, so help me God. He then kisses the book and signs the oath.

THE END.

Printed by R. Gilbert, St. John's-square, London.

itself *(toujours la bonté même*, original), immediately formed her determination, without explaining it to any one; she gave orders to the captain to set sail, that same evening, for St. Jean d'Acre, where we arrived on the 6th. The Princess went herself to the governor, and urged him to grant permission to all the suite to travel to Palestine. He at first started many difficulties. They were, however, gradually overcome by the sight of some rich presents exhibited to him, which operated on his avarice—a vice so powerful among his fraternity that they cannot do other than yield to it, even at the hazard of their lives and favour. Thus, to travel amongst the Turks, it is not only necessary to be well provided with money, but also to be liberal of it; and it is only with this metal, or with presents, that what is desired can be obtained from them. The governor, not wishing that the real motive which tempted him to deviate from his duty should be known, told the Princess, through the medium of his interpreter, that as he had received great obligations from, and felt that gratitude was due to, the English, for the services rendered to the city, he was resolved, at all hazards, to grant this indulgence to their sovereign : he was even generous in return, for he made her Royal Highness a present of five linen tents, a zetique, similar to those used in Sicily, and as many horses as were necessary for the journey; also an escort of officers of the guard, guides to conduct us, and camels to transport our baggage.

# JOURNAL

### OF

## THE VISIT

### OF

# HER MAJESTY THE QUEEN,

### TO

### TUNIS, GREECE, AND PALESTINE;

#### WRITTEN BY

## LOUISE DEMONT.

#### WITH OTHER CORRESPONDING PAPERS, COLLECTED IN SWITZERLAND, AND TRANSLATED

#### BY

## EDGAR GARSTON.

———

### LONDON:

### PRINTED FOR T. AND J. ALLMAN,

#### BOOKSELLERS TO HER MAJESTY,

PRINCES-STREET, HANOVER-SQUARE.

### 1821.

BARNARD AND FARLEY,
Skinner-Street, London.

# INTRODUCTION.

THE public curiosity has been considerably excited, respecting a Journal* of the Visit of her Majesty the Queen to Tunis, Greece, and Palestine, written by Mademoiselle Demont, in consequence of references made to its contents in a letter, addressed by her to her sister, which was produced, and read at the bar of the House of Lords, during the late proceedings against her Majesty, and of her examination as to its contents, consequent upon the production of the letter. It might therefore reasonably have been expected, that

---

* I believe that, though in the examination of Demont, the Journal was only spoken of as a Journal generally, without specification, it was a general impression that it related particularly to the ". long voyage," as it was termed, " par distinction."

such a public feeling would have been grati_
fied, by the production of the Journal, either
by the lady herself, or some one of her friends,
unless there existed powerful motives for its
abstraction from public notice.

Into the existence or nature of these motives, I do not pretend to enter, but, as it appears certain, that by her or them the Journal
will not be brought forward, I have myself
determined upon giving to the public a copy
of it, which circumstances placed in my possession some time back.

After having acted as interpreter on the
behalf of her Majesty, at the bar of the House
of Lords, during the production of the evidence, or allegations against her, I had the
honour of being called upon to assist, on the
continent, in the preparation for the defence ;
and for purposes connected with it, about the
middle of September last, visited the neighbourhood of the Lake of Geneva, in com-

pany with Mr. Tyson, law agent to her Majesty.

During our stay there, we directed some
inquiries and researches to the existence of a
Journal, as above stated, the result of which
was, the ascertaining that the manuscript had
been generally circulated throughout the Canton de Vaud, and that in some instances
copies of it had been taken by those to whom
it was lent.   At Colombier, Demont's native
village, we were further informed, that the
original manuscript had been carried to England, either by Demont herself, or by an
Englishman, who, since her departure, had
been over at Colombier to take out some
papers respecting her; but, that a copy of it
was in the possession of Madame Gaulise, a
lady, whose mansion is on an eminence close
by the village. This information, combined
with the circumstance that this lady is named
in Demont's letter, (already alluded to, and a
copy of which is annexed to these sheets) as

BARNARD AND FARLEY,
Skinner-Street, London.

# INTRODUCTION.

THE public curiosity has been considerably
excited, respecting a Journal* of the Visit of
her Majesty the Queen to Tunis, Greece, and
Palestine, written by Mademoiselle Demont,
in consequence of references made to its contents in a letter, addressed by her to her sister, which was produced, and read at the bar
of the House of Lords, during the late proceedings against her Majesty, and of her examination as to its contents, consequent upon
the production of the letter. It might therefore reasonably have been expected, that

---

* I believe that, though in the examination of Demont, the
Journal was only spoken of as a Journal generally, without
specification, it was a general impression that it related particularly to the ". long voyage," as it was termed, " par
distinction."

such a public feeling would have been grati_
fied, by the production of the Journal, either
by the lady herself, or some one of her friends,
unless there existed powerful motives for its
abstraction from public notice.

Into the existence or nature of these motives, I do not pretend to enter, but, as it appears certain, that by her or them the Journal
will not be brought forward, I have myself
determined upon giving to the public a copy
of it, which circumstances placed in my possession some time back.

After having acted as interpreter on the
behalf of her Majesty, at the bar of the House
of Lords, during the production of the evidence, or allegations against her, I had the
honour of being called upon to assist, on the
continent, in the preparation for the defence;
and for purposes connected with it, about the
middle of September last, visited the neighbourhood of the Lake of Geneva, in com-

pany with Mr. Tyson, law agent to her Majesty.

During our stay there, we directed some inquiries and researches to the existence of a Journal, as above stated, the result of which was, the ascertaining that the manuscript had been generally circulated throughout the Canton de Vaud, and that in some instances copies of it had been taken by those to whom it was lent. At Colombier, Demont's native village, we were further informed, that the original manuscript had been carried to England, either by Demont herself, or by an Englishman, who, since her departure, had been over at Colombier to take out some papers respecting her ; but, that a copy of it was in the possession of Madame Gaulise, a lady, whose mansion is on an eminence close by the village. This information, combined with the circumstance that this lady is named in Demont's letter, (already alluded to, and a copy of which is annexed to these sheets) as known. It is from this copy, now in my possession, that the following translation is made.

After giving it up to me, Madame Gaulise expressed the utmost astonishment at the part which Demont had acted, she having always spoken of her Majesty with the highest respect, and in terms of unhesitating praise, whenever her name was mentioned during the visits, which, in consequence of her having held a place about her Majesty's person, and of the false colouring given by her to her return home, she was invited to make at her mansion. She was at a loss to account for it otherwise, than by ascribing it to the influence exerted over her by the Italian who conducted her to Milan\*. These sentiments, I

---

\* Her journey to Milan sunk her so much in the estimation of her friends, that it caused many to discontinue her acquaintance. The Demoiselles Jaqurod, whose names were mentioned in Martigny's testimony, were of this num-

already knew, were not confined to Madame
Gaulise: they were as general as had been
Demont's expression of her opinions, unreservedly and unequivocally avowed by her,
to all those who received her after her return
from the service of the Queen : these, equally
with Madame Gaulise, had compared them
with her after-declarations at the bar of the
House of Lords. This feeling of astonishment at her conduct, and persuasion as to its
immediate cause, were perhaps most strongly
felt by those, who not only had heard her
opinions verbally expressed, but had perused
her Journal, and still remembered passages
in it, more particularly one introduced with
the description of her Majesty's entry into

---

ber, and gave her an intimation to that effect, through the
medium of one who even then remained a friend to Demont. I mention their names with this circumstance, because they were much distressed at the idea of being connected, in the eyes of the world, with Mademoiselle Demont, in
consequence of the testimony of Martigny.

Jerusalem, which, equally with her **verbal** expressions, and more gratuitously **than they,** belied her after declarations.

· It may be proper here to remark, **that in** the letter of Demont, produced in the **House** of Lords, and already alluded to, she **herself,** mentioning her Journal, says, " *on se l'est pour ainsi arraché.*"

It is true, true in its fullest extent, **that, as** she writes in that letter, at the time the Journal was first circulated, it was read with the utmost avidity; not only by those who were actually acquainted with her, and her family, but both at Genoa and Lausanne, by those who were acquainted only with the circumstances of her life, and with her name and origin. The correctness of the allusion made to the Journal in that letter, will be recognised on a perusal of it—and if the perusal of her actions were as easy, it would be as easily known, that that letter, which she ex-

plained as a tissue of deception, was written
in full sincerity, for every sentiment which it
contains, relating to her benefactress, has its
prototype among those which she, uttered,
without reservation, amidst her friends, where
deception, and " doubles entendres," would
be difficult and useless.  Her conduct is so
revolting to the upright and manly feeling of
the true-hearted Vaudois, that they regard
her as a dishonour to their canton in the eyes
of the world.   In truth, it appears that her
conduct must exclude her for ever from Colombier as a home, and from again associat-
ing with the friends of her early days.

I must here state, that at Morges, a
small town, distant about a league from Colombier, on the banks of the lake, I obtained
a copy of a Journal of the same voyage and
travels of her Majesty, on a more extended
scale, which was circulated by Demont after
her return to Colombier.  This Journal cor-
responds for the most part minutely in the

b 2

facts, dates, and remarks, with the one now
given, with this difference, that the style of it
is superior, and the classical and geographical
notices so much more correct and extended,
that they must have been the result of subsequent labour and reflection on the part of
Demont.  The arrangement is not that of a
Journal made " en route," and the descriptions of towns and their dependencies are
rather the fruit of reading, than of a day or
two's hurried visit.  I have thought that extracts from this more elaborate performance
would not be inopportune, where they might
contribute to throw more light on the actions
of her Majesty, or on the sentiments of the
writer.  It should be remarked that this was
not circulated till after Demont's return
home; the other was received at Colombier
before that time.

Respecting the faithfulness of the translation I need say nothing, as a comparison
with the Journal in its original language,

which will be its companion to the press, will speak for itself: respecting the style I merely have to observe, that the cause of, and apology for, its stiffness, rest alike in its faithfulness to the original.

My last remark is, that in offering this Journal to the public, I have conceived it to be no part of my duty, to deduce any arguments from its contents, or to make any observation upon its bearing or effect upon any of the questions agitated in the recent proceedings at the bar of the House of Lords. The intelligent and impartial reader will make his own reflections on these points.

EDGAR GARSTON.

*Surry Street, Strand,*
  *15th January,* 1821.

# LETTERS

---

*Letter from Louise Demont to her 'Sister Mariette,*
*dated Colombier, 8th Feb.* 1818.

" Dear and good Mariette,—Although you have not said
four words in your last letter, yet I love you too well not to
pardon you for it; and it is with real pleasure that I reply to
you. I hope, my dear sister, you are perfectly happy; but
I ought not to doubt it, so well as I know the extreme
goodness of her Royal Highness, and of all those with whom
you have any thing to do. Endeavour always to deserve such
kindness, by continuing the same way of life which has
procured it for you, that experience may not be useless to
you. Keep always before your eyes the trouble which
arises from rashness and inconsistency; you have lately
had sufficient proofs of that.

" You will no doubt be very desirous of knowing what is
my situation in our little country; I assure you, my dear, I
have been received in such a manner as you would have no
idea of. I have been every where sought after, and received
with the greatest cordiality at Lausanne, at Morges, and at

Cassonay. I passed a whole month at the last town, where every possible amusement was procured for me. You know how fond I was of sledge-riding; well, every day we made a party for it. At the beginning of the new year we had a delightful masked ball; last week two more, the best that have been seen in this town, and a number of other evening parties given by a friend of mine : in short, every day brought some new invitation. Conceive to yourself how, in the midst of all these numberless pleasures, I was sad and silent; every one quizzed me on my indifference : I, who used to be so gay before my departure. I was not insensible of my dulness, but, spite of all my endeavours, could not get the better of it.

" Can you not, my dear, divine the cause of all my sadness ? Alas! was it not the regret of having quitted her Royal Highness, and of knowing that she suspected my character, and taxed me with ingratitude? Oh, God! I would surrender half my life, could she but read my heart; she would then be convinced of the infinite respect, the unlimited attachment, and the perfect affection, I have always entertained for her august person.

" I should have wished, my dear Mariette, to have written to the Count, to thank him for the kindness he has shown me, but I was afraid to trouble him; tell him one line, if he would but have the goodness to write to me, would afford me a little tranquillity, since it would make me hope for pardon.

" I was afraid her Royal Highness would be displeased at the course I have taken in my journey. Judge, then, of my happiness when I learned that she was not at all angry at it; but, on the contrary, gave me leave to take it. In truth, this pretence has been very useful to me; for you are sufficiently acquainted with the world to suspect that I have been assailed with questions, particularly by great folks—for I am not vain enough to think that I have been sought after only on account of my beautiful eyes—and that a little curiosity has had no part in the desire to see me. Ah! why was not her Royal Highness at my side? She would then have found if I were ungrateful.

" How often, in a numerous circle, have I with enthusiasm enumerated her great qualities, her rare talents, her mildness, her patience, her charity; in short, all the perfections which she possesses in so eminent a degree! How often have I seen my hearers affected, and heard them exclaim, that the world is unjust, to cause so much unhappiness to one who deserves it so little, and who is so worthy of being happy!

" You cannot think, Mariette, what a noise my little journal has made; it has been, if I may use the expression, snatched at. Every one has read it. —— begged me to let her carry it to Lausanne: all the English who were there wanted to see it immediately. I have been delighted at it, for you know I say in it a great deal of the best and most amiable Princess in the world; I relate in detail all the traits of sensibility and of generosity which she has shown; the manner in which she has been received, applauded, cherished, in all the places we have visited.

" You know that where the Princess is my subject I am not barren; consequently my journal is embellished with all the effusions of my heart, my greatest desire having always been that the Princess should appear to be what she really is, and that full justice should be rendered to her. I assure you, that although distant, it is not less my desire, and that I shall always endeavour with zeal that such 'may be the case, and as far as my poor capacity will allow. You may judge 1 shall not make a ·merit of this, since she will be ignorant of it, and even suspects me of ingratitude; but it will be only to content my heart, which would find a sweet satisfaction in this charming success.

" But 1 had almost forgotten to confide to you a thing which will surprise you as much as it has me. The 24th of last month 1 was taking some refreshment at my Aunt Clara's, when I was informed an unknown person desired tó deliver me a letter, and that he would trust it to no one else. I went down stairs and desired him to come up into my room; judge of my astonishment when 1 broke the seal : a proposal was made to me to set off for London, under the pretence of being a governess. I was promised high protection, and a brilliant fortune in a short time. The letter was without signature, but, to assure me of the truth of it, I was informed I might draw on a banker for as much money as I wished. Can you conceive any thing so singular? Some lines escaped from the pen of the writer, discovered to me the cheat, and I did not hesitate to reply in such terms as must have convinced him I was not quite a dupe. Notwithstanding all my efforts, I could draw no eclaircissement from the bearer ; he acted with the greatest mystery.

" You see, my dear, with what promptitude the enemies of our generous benefactress always act. There must be spies constantly about her; for no sooner had I left Pesaro than it was known, with all its circumstances, in the capital

c

of Europe.  They thought to find in me a person revengeful
and ambitious: but, thank God, I am exempt from both
those failings, and money acquired at the expense of repose
and duty will never tempt me, though I should be at the last
extremity.  The Almighty abandons no one, much less
those who act agreeably to him.  A good reputation is better than a golden girdle.

" Since I have introduced the subject of money, my dear
sister, I must give you some advice.  Economize as much
as possible, retrench every superfluity: did you but know the
pain I feel in not having done so!  I do not think I ever
was guilty of extravagance, but I have not deprived myself of
many things which were almost useless.  You know that
every one here, as elsewhere, fancies the Princess of Wales
throws her money out of the window, and supposes me possessed of a large fortune: from a species of self-love, and
to prove still more her generosity, I do not try to undeceive
any one; consequently, though I have great need of money,
I don't dare to ask my guardian for any.  I know how to be
moderate, and am at no expence.  I have often reflected,
that if I had always acted in the same way, I should not be
in the situation in which I am.

" Every one should economize as much as possible; one
can gain by no other means.  Profit by the lesson I have
just given you; be assured that it will be salutary to you, for
I speak from experience.  M. ——— has not sent the
packet; I wrote to him at Milan and at Paris.  I expect
his answer one of these days.  If it should be lost, it will be
very disagreeable, as the cloth cost a great deal.  If I had
known, it should not have been purchased, as my mother
had a good spencer, and might very well have done without

it. I regret the velvet very much, as I want it for my hat; besides, we did not get that either for nothing; and three louis are well worth lamenting, without reckoning the other baubles. Money will not come by whistling for it. A sous here and a sous there soon make a livre, and twenty-four livres make a Napoleon. You see I am become an adept in arithmetic. I will answer for it, however, that Mr. —— will make all good, if he has lost any thing. I shall show him no favour, and have written to him in such a manner as sufficiently shows I am not very well satisfied with his negligence.

" But, my dear Mariette, I perceive I have almost finished my letter without speaking a word of our dear parents. Our good mother is tolerably well, though her asthma, and complaint in her stomach, torment her sometimes, but nothing compared to what she has suffered this summer; my father is very well; Henrietta is always charming. I give her every day lessons in writing and reading. She sews very well, and *repassie* as well; she has already worked several frills for me, and some gowns, with which I am very well satisfied. Her desire of travelling is the same; pray try to get her a situation; I am convinced she will give you no cause to regret it. She is much altered for the better; she is gay, and always in good humour, mild, obliging, in short, of a character to make herself beloved wherever she goes; for she has an excellent heart, and knows how to be contented in all situations. Margaret is entirely amiable, of a pretty figure, and so lively, that she makes one half dead with laughing. Louisa is very genteel. I assure you, dear Mariette, they are all changed very much for the better, and I am quite contented with them.

" I have been for this month past in my favourite chamber

at Colombier, where some repairs have been done; for example, a good chimney, and a small cabinet, wherein I sleep
I make little excursions often in our environs; and frequently
receive visits, which afford me amusement.

"I think I hear you say, ' Well, dear Louisa, what do you
mean to do? Won't you marry? What does —— do?' I
will tell you word for word.  I every day feel more and more
repugnance to marriage: —————— has done all in his power
to induce me to accept a heart, which, he says, he has preserved for me these seven years; what heroical constancy,
and little worthy of the age in which we live! I shall not,
however, be dazzled by it; and, although he be rich, charming, and amiable, I do not wish to retract the refusal I gave
him four years ago.

"If this amuse you, I will tell you of several other
lovers, not less desirable than he.  I am very foolish, perhaps, to refuse them; for they are infinitely better than I am—
perhaps I may one day repent it.  You know the proverb,
'He who will not,' &c.  But I cannot do otherwise.  Recent
events have created in me a sort of antipathy to men; I can
have no connexion, no communication with any of them.
I love and cherish sweet liberty alone, and wish to preserve
it as long as I can.

"Dear Mariette, I conjure you imitate my example, and
never think of marrying.  My mother and I forbid it, as long
as her Royal Highness shall wish to keep you in her service.
You can have no greater happiness.  It is impossible! Be-
ware of forming any attachment—you are too young—remain free.  Be assured you will be a thousand times more
happy.

" I do not recommend prudence to you, because I know
you too well to distrust you; but, although it may be said
of me that I would die rather than abandon it for an instant,
and deviate from the strict path of virtue, the most precious
good we possess, yet I have known some persons suspect my
conduct. But I have God and my own conscience for witnesses. Are they not sufficient for my peace? no one can
deprive one of that. No, I have nothing to reproach myself
with on that head, and you know, therefore, I can give you
such advice as you should follow, especially as it is also that
of our mother.

" Dear sister, if you dare, place me at the feet of her
Royal Highness, beseeching her to accept my humble respects: do not fail, I entreat you, when she speaks of me,
to endeavour to convince her my repentance is still the same;
that I conjure her to restore me to her favour. Tell me if
her Royal Highness is still so enraged against me, and if
there is not any appearance of a pardon; but tell me always
the truth. Try also to persuade her Royal Highness that I
am and always shall be so entirely devoted to her, that no
sacrifice I could make for her would appear too great, and
that she may even dispose of my life, which shall for ever
be consecrated to her service. Tell the Baron also that I am
very sensible of his remembrance, and beg him to accept the
assurance of my perfect acknowledgment. Embrace for
me the charming Victorine; repeat also my thanks to the
Count, and assure him I shall never forget his kindness.
Remember me to the Countess, Madame Livia, and Mr.
William, begging them to receive the assurance of my sincere friendship.

" If I were to tell you all those who send you salutations,

I should want two more pages; for every one is interested for you, and they never cease to wish for your happiness. Believe, however, the most sincere wishes are made by us.

" You will tell Mr. Hieronymus that John is quite well, and that Mr. ——— is very well pleased with him in all respects. His board is not paid for; and tell Mr. Hieronymus, on the receipt of this letter, I beg he will immediately send an order to —— for six months' pay, and address it to me. He must not delay, for I have no money.

" You will not do wrong if you send at the same time the two Napoleons, to make up the twenty-five, if you can. It is I who send you the gown: instead of lace, you should trim it with muslin. Make my compliments to Mr. Hieronymus, and tell him the first time I write again I will give him more particulars respecting his son, because I hope to have more room. I wish very much to know how ink is made with that powder which he gave me, and what he has done with the two pictures I sent him at the Villa d'Este.

" Adieu, dear and good sister. We embrace you cordially. A reply at once if you please.

                                    " LOUISA DEMONT."
    " 8th February, 1818.

" A Mademoiselle Mademoiselle Mariette Bron, à Pesaro."

———————

*Letter from Mademoiselle Demont to the Queen, dated Rimini, 16th November, 1817.*

" It is on my knees that I write to my generous benefactress, beseeching her to pardon my boldness, but I cannot resist my feelings. Besides, I am convinced that if her

Royal Highness knew the frightful state into which I am plunged, she would not be offended at my temerity. My spirits cannot support my misfortune; I am overwhelmed by it, and I am more than persuaded I shall sink under it. I feel a dreadful weakness: a mortal inquietude consumes me internally, and I do not feel one moment of tranquillity. A crowd of reflections, ' on the-past goodness of her Royal Highness,' and ' on my apparent ingratitude,' overwhelm me. May her Royal Highness deign to take pity on me; may she deign to restore me her precious favour, which I have unhappily lost by the most deadly imprudence; may I receive that soft assurance before I die of grief; she alone can restore me to life.

" I dare again to conjure, to supplicate, the clemency and compassion of her Royal Highness, that she will grant me the extreme favour of destroying those two fatal letters; to know that they are in the hands of her Royal Highness, and that they will constantly bear testimony against my past conduct, kills me. The aversion which I have merited on the part of her Royal Highness, instead of diminishing, would be increased by reading them.

" I permit myself to assure her Royal Highness, that it is only the granting of these two favours which can preserve my life, and restore to me that repose which I have lost. My fault, it is true, is very great and irreparable, but love is blind. How many faults has he not caused even the greatest men to commit! I dare flatter myself this is a strong reason why her Royal Highness should condescend to grant me the two favours which I take the liberty of asking of her.

" I allow myself to recommend to the favour and protec-

1

tion of her Royal Highness my sister Mariette, and also her who is in Switzerland. Her Royal Highness gave me to understand that, perhaps, she might be allowed to supply my place. The hope of this alleviated my distress. It would be an act of charity, for my sisters have only moderate fortunes, and in our small poor country they are not to be acquired. I am certain her Royal Highness would have no cause to repent her great goodness and extreme kindness towards a young girl who has always gained the esteem and friendship of all to whom she has been personally known.

" I cannot sufficiently thank her Royal Highness and the Baron for their kindness in sending Ferdinand to accompany me; he has paid me all the attention and taken all the care of me imaginable; I know not how to acknowledge so many benefits; but I will endeavour by my future conduct to merit them, and to regain the favourable opinion which her Royal Highness entertained for me during the days of my good fortune.

" It is with sentiments of the most entire submission, and the most perfect devotion, that I have the honour to be,

" Her Royal Highness's most obedient Servant,

" LOUISA DEMONT."

# JOURNAL OF THE TOUR,

## &c. &c.

———————

We set out from the Villa d'Este the 18th of November, 1815, and slept the same night at Milan, that of the 13th at Nuovi, and on the 14th arrived at Genoa, where we embarked immediately on board an English ship of the line, of eighty-five guns, and five hundred men, called the Leviathan, after the most bulky inhabitant of the deep. The wind being contrary, the vessel could not put to sea the same day, and we were in considerable peril, from her touching several times upon banks.

The wind became so violent, t
sible to put out a boat; but on the 17
rated, and we set sail the same day:
we passed the isle of Capraja, near to the Gulf of Naples, on which the Roman Emperor Tiberius

ended his days*. We afterwards came in sight of
the island of Corsica, the capital of which, Ajaccio,
gave birth to Napoleon. In the evening we reached
Elba, and came to an anchor in Porto Ferrajo ; and
on the following day, the 19th, we disembarked,
and paid a visit to the house of Napoleon, or
rather to his prison, for it is as ill-situated and in-.
convenient a building as can be imagined. There
are eight very small chambers below, and above is
a hall, in which the portrait of the great Napoleon,
painted as at his coronation, is preserved. There
are, besides, three small apartments, which were
occupied by the Princess Eliza, his sister; and by
the side of the house is a garden, which was laid
out by Napoleon, as also a theatre, in which his
officers performed plays for his amusement. The
town of Elba is pretty and neat, though small, and
is paved throughout with cut stone: it was much
improved by the care of Napoleon, who formed a
fine road to it four leagues in length, and caused
the discovery of mountains, productive of iron, and
other minerals. Whilst Napoleon was there, he
circulated money freely ; and every one in the

* Capraja, between Corsica and Tuscany, confounded with
Capri, in the Gulf of Naples.

place still·laments the loss of this man, so renowned in every way—of this incomprehensible
genius, whose like will never again be seen.

On the 20th we re-embarked on board our vessel;
but the wind being contrary, we got out to sea on
the 22d only. The island of Pianoza is close by
that of Elba; it is flat, and low, and was used by
Napoleon as a receptacle for his horses. It was
here also that Jonah, on his way to Nineveh, was
driven by storms, and remained three days, and as
many nights, in the belly of a whale. On the
24th we passed the isle of Montechristo, and on
the 26th arrived at Palermo, the capital of Sicily.
The town is rather extensive, very dirty, and without any remarkable object of curiosity. The public
gardens are the most pleasing which it presents.
The place is well situated, and the climate excellent, as may be suppo           I state,
time we were there, t
the month of May in

On the 4th of Dec
evening, we quitted this city, and
ing passed the Lipari Islands,

and the island of Stromboli. The latter is a mountain, which constantly throws out flames; and the
following very singular, and equally true, anecdote
was related to me respecting it. The servant of an
English gentleman was taken by the impress, and
carried on board a brig, out into the Mediterranean.
At the distance of three leagues from Stromboli,
whilst the officers of the brig were observing, with
a glass, the fire which issued from the mountain,
they suddenly saw a carriage with six horses pass
by,—an object which had never before been seen,
on this isle.   The coachman of the English gentleman looked, and assured them that it was his master's carriage, with his arms upon it, and that he
recognised him in the vehicle.  All were greatly
struck with the circumstance.  In every English
vessel a book is kept, in which all extraordinary
occurrences are noted down; and this book, at the
end of every voyage, is inspected by the Admiralty
of England.  The officers of the brig noted, in their
book, the circumstance, and the day and hour in
which they had observed it.  Afterwards, on his return to England, the coachman went to seek his
old master :—how great was his surprise, when told
that he had died precisely on the same day, and in

the same hour, in which he had seen him pass by
on the mountain. The story circulated,—the friends
of the deceased, who were people of quality, much
incensed at it, cried out for justice.—A council of
war was assembled,—the book was brought,—all
the officers appeared, and confirmed what had been
related. The relations were ashamed that one connected with them should have gone to hell, and
that convincing proofs of it should exist. This
mountain is particularly remarkable, for though
much smaller than other volcanos, it burns incessantly.

The 5th of December we entered the straits of
Messina, and that same evening reached the town.
We disembarked on the 10th, and quitted our delightful vessel, to return to it no more; we had
been so happy whilst in it, that we left it with
much regret. Her Royal Highness took a house
a little out of Messina. Messina is, in rank, only
the second town in Sicily, but, in reality, is prettier
and cleaner than Palermo. Opposite to Messina
is Calabria, and St. Jean de Roviegio may be
seen. Near this town is the plain where the fa-

mous Achilles encamped his army, when on his way to the destruction of Troy.

On the 6th of January, 1816, we departed from Messina, and embarked on board the frigate Clorinde. Catania is but seven leagues distant. When we were on the very point of landing, the wind became so violent and contrary, that it rendered it impracticable. It is a dangerous spot, because there is no *port*, but merely a small open road. The gale continued so heavy that we were in great danger. The sails could not withstand its force; but, as soon as set, were rent into a thousand fragments. During an entire day but one sail could be set, and the vessel was tossed about with so much violence, that it was impossible to remain standing. Four days we were in the same spot, with this terrific contrary wind, expecting every moment that our frigate would upset. At length Providence had mercy upon us, and on the 10th of January we entered the port of Syracuse.

Syracuse is, at present, a small town, but was formerly much celebrated, and governed by its own

kings. It is very ancient, having been founded by
Etolus (one of the descendants of Noah), 320
years after the deluge. It possesses many antiquities worthy of remark; among others, Dionysius's
ear; it is a grotto, hollowed in the rock in the form
of an ear, and was constructed by Dionysius, the
famous tyrant. The echo is surprising; a pistol
fired in it produces the effect of a cannon-shot;
and words uttered in a very low tone, are repeated
distinctly by the echo. It was here that the unfortunate victims of the tyrant's brutality were
confined! He had caused a small chamber to be
constructed above, in which all the complaints of
the prisoners below could be heard. He placed
a sentinel there, who, in the morning, related to
him what had been said against himself during
the night; and influenced by a fear, that the sol-
dier might disclose the secret of the small chamber,
he strangled him : every evening he caused a fresh
sentinel to be placed there, and every morning he
was, himself, his assassin. It was the same tyrant
who would not suffer himself to be shaved, from a
fear that the operator might cut his throat with the
razor: he compelled his daughters to take off his
beard for him; but, afterwards, suspecting even

them, he had it burnt away. At Syracuse are
shewn, also, the catacombs, or vaults, in which were
the sepulchres, and into which, the old men,
women, and children, fled in time of war. Formerly, it was possible to go under ground to Catania, distant forty miles ; but at present they are practicable only about fifteen. They consist of many
narrow passages, which lead in different directions,
with large chambers at intervals ; and are visited
always with lighted flambeaux : the gloom, and
the feeling which it excites is horrible ; and the
atmosphere very noxious. There exist still,
at Syracuse, the ruins of many temples, sacred to
the gods and goddesses, whom the Syracusans of
former ages worshipped. The temple of Minerva is the most ancient ; it is now converted into
the great church, and is said to be the most ancient structure in the world. The fountain of
Rotuza is to be seen, the waters of which, though
fresh, come from the bay, and return to it. The
ruins of the houses of the Saracens are still visible ;
they were hollowed out in the rock ; the tables
and chairs were also formed of rock. Syracuse
formerly possessed four considerable cities, all of
which are now reduced to ruins : it gave birth to

Archimedes, the most illustrious of geometricians, and the one, who invented burning glasses to destroy the vessels of the enemy. The climate of Syracuse was delightful; not a window or door in the house would close well, and still we never experienced the least inconvenience from cold.

We quitted this town the 29th of January, for Catania, in suspended chairs, a horse before, and another behind, it being impossible to travel in carriages, on account of the narrowness and rockiness of the roads. The same evening, we slept at Albentina, a small ruined town of great antiquity; and on the 30th we reached Catania, a very pretty town, at the foot of Mount Etna, a volcano, most formidable during its eruptions: the town has already been destroyed, and rebuilt, several times. This mountain is excessively high, as may be supposed from its being covered with snow in the month of August, at which time it is difficult to ascend it without suffering from the frost; a circumstance not a little surprising, on a mountain whose interior is a glowing fire. It was here, according to story, that Vulcan had his forges, and that the Cyclopes (who had but one eye, in the

c

middle of the forehead) wrought the instruments of hell. Catania is very clean; the streets, for the most part, are straight, and the houses well built, and new. About it are scattered masses of fire-stone, in size equal to cottages, and in colour like coal, which have fallen from Mount Etna. Formerly there was a port, which the lava has now choked up. The ruins of the old port, where Ulysses anchored his vessels, on his way to the destruction of Troy, are still to be seen.

On the 25th February we left Catania, and arrived in the evening at Augusta, a small town, with nothing remarkable except the harbour, which is safe and good. On the 26th March, the small vessel, called the Royal Charlotte, belonging to her Royal Highness, arrived. We embarked the 1st April, and steered for Girgenti, a town of great antiquity; but which we were unable to visit, on account of the shallowness of the harbour. The island of Sicily is the largest in the Mediterranean, and very fertile; the land yielding every sort of produce spontaneously: the seeds are put into the earth, and left without any culture until the harvest. We saw the corn springing amidst stones and briars, in the middle of the month of January, and the country as green and luxuriant as in the middle of May in Switzerland. Notwithstanding this, the people are very poor: their poverty, doubtless, arises from idleness, or want of exertion.

The 3d of April we set out on our passage from Europe to Africa, which we accomplished very rapidly, having run 160 miles in one night. The wind was so strong that it was impossible to stand; for when up, instead of walking, we were obliged to drag ourselves along by our hands; or, if lying down, were unconsciously rolled out of our births. It seemed as though the whole fraternity of devils were in and about our vessel: plates, glasses, and bottles, all rolled about with a frightful uproar. The mountains of water were higher than the masts, and dashed with fury from one side the vessel to the other;—if any one were induced, by fear, to put his nose (orig.) through the window, paf (orig.) came a wave, which dashed over, and drenched him. The tables, chairs, and beds were tied with strong cords, and even nailed down. At one instant, the vessel rose on the bosom of a wave, and then again sunk so rapidly, that one's breath was checked by the shock; she was dashed, also, violently from side to side, so that to have a moment's rest was impossible. Those who have never seen the sea, cannot possibly form to themselves an idea of its impetuosity. To me it is a most magnificent spectacle, so long as it can be contemplated with tranquillity, and without dread; nevertheless, it is not quite prudent to throw one's self at the mercy of two elements so inconstant as the winds and the waves. For myself, I have always thought that He who had the power of creating, has also the power of stilling them, and preserving us: I ever reposed my confidence in God, our good preserver; and remained perfectly at ease in the greatest dangers, resigning myself to all which it should please Him to send us—whether life or death. The dawn of day, and the view of land, were, however, impatiently expected; never did night appear so long! The darkness was so deep, that it was necessary for the vessel to lie to, lest she might ground too violently (trop fort), which would have been destruction to us. At length, the weather cleared up, and day-break appeared: what delight! we were in view of land, and of the

shores of Africa! We did not, however, get into
the roads of Tunis till night. "Happy is he
who gets into port after a storm."

On the 4th of April we disembarked at the Goletta. (Note *a.*) After passing the Mole, there is
a small lake, between the Goletta and Tunis, twelve
miles in length, from which the town presents a
delightful view. At Tunis it is customary to walk
out on the roofs of the houses, and there are ter-
races, upon which it is practicable to make a tour
of the town; but the streets are very dirty and
narrow. Women, of a certain rank, never step beyond their own doors: when their husbands go out,
they lock them up, like slaves, and carry the key
in their pocket. Occasionally, but very rarely, a
few women of the lower class are met with; they
wear ample cloaks upon their shoulders, and two
handkerchiefs over the face, disposed in such a
manner, that merely the point of the nose, and the
eyes partially, can be discovered: they have the
feet always naked, wearing only an undersole of
wood; very wide trowsers are worn by some, pet-
ticoats by others. If a husband meet his wife in
the street, he cannot accost her, under pain of

death. Some Turks have so many as ten or twelve
wives; the first is compelled to serve the second,
the second the third, and thus with as many as he
may have. If one of them have the misfortune to
displease him, even in the slightest particular, he
takes off her head without ceremony; the Turks
being absolute masters in their own houses, and having it in their power to take away the lives of their
wives, their children, and their slaves, without being called to an account for it. *(b.)* The women
never go out; they have wooden gratings before
their windows, to prevent their seeing any one,
except their husbands, who treat them more se-
verely than Christians their beasts. If a Christian
be tempted to converse with a Turkish woman, he
loses his head, and the woman is tied up in a sack,
and thrown into the sea. After they are married,
the women are allowed to see none of their relations, not even their brothers. The Turks have a
fixed hatred towards us, whom they call Christian
dogs: when it is in their power to kill a Christian,
it is esteemed an exploit so to do, and no one con-
demns it; thus one's safety is very precarious
amongst these barbarians. They have a profound
veneration for their prophet Mahomet. The men

have constantly in their hands a chaplet of seeds, and count them, saying over every seed, " God is God, and Mahomet is his prophet." They pray every two hours, and never without washing their hands, feet, and ears. Their mosques are very lofty, and without bells; at an appointed hour, a man, whose duty it is, stands in a box, over the centre of the mosque, and cries out that it is the hour of prayer. The women never go to the mosque, or church, but pray at home. They have no chairs in their houses, and remain all the day stretched out on the floor, with long pipes in their mouths, drinking incessantly thick coffee, without sugar; which is, in truth, the most horrible composition that can be swallowed. The Turks eat with their fingers, and neither the great nor the vulgar are possessed of knives and forks. Before each repast, they wash their feet and hands, and after it repeat the same ablution.

On the 12th her Royal Highness went to pay a visit to the Bey (c.), at his country residence. All the Turkish officers accompanied her, and on the road went through a very pretty manœuvre to entertain her. They galloped forward with their horses, which seemed rather to fly than to run ; when advanced to some distance, they wheeled round, and returned with the velocity of lightning, discharging their muskets, and exhibiting a sham fight together. It is difficult to conceive how a man, mounted on a fiery horse, swift as the wind, can load his piece, and discharge it with so much facility ; but such is their manner of carrying on war. In other respects they are very cowardly, and a Christian need not fear an encounter with thirty Turks. Their uniform made us nearly expire with laughter; they looked like so many old women ; some had white head-dresses (à papillons), others had gray handkerchiefs fastened on the head, and cloaks made like mantillas on their shoulders, with large wooden boots on their legs. During a journey of three miles we were much diverted with this masquerade. We then arrived at the palace of the Bey, who received her Royal Highness. Her Royal Highness had the kindness to present us to him; after a short conversation (they conversed in Italian), he took the Princess by the hand, and conducted her into his seraglio. She commanded us to follow her ; the gentlemen remained in the hall, it being forbidden for any man

to enter the seraglio, under pain of death. We
were introduced into a magnificent room : the women were dressed with incredible splendour, being
loaded with gold, diamonds, and precious stones ;
their legs were uncovered, and their ancles encircled with diamond chains, their fingers covered
with rich rings, and the tips of them painted black.
The Princess seated herself with the Bey and his
first wife, upon rich cushions ; five wives, of the
rank of slaves, presented napkins, wrought with
gold ; and afterwards the richest collation that can
be pictured was served to them ; there were full
two hundred different dishes, all served upon gold.
After the repast, the slaves brought their finest
perfumes, and sprinkled us with them from head to
foot : our dresses have not even yet lost the scent. The
Bey ordered music to be brought. Six old women
commenced playing a sort of charivari, which dea-
fened our hearing, but it was the most excellent
melody of the Turkish court ; and the old women
were the most perfect of its songstresses. Afterwards the eldest son of the Bey (he who is now
reigning), took her Royal Highness by the hand,
and conducted her into his own seraglio, whither
also we followed her. That of the son is more ex-

D

tensive than that of the father, and contains more
women ; but they were not so richly dressed, with
the exception of his wife, who was very beautiful,
as was also that of the second son. The ceremonies
with which we were received in the first seraglio
were repeated in this ; the women crowded round
us, and appeared delighted to see us.   Unfortunate
creatures! we were undoubtedly the first strangers
whom they had seen since they were first immured,
like encaged birds, in these cloisters.   When once
the doors of the mansion are closed upon them,
they step forth no more, and meet the eye of no
one, save the princes, by whom they are treated
like slaves. When the princes enter, they all hasten
to kiss their hands ; it is the only favour enjoyed
by them.   They are enormously fat, and those who
are the most bulky are esteemed the most beautiful ; those who are slender are lightly valued, and
even scarcely looked at.   They are constantly
guarded, and watched by eunuchs ; thus I look
upon them as buried alive.   It is said that there
are five hundred in the palace of Tunis.

After having viewed all, we returned to Tunis,
where we resided in a magnificent palace belong-

ing to the Bey. The poor old man showed great
politeness to the Princess. Every day he had a
dinner prepared for her, and for the whole of the
family, the cost of which it was said was thirty
louis per day. She was attended with the state of
a queen, in her own palace; we never went out
without the attendance of a guard of honour, which
remained constantly in the palace, awaiting the
commands of her Royal Highness. We made several small excursions, in which the Bey provided
us with horses, and we usually slept at some one
of his country houses, where every thing was pre-
arranged for our accommodation. Her Royal Highness visited Utica, celebrated for the self-destruction
of Cato, the last of Roman republicans. She went
also to Saroine, where there are many vestiges of
ancient days; among others the celebrated aque-
duct which supplied Carthage with water; it is
sixty miles in length. The roads are so horrible
that it requires no slight degree of courage to pass
them in a wheeled vehicle. At one time we had
to descend, as it were, a ladder, and ford a river;
at another, we were compelled to pass over precipices, and fragments so high that the carriage was

jolted quite off the ground (sautait en l'air). We were, notwithstanding, quite devoid of fear.

We afterwards visited Carthage, so much celebrated for its antiquity, and for having been long the rival of Rome. It was founded by Dido, sister to the king of Tyre. This city, the birth-place of the renowned Hannibal, was once beautiful, and the emporium of commerce, but was afterwards thrown down, and reduced to ashes by the Romans; and on its site is now to be seen nought but a few old miserable houses.

On the 22d of April we quitted Tunis (d), and on the 24th, made sail for Greece. On the 28th we passed the island of Pantalania, and on the 29th that of Gozo, where Ulysses, on his return from the Trojan war, was detained seven years by the goddess Calypso, who sought in vain to enslave him for ever. Telemachus, his son, was shipwrecked on the same isle, and was also well received by the goddess. Gozo is very near to the island of Malta, on which the Apostle Paul was wrecked, during his voyage to Greece. We en-

tered into the harbour ; but, as arriving from Tunis,
could not land without performing quarantine.—
The town, when seen from the harbour, appears
pretty ; but the streets are all up-hill. On the 31st,
the wind becoming favourable, we continued our
voyage, and during three days had sight of no other
objects than the sky and the sea.    Nothing is more
melancholy ; one feels as if exiled from the rest of
the world!    Proportionably great was our joy on
coming in view of the isle of Cythera.    It is the
first of the Archipelago, and the one where Venus
was produced from the foam of the sea.    Formerly
she had her temples there, and was adored as a di-
vinity.    The number of the rocks around it render
it dangerous ; among others, is a large one in the
form of an egg: any vessel so unfortunate as to
strike upon it is inevitably lost.

On the 4th we reached Milo, an island having an
excellent harbour, and a small village on the heights
of a mountain.    The women of this isle are re-
markably beautiful, and still wear the costume of
ancient Greece, which is much more elegant than
the modern dress.

On the 5th, we left Milo, and set sail for **Athens**, where we arrived on the 8th ; we landed immediately, from a desire to gratify ourselves with a view of this city, which was formerly so famous and so interesting, and in which so many illustrious men have flourished. It was in being 1600 years before Christ ; and many beautiful monuments of its ancient splendor still remain (e). Athens is distant from the port about four miles, and it is customary to travel that distance on horseback. On the 9th, we commenced our visits to the most remarkable antiquities ; among which is the temple of Theseus, the hero of Athens. It is the best preserved monument, not only in the city, but in the world. It consists of thirty-six columns of white marble, of the Doric order; the columns are eighteen feet in height, and are ornamented with bas-reliefs of the exploits of Theseus : at this time the temple is converted into a church, for the use of the Greeks, and is dedicated to St. George, their protecting saint*.

---

* What follows is an unconnected catalogue of existing monuments, taken promiscuously and unconnectedly.

Pricho, where the public assemblies were held,
and where Demosthenes and other orators ha-
rangued. There was an extensive space of ground,
where the audience were seated, and above was
an eminence, the ascent to which was by a flight
of marble steps, still visible. There the orator
spoke, and thence was he, with facility, heard by
those around him. Below this eminence are the
excavations, in which the Athenians made offerings
for any blessing granted to them. Above, is the
Areopagus, at this time an extensive plain ; and on
the hill, called Musée, is still seen the Philapapus,
a monument of marble, constructed by the Emperor
Hadrian, which is now reduced to a few mutilated
statues and horses in bas-relief. Beyond this hill
is l'Agro Corinto, and Mount Elicon. Beneath,
still exist the gloomy prisons of the Areopagus,
constructed entirely of marble. They had no
doors ; and the entrance into them was by an
aperture in the roof. It was in them that Socrates
was condemned to drink the fatal hemlock, because
he had dared to speak of the one true God, whom
the Athenians absolutely refused to acknowledge,
preferring rather to remain in the darkness of
ignorance, and the worship of their false deities.

The temple of the four Winds is extremely well preserved; and the exterior is ornamented with figures, descriptive of the powers to which it was sacred: this temple is at present converted into a mosque, and in it the dervises perform their extravagant ceremonies. Never was any scene more frightful! In the outset the premier sings, and the rest repeat after him; they then take him by the hand, and utter such violent cries that they lose their breath, and appear on the very point of suffocation. Two of them then strip off their gowns, their shoes, and their turbans, beat their bosoms, tear up their dishevelled hair, like furies, from every part of their heads, shriek again till they are out of breath, and then turn rapidly round, until their eyes grow dim, and they fall to the earth. Afterwards, comes forward another, with his hair wild, his dress half stripped off, and a knife grasped in his hand, which, after many horrid gestures, he plunges into his own bosom: the rest wipe up the blood with their hair; one takes a drop and smears it on his face, and the others lay hold of him, and toss him about violently till he becomes senseless and falls. All then throw aside their turbans, the music commences, and

they turn round as if distracted, kneel, kiss the
earth, and rise again. The chief priest holds a
crown in his hand, and cries "Nolan la Mahommed, Nolan la;" the rest repeat the same words,
in different tones, and the most confused manner.
The priest turns himself in the direction of
Mecca (where lies the tomb of their false prophet,
Mahommed,) and bows repeatedly, and profoundly;
his example is followed by the others, who bow
in the same manner, and turn round again to the
sound of a sort of music, which is little better than
the striking together of a pair of sandals. They
conclude by embracing each other, and, kneeling,
kiss the earth. It is impossible, without witnessing
the scene, to form an idea of the sensations which
are called forth by it: at one moment it is difficult
to repress laughter; at another, pity and dread
contend for the mastery. I was so overcome by
terror, that I involuntarily seized hold of a gentleman who was at my side, and trembled from head
to foot. It is forbidden to be a spectator of these
ceremonies, but her Royal Highness had asked
permission, and obtained it as a high favour.

In Turkey, if a person become mad, he is looked

E

upon as a saint, and rambles through the streets,
his head covered with flowers, and his body with
ribbons.   After his death he is held ˙in great
veneration ; a tomb is erected over him, and˙ he
is invoked as a saint :—a circumstance, which,
exhibits strongly the stupidity and ignorance of
this uncivilized people.

The lantern of Demosthenes is still· to be seen
in Athens ; it is a monument of marble, and is
ornamented with many fine bas-reliefs.   Music is
at this time performed in it.

The fortress, or Acropolis, in which is the statue
of Icide, and. the fountain of fresh water, which
was created by Neptune, when disputing with
Minerva.   The grotto of Diapanne Propiles, or
the citadel ; in· it is the temple of Minerva, the
magnificence of which consists in the number,
height, and massiveness of its columns, of white
marble, and of the Doric order : there are various
bas-reliefs, and five statues on the front.   At the
fortress still remains the portico, consecrated˙ to
Neptune Erecteus, with five columns in front ; it
is now used as a powder magazine.   In the same

place is also the olive tree, which Minerva commanded to spring from the earth, during her dispute with Neptune. The ruins of the temple of Victory. The temple of Minerva, protectress of the ancient Athenians, constructed wholly of white marble, and encircled with a double portico, supported by two rows of beautiful Doric columns. The length of the temple is one hundred and twenty-seven feet, the breadth one hundred, the height sixty-nine. This also is now used as a powder magazine.

In the wall of the fortress is a head of Socrates, supposed to have been once very fine, but now scarcely to be recognised, so much has it been consumed by time. Below, are the ruins of the theatre of Herodotus Atticus; besides them, those of the theatre of Bacchus, in which, during the festivals of that god, seven pieces were at times represented in the course of a day. There was room in it for thirty thousand spectators; but if any rain fell, they were obliged to quit the performance, because the place was entirely exposed. The triumphal arch of Adrian. Near it is the temple of Jupiter Olympus, or the Pantheon; of which there are now but thirteen columns remaining, out of the one hundred and twenty which it formerly possessed ; they were sixty feet in height, and nineteen in circumference, of beautiful marble, and of the Doric order.

The Ilissus, the celebrated Athenian river, over which was formerly a fine bridge, near to this temple, now in ruins. We were told that there had not been water in its bed during forty years, and that it had reappeared only this year. Here was the promenade of the beautiful Grecian ladies.

The stadium, in which were exhibited the wild beast combats, and where, every five years, the ancients celebrated the Olympic games; it is of immense extent, and in the form of a horse-shoe. Under the mountain is the enclosure, whence the chariots issued, for the race in the arena, and into which, when concluded, they returned. After the games, crowns, formed simply of laurel, were distributed to the victors, who were more gratified than if a kingdom had been bestowed upon them. It is related, that, on one occasion, a fond mother

expired with excessive joy, on seeing her son proclaimed victor.   This amphitheatre would accommodate one hundred and fifty thousand spectators :
the site, and the grass, which flourishes on it, are
all that now offer themselves to the eye.   .

At a short distance, are the ruins of the temple
of Ceres, goddess of agriculture ; as also, the fountain of Galiochéa, now dried up.   In the town is
the temple of Jupiter, at present converted into
a Greek church ; and, likewise, the temple of Au-
gustus.

Mount May is still pointed out, as the spot
where St. Paul preached to ten thousand Athenians, who became converts the same day.

Outside the town are the tombs of Transiles,
and of Pericles, the best, and most illustrious
monarchs of those days.   The house of Plato, the
great philosopher.   The temple of the Furies, in
which Œdipus died of despair.   This young man
having killed his father, without knowing him,
became so wretched, that he quitted Athens, and
never returned to it more.   The temple of Venus,

in which is a myrtle, said to have been cut, and even burnt down to the root so often, that its reproducing itself is inexplicable. It, surely, must be an exertion of the power of the goddess, protectress of love, of which the myrtle is emblematic; and consequently, demonstrates, that it is vain to attempt to exterminate and destroy (qu'on a beau couper l'amour jusqu'à la racine, et faire tous ses efforts pour le détruire) love: it always resumes its post.

On the Piræus is the tomb of the famous Amazon, wife, it is said, of Theseus. In truth, on whatever side one bends one's steps, it is over the ruins of this ancient and beautiful city, which formerly ranked among the most celebrated in the world. It is now much changed, being small and wretched, without trade, and without industry.

The mountain, from which the ancients obtained all their fine marble, still remains; but marble is found in it no longer. Opposite to it is Mount Hymettus, productive of excellent honey.

From the fortress, the small town of Athens

presents a beautiful prospect; it is situated in a
rich plain, planted with olives, the fruit of which
yields an abundance of oil.

The Athenian women are not beautiful, nor yet
is their costume; they suffer their hair to float at
length, and those who have not a sufficient quan-
tity, add to it silk, painted the same colour: they
conceal the greater part of the face (f).

(g) Her Royal Highness gave two balls to the Grecian ladies: their manner of dancing is insipid to
the last degree (pour mourir d'ennui). They are
not permitted to dance with the gentlemen, but
merely among themselves; and their dance consists of nothing more than taking each other's hand,
and turning, The first, or the one who dances
best, holds a handkerchief in her hand, which she
constantly waves; the accompanying music is
simply, là, là, là, là, là, là, and là, là, là, without
variety. Added to this, their want of grace makes
one fancy them puppets, moved by wires. The
lower rank of women wear a head-dress, composed
of a silver coin, called barras, which is equivalent
to a raps of Switzerland; they have also necklaces

of the same materials : the coins are pierced in the centre, and placed on an iron wire. The women who are more wealthy, wear gold coin in the same style, and in great profusion. Both the poor and the wealthy unstring them, when they have no other money, or in preference to borrowing, and distribute to the many poor who offer themselves every where, and invariably limit their petition to a barras *(h)*.

After having examined every object of curiosity, and interest, at Athens, we quitted it, on the 24th, to proceed on our voyage, and on the 26th, arrived at Corinth *(i)*, a very insignificant town, with respect to size, but of great antiquity. We resided in the palace of the Bey, which is very extensive. Corinth offers no objects of curiosity, save its castle, in a commanding situation ; a few columns, which are said to be the wreck of a temple of Neptune, god of the sea; and a tomb, pointed out as that of the children of Medea, slain by her own hand.

On the 28th we resumed our journey, after having visited the Seraglio, in which there are many

women. The port is six miles distant from the old
town, agreeably with the system anciently pursued
by the Greeks, through motives of policy, of con-
structing their ports at a distance from their cities.
On the 29th we set sail, and the following day the
wind became so violent, that we were obliged to
come to an anchor off Cape Colonne. On a
mountain above the road are the ruins of an ancient temple of Minerva Poliades, built of splendid
white marble : there still remain fifteen columns,
which we visited.

The first of June, the wind being again favorable, we set sail, and on the 3d reached the isle of
Tenedos, opposite to the plains of Troy. It was
thither that the Greeks retired, whilst the wooden
horse, with ten thousand men enclosed in it, was
introduced within the walls, for the purpose of destroying this great and beautiful city, after it had
withstood a siege of ten years. There is no longer
a stone to be seen of its once proud edifices, and
its site is an unbroken plain, planted with olive
trees. We twice passed the Scamander, which
formerly crossed the city. At a trifling distance is
New Troy, built by Alexander the Great. The

town is not, in any way, remarkable. Close to it
is the Strait of the Dardanelles ; the rapidity of the
stream renders the entry into it very difficult, and
without a very stiff breeze to overcome the current, it frequently occurs, that vessels are detained
six weeks without being able to get through it. At
the entrance are two fortified castles; on the left
that of Europe, and on the right that of Asia, as
also a pretty little village. A little further up we
saw the ruins of Sestos in Asia, and of Obisto in
Europe.

On the 5th of June we passed Gallipoli, at the
entrance of the Sea of Marmora, and on the 7th, at
four o'clock in the morning, entered the port of
Constantinople. From the port this immense city
forms a magnificent view. It is built in the form
of an amphitheatre, and is divided into three districts, Pera and Galata, the residences of the Christians, and Constantinople that of the Turks. The
houses are all constructed of wood, which is frequently the cause of great conflagrations, extending even to three or four thousand houses. If a fire
break out, no attempt is made to extinguish it,
unless the Grand Seignor be present; and if he

1

were at a distance, the town would be suffered to
burn down, whilst awaïting his arrival.  On the
day of our arrival, we disembarked, and went to
reside at the spacious palace of the British ambas-
sador.  When within the city, it appears far from
beautiful, owing to the narrowness and dirtiness of
the streets.  Her Royal Highness, her lady of
honor, my sister, and myself, went up in a sort of
car on two wheels, drawn by oxen, which is the
best equipage the country affords ; the rest of the
household were on foot.  It is said that the Mosque
of St. Sophia is splendid, but no Christian is allowed to enter its precincts ; the Turks themselves
enter barefoot.  Every Friday the Sultan goes to
prayer, accompanied by his guard.  His palace is
very beautiful, and is surrounded by cypress trees ;
this tree appears to be the favorite of the Turks,
for before every house there is one,—the effect of
which, in this great town, is strikingly pleasing.

The plague breaking out here, her Royal Highness was under the necessity of taking a country
house.  On the 14th, we went to Biutiere, fifteen
miles distant from Constantinople, upon the Bos-
phorus.  Nothing can be imagined more enchant-

ingly beautiful than this canal, which unites the
Black Sea, and the Sea of Marmora.   The mountains, on either side, are sprinkled with villages
and villas, and the canal with vessels, laden with
merchandise, passing from sea to sea.   We occasionally made excursions on the Black Sea, and in
one instance we breakfasted in Asia, and dined in
Europe.   On the banks of the Black Sea are many
fortresses, and in a small garden is seen the tomb
of a giant, who is said, in days of yore, to have
been the King of that country—it is sixty-four
feet long.   Near it is a temple, consecrated to Bacchus, God of Wine.

The Grand Seignor sent rich presents to the
Princess, though he is by no means fond of seeing
any distinguished personage within his dominions.
The boats, on these seas, are not broader at the
bottom than the hand, and to prevent being upset,
it is necessary to sit down on the planks; even
then they are dangerous.   They are very long, and
go like the wind.   In Constantinople, seven or eight
women may often be seen taking an airing together
in a chariot, drawn by oxen.   They are invariably
escorted by Turks, to prevent them conversing

with any Christians, if they should take a fancy
so to do ; this is by no means an improbable occurrence, as the Turkish women entertain a great admiration for Christians.  It is said that they are
beautiful, but with regard to them, we must not,
like Thomas, decline to believe, without ocular
demonstration ; in that case, we should always remain in doubt, for they never unveil their coun-
tenances.

On the 16th of June we quitted Biutiere to
embark, and sailed on the 17th.  The current
carried us rapidly out of the Dardanelles.  The
22d we passed Mitylene, and the 23d landed on
Scio, a beautiful and well cultivated island : the
women are exceedingly beautiful.  Ten miles distant from the town of Scio, is seen the spot on
which was the school of Homer ; also the chair of
Peter, on which are carved a lion, and a lamb.  We
left the same day, and arrived at Scala Nuova, distant ten miles from the ruins of Ephesus, a town,
formerly of great importance, but of which now
not a house exists.  It was at Ephesus, that St.
Paul the Apostle wrote so many letters.  The ruins
of the celebrated temple of Diana,

Chase, are still to be seen :—two hundred years
had been employed in building the temple, and a
fellow, of the name of Erostratus, destroyed it by
fire in a day. When asked why he had committed
the act, he replied, that it was to render his name
immortal !!! Three miles from Ephesus, is the
grotto of the Seven Sleepers, who were perse-
cuted, on account of their religion, by a tyrant,
king of that country. They were cast into the
grotto, and awoke after a sleep of two hundred
years' duration. They were much astonished, on
awaking, to find that every thing was changed ;
that the true religion was established, and that
their tyrant and his descendants were dead. They
supposed that their sleep must have been of more
than ordinary duration, and that a considerable
lapse of time must have taken place, left their
grotto, and went into the town. I am ignorant in
what manner they lived there afterwards.

On the 25th we quitted Scala Nuova, and
passed the islands of Rhodes and Cyprus, so productive of good wines. We did not dare to dis-
embark, on account of the malignant fevers, which
prevail there in the month of June, the effect of

continued rains.  The 2d of July we landed at St.
Jean d'Acre, a town equally celebrated in ancient
and modern history.  The anchor was cast exactly
in the spot where Richard Cœur de Lion, King of
England, was detained, on his return from the crusades in the Holy Land.  The tower, where he was
imprisoned, still remains in the state in which it
then stood.  It is in the centre of the roads.  It
was here, also, that Napoleon the Great first gave
battle on his campaign into Egypt.

He was compelled to raise the siege, by the arrival of the English, under the command of Sir
Sidney Smith.  There were eight hundred French
in the town, who retired to a tower, in which
they defended themselves gallantly, until compelled to yield to numbers.  The barbarous Turks
cut off their hands and feet, and putting them
into bags, cast them into the sea, subjecting them,
also, to numerous torments, before putting an end
to their lives.  What a striking proof is this of the
barbarity of this ferocious nation towards the
Christians, and of the melancholy effects of the
ambition of a chief, who feels no compunction for
exposing the lives of his brave soldiers!!  St.

Jean d'Acre is a small and convenient town, but, like other Turkish towns, constructed of wood. We went with the intention of visiting the old fortress, where Napoleon fought; it is now destroyed, but the English have built another in its place.

On the 5th we set sail for Jaffa, which is distant but half a day's journey *(k)*. Her Royal Highness purposed going thence, by land, to Jerusalem ; but, as we were unprovided with passports, the Bey refused to let more than five persons proceed. We were, therefore, under the necessity of returning, on the 6th, to St. Jean d'Acre. The Bey there was exceedingly polite, and granted us passports, and as many horses as we had need of, five linen tents for the journey, and a guard of Turkish officers to escort us, the country being infested with robbers and banditti.

On the 8th we commenced our pilgrimage to the Holy Land : our company consisted, in all, of two hundred and eighty individuals, and presented the appearance of an army *(l)*. On the morning of the 9th we arrived at Nazareth, now a small

village, built of stone. After having taken some
repose, we visited the church, which is built upon
the spot where formerly stood the house of the
Virgin Mary; there are some fine paintings in the
church. On the evening of the same day, we set
forward again, and arrived on the morning of the
10th at Clon, which stands in an extensive plain.
We reposed under our tents, but the heat was so
excessive, that it prevented us sleeping; at five
o'clock we dined, and the caravan again continued
its route. On the 11th we arrived, in the morning,
at Rama, where we slept in the convent of Capuchins. As far as Rama the road had been very
narrow and rocky, filled with brambles, and constantly up and down hill, so that many of the
company, partially overcome by sleep, fell from
their horses. In the evening, after having slept
and eaten, we resumed our journey. On the
morning of the 12th we again slept under our tents,
pitched in the open air. The road became more
practicable than before. At three o'clock in the
afternoon we broke up our tents, and the same
evening, at nine o'clock, reached Jerusalem. At
our entry, the people assembled in crowds to see
the Princess of Wales, who rode upon an ass.

G

This circumstance recalled to me strongly the Day of Palms (Palm Sunday), on which our Saviour made, in the same manner, his entry into Jerusalem. I imagined I beheld him, and inwardly made comparisons : for assuredly, if any one can in any way resemble our great Saviour, it is this excellent Princess. She is, like him, charitable, mild, and beneficent to all ; she has suffered much, and always supports her misfortunes with great patience and resignation ; and, like him, she has not deserved them.

Jerusalem is unquestionably, to every true Christian, the most interesting town that can be visited, having been the centre of the actions of our Saviour ; it was in Jerusalem that he gave the most powerful testimony of his truth. Jerusalem was also the land promised by God to his elect, and was the scene of the lives of many prophets and illustrious men. It is very different now from what it formerly was, and, like many other cities, has been laid in ruins. In contemplating these ruins, one has a melancholy example of the fragility of human greatness. Cities which were once the most brilliant and the most beautiful, are now but heaps

of stones; and that which was, coevally with their
splendour, passed over as unworthy of notice, is
now, in their stead, brilliant and beautiful. If the
great men who then flourished were to come forth
from their tombs, how great would be their astonishment to behold the order of things thus
changed! Reflections such as these should convince us of the futility of fixing our affections on
earthly objects, and instruct us to bestow them
rather on our true habitation, which is above; considering ourselves only as travellers and strangers
here below.

We took up our abode at Jerusalem in a convent
of Capuchins, and the following morning set out
on our visit to the curious and interesting objects
which abound there. We began with the church,
which was built by St. Helena. This virtuous
Queen of England followed her husband to the
crusades, and founded, it is said, five hundred
churches, and as many hospitals. A more beneficent Queen it is impossible to imagine. She died
in endeavouring to save the life of her husband,
who had been wounded in the arm by an enve-
nomed arrow; she extracted the poison by sucking

the wound, and thus saved him, but was herself the victim of her excessive tenderness. Her husband caused her body to be transported to England, and on each spot where the vehicle which bore it rested, he erected a cross. The crosses still remain. The Queen was classed among the saints. The church is magnificent, and enriched with paintings ; it is built exactly on Mount Calvary. On entering it, the attention is directed to the spot where Joseph of Arimathea embalmed the body of our Saviour, and afterwards to his holy sepulchre, which is of an oblong form, covered with scarlet velvet, embroidered and fringed with gold : the interior, in which three persons might be placed, is ornamented in the same manner. Within are forty-four silver lamps, constantly burning, maintained at the expense of the different courts of Europe: each one has its mark. The stone which covers the opening is beautiful white marble.

What sensations can be supposed to arise from being in a spot so holy ; from having it in one's power to put up prayers to God, at the very tomb in which his son was buried ! I imagine I see him issue forth from his tomb, covered with the wounds

inflicted on him, and exclaiming to me, " If thou
followest my precepts, and doest the will of God,
*my* Father and *thine*, thy sins shall be forgiven
thee, and thou shalt be received into grace." We
quitted the sepulchre, filled with devotion. At the
entrance is the spot on which the angel rested,
when the women came to weep, seeking for Jesus.
Afterwards we touched the column, to which our
Saviour was bound when scourged, and visited the
place where he was crowned with thorns. All
persons are prohibited from touching, or even seeing, these objects ; but through the interest of her
Royal Highness we obtained the privilege of doing
both the one and the other. We saw the prison in
which he was confined. From thence to Mount
Calvary the ascent is entirely by steps, by which
we went up, and viewed the very spot where he
was nailed to the cross, and where his mother, conscious of her son's guiltlessness, stood weeping.
We touched the cavity into which the cross was
fixed—the cross on which the Son of God expired
for *our* sins ! Can we do other than abjure our
sins, where *He* died ; reflecting how great God's
abhorrence of *those sins* must be, when he willed

that his Son should suffer, and die to expiate them?
Ah! let the incredulous only visit Jerusalem, and
I am convinced their conscience will be moved,
and they will not disavow a religion established by
proofs so many and so overpowering, that it is im
possible to doubt its truth.   Close by are between
the clefts of the mountain, which was rent at the
moment when our Saviour expired.   Below the
church is the site where St. Helena (inspired un
doubtedly by the spirit of God) found the holy
cross, which was dug for by her order, she herself
watching throughout the day at a window, from
which she distributed money to the workmen.—
The Jews, who had carefully hidden the cross, as
well as those of the two thieves who were crucified
with him, little imagined that one day they would
be discovered. There were, however, three of them.
In order to ascertain which was that of our Saviour, they were placed on the tomb of a dead
man ; the two first produced no effect, but as soon
as the third was brought near, the dead man arose.
This cross was carried to Rome, where, to this day,
it remains.   In the church are still the tombs of
Nicodemus, and of Joseph of Arimathea.

On the 14th we went to visit the chamber in which Jesus instituted the holy sacrament. I must just observe, *en passant*, that the Pope repeats a similar ceremony, every year, on the same day.— Twelve of the poorest priests in the Roman states are selected; he sups with them, and afterwards washes their feet and their hands, as Jesus did to his disciples. The Catholics assert that the Pope is the representative of Jesus Christ upon earth. It was also in the same chamber that the Holy Ghost descended upon the apostles, on the day of Pentecost. In the same house is the tomb of King David; but the Turks absolutely refuse to let it be seen. We went thence to the house of Caiaphas; the entrance is through the court where Peter denied Jesus thrice, and where the cock crew.— Within is the small room in which our Saviour was confined, whilst Caiaphas was deliberating what should be done with him. In it is the same stone which was rolled by the angel from before the sepulchre, and which has been carried thither: we touched it. At this time this house is converted into a church. From it we went to the prison of St. Peter, where the angel burst open the seven gates of iron, and released him. Close by is a

beautiful church, used by the Armenians, in which
are the sepulchres of the four evangelists. On our
return we saw the house of King David, and the
window in which he played upon the harp ; a lamp
is constantly kept burning in it. The same day we
traced the steps of our divine Saviour, when bearing the cross, and the spot where he fell from fa-
tigue. Further on are the remains of the famous
Temple of Solomon : there are yet seven gates remaining ; among them, that through which Simeon
entered with the infant Jesus is in an excellent
state of preservation. All the stones of this temple
were cut with a ring, sent by the Deity expressly
for that purpose. In the interior the Turks have
now erected a superb mosque ; for which reason no
Christian can enter, under pain of death. Our
only resource was to look into it through a window,
which is opposite. The place is vast in extent,
and I am not surprised that this temple was esteemed one of the wonders of the universe. It
was here that Abraham showed his profound obedience to the commands of God. We went to the
Mount of Olives, and visited the grotto in which
Jesus sweated drops of blood, and prayed with so
much fervour ; the place whence he ascended to

heaven in view of his disciples, and the sepulchres
of Mary and Joseph also.

On the 15th we departed for Jericho. The road
being very perilous, on account of banditti, the Bey
gave us an escort of two hundred soldiers, of
whom the chief, as we were, fortunately, not till
afterwards informed, had been condemned to death
but a year before, for having headed a band of
robbers. Consequently, if we had cause of alarm,
it was from him, and from the character of the
soldiers, by whom we were surrounded. They
all had the air of fugitives from the galleys, or
something even more horrible. One had a gun,
another a club, another a bar of iron, and a fourth
a sort of fork, as a weapon. Their dress was not
more uniform, and they themselves exactly the
colour of the chestnut. On their head they wore
a small turban, with which, you would have said,
they had wiped the spit for a week; and the rest
of their dress was equally clean. Such are the
men under whose protection, in the deepest
darkness, we accomplished this journey, in the
deserts of Palestine; in the midst of frightful
precipices, and on a road, known by us to be

infested with robbers, and on which not a cottage
was visible. Notwithstanding all this, I did not
bestow a thought on the danger, but slept as well
as if in a good bed; it was not till they were past
that we reflected on the perils to which we had
been exposed. These are the advantages of
travelling! one acquires courage and firmness!
On this route we passed the house where Jesus
raised Lazarus from the dead: the tree on which
Absalom, son of David, was caught by his hair:
the potter's field, bought with the money which
Judas had taken as the price of betraying Jesus:
the cave, in which Jeremiah wrote his book: and
many other trifling objects, which it would be
tedious to name. On the 16th, early in the
morning, we reached the Jordan, and went down
to it in the same part where our Saviour constrained
John the Baptist to baptize him, and where the
dove of fire descended from heaven. On the other
side is the desert, in which St. John preached. It
was also over it that the Almighty commanded the
sun "to stand still," over the heads of the
Israelites, under the guidance of Joshua (m). We
arrived at Jericho, that once noble city, of which
but a few ruins now remain: It was there that

Joshua, being unable to enter with his army, implored the intervention of the Most High; immediately the walls fell untouched, and the Jews entered the promised land, after forty years' slavery in the deserts of Egypt (n). Our tents were pitched there, and we slept under them the whole day. The heat was excessive, and almost insupportable; we were perishing with thirst, and had nothing to allay it, save miry water. At length, after having refreshed ourselves by eating, we returned to Jerusalem. The Mount of Olives, as well as the valley of Jehoshaphat, are on this road.

On leaving Jerusalem I could not avoid reflecting, that it was much to be deplored that so many nations, calling themselves Christians, and who wage war with each other for an acre of territory, or a slight provocation received, should not employ their arms in a manner which would be far more useful; and would tend to strengthen the true religion. In truth, is it not a reproach, that the land reserved by God for his chosen people, the land in which his only Son gave to men his holy religion, and in which he died to confirm it, should

be in the power of *his* and *our* most mortal foes?
No Christian can go to the holy sepulchre without
paying to, and craving the permission of, the
Turks: if it do not please them to grant it, they
flatly refuse, and there is no remedy in complaint.
The holy sepulchre itself is guarded by a Maho-
metan : so also is the church, of which he carefully
conceals the key.   Five different religions are
professed there, viz. that of the Christians, Turks,
Greeks, Armenians, and also of the Gotz ; each
separate sect, or religion, has its chapels and
apartments.

The few Christians who reside at Jerusalem,
particularly the prophets, are ill treated, poor, and
wretched.   Her Royal-Highness bestowed many
charities upon them, and left them fifty louis per
year for the maintenance of their convents.   If
some nations would rouse themselves, and institute
another crusade, as in days of yore, expel the
barbarous Turks from that which belongs to us,
restore Jerusalem, and give it to him whom they
affirm to be the representative of Christ, our
Lord, to fix his residence there ;—this war would be
truly useful and praiseworthy in the eyes of God,

But, alas! St. Louis, and all those who had religion at heart, are now dead; and in the present day, all think much more of their own interest than of the glory and advancement of our holy religion. It would seem as though this perishable world were their everlasting dwelling-place!

At length, on the 17th, we quitted Jerusalem, our hearts touched with the objects which we had seen there; the remembrance of which can never be effaced. We slept once more at Rama, and on the 18th arrived at Jaffa, a small town. Our vessel was in the bay, and the wind being favourable we put to sea the same day. Her Royal Highness had an intention of visiting Alexandria, and going thence into Egypt; but her design was rendered impracticable by the plague, which was making great ravages there. We were within ten miles of Alexandria; thus we may say, that we made the tour of the Mediterranean, traversed the sea of Marmora, and had been upon the Black Sea. I omitted to mention, that near to Jericho is the Dead Sea; so called, because the water that flows into it does not again issue from it. On the 27th we passed Cyprus a second time:

we were three days in sight of this island, which
was at that time the resort of the pirates.  It is a
very dangerous spot, and many vessels have been
wrecked upon its shores.

Our provisions began to fail us, and we were
obliged to steer for the isle of Rhodes, whither we
arrived, after passing Caramania, on the 1st of
August.  This island presents a beautiful coup
d'œil; the town is clean, and in it yet remains the
palace of the Knights of Malta, who made it their
residence, when of old they were possessed of the
island.  The ruins of the famous Colossus are still
to be seen; it was esteemed one of the seven wonders of the world, because lofty enough to admit
the passage of the largest vessel between its legs.

On the 3d we departed thence with a light
breeze, which, in the evening, freshened up, and
became so violent, that we were in great danger;
it was contrary, and drove us backwards from our
course.  On the 4th we came in sight of Candia,
(anciently Crete) and of Mount Ida: on this mountain Jupiter, god of all the gods, was born.  We
were four days in passing the island, the wind be-

ing either constantly unfavourable, or dying away
to a dead calm. On the 8th we made sail for
Zante; but as the wind continued still contrary, we
changed our course for Sicily. We did not enter
the port of Syracuse till the 20th; this was the
first Christian town we had for a long time seen.

We there offered up our thanks to the God of
mercy, for the manifest protection which he had
extended to us, throughout our journey: for, assuredly, it was his all-powerful hand, that preserved
us, in safety, from the dangers which had threatened us. We had escaped the plague, robbers, assassins, and what is even more formidable than all
these,—the corsairs. Every one is aware of the
massacres which took place in Tunis after we left,
and that five brigs of war were fitted out, from the
Goletta, for the express purpose of piracy. These
pirates well knew that the Princess had many diamonds, and much money, in her possession, and,
in consequence, were continually in pursuit of us.
Had they overtaken us, we could not have defended ourselves, having only six guns on board,
whilst they had, each of them, thirteen. The
Princess expressed a hope, that, in case of attack,

they might be satisfied with our property only ; for these wretches, usually, after having carried off all the valuables, massacre those who are on board, or with shot sink the vessel. Once in their power, one's only escape is by a cruel death. They approach so quietly, that, when perceived, it is too late to think of escape. They were always in pursuit of our vessel, and it is difficult to comprehend how we escaped them. We must have been protected by a veil, which hid us from their search.

.One of the brigs had been captured at Scio, and two others at St. Jean d'Acre ; thus there were two still at sea, and these were committing great ravages. Whilst we were off Cyprus, an English brig was brought in, which had been taken possession of by these wretches ; all on board had been decapitated, and the vessel was driving about at the mercy of the sea. When we were between Zante and Candia, one of these corsairs was seen in chase of us : our consternation may be more easily imagined than described ! instantly every light on board was extinguished, to prevent them keeping sight of us in the dark ; they lost us, and,

in the morning, we were greatly delighted to find
they were no longer in sight.

At the time her Royal Highness left Tunis, she
was conjured by every one not to go among the
islands of the Archipelago, because they were infested by pirates, even more to be dreaded than the
corsairs. These pirates have two or three large
boats, with twenty-five oars; when the breeze,
amidst the islands, dies away, they conceal themselves, and, during the obscurity of the night,
move so rapidly with their oars, and under their
black banners, that nothing can escape them. They
board the vessels, wound and massacre all whom
they meet, carry away every thing they discover,
and leave the barks to the mercy of the waves. We
ourselves saw some barks at Milo, that had been
treated in this manner, and were picked up by a
French brig. Her Royal Highness, who, as I have
before observed, is highly courageous, was not terrified by these recitals, and thanks to God, we escaped all the threatened dangers.

We have, besides,
a spectacle, of which

adequate idea, without having seen it, and which
we cannot recall to our memories, without shud-
dering. It is, notwithstanding, a most magnificent object of contemplation,—the vast expanse of
water,—the foamy waves dashing in uproar around
the vessel, whilst they form an abyss which seems
about to engulph her. How often, seated at my
scanty window, have I, with emotion, gazed upon
so surprising a scene, and said within myself:—
How can any one be so senseless as to deny the
existence of an Almighty God! Who could create
this, except such an one? who could support, and
preserve from destruction, so frail a vessel, at the
mercy of the waves, and tossed about by the
reckless winds, save a God who has created them?
It is he who rules our destiny, who places us in
dangers, and who afterwards releases us from them,
if such be his good pleasure, and for our advantage.
Let us then submit to all which it pleases him to
ordain, reposing our trust in him. After such reflections, I felt perfectly at ease, and, if in peril,
offered up my prayers to God, recommending my
soul to him, and awaiting his pleasure.

Our voyage was now nearly concluded; but we

2

were not suffered to land, or to touch any one. All
vessels, coming from the Levant, are compelled to
submit to quarantine, on account of the plague.
At Syracuse we had a small spot of land appropri-
ated to us, and every one fled from us, as from wild
beasts, with which we were diverted not a little.

On the 27th we again set sail, again to encounter new dangers. We had been told, that
some Algerines were cruising off Sicily, and that
they even chased, for three hours, a small vessel, which took shelter in Syracuse; and, in consequence, her Royal Highness engaged an Austrian
frigate to convoy us. By an unparalleled good fortune, when we passed Catania, these corsairs were
short of water, and had gone on shore to procure it,
and thus we escaped them once more. As they
were at war with the English, it would have been
a master-stroke for them, to have captured the
Princess.

At length, on the 31st, we entered the Straits of
Messina, and in the evening cast anchor in the port.
We had flattered ourselves, that we should be suf-
fered to land without performing quarantine; but

flattered ourselves in vain ; so on the 7th we again
made sail, and coasting the shores of Calabria, on
the 14th came in sight of the isle of Capri, in the
Bay of Naples. Whilst we were there, Vesuvius
was burning, but faintly. We did not land at Naples ; but as I have before been there, I cannot pass
so interesting a town unnoticed.

Naples is extensive, but very dirty ; the Strada
Toledo, which is three miles in length, is the only
part worthy remark. The public gardens, on the
sea-shore, are delightful. The theatre of San Carlo
was extremely beautiful, but the greater part of it
has been destroyed by fire. There is rich store of
antiquities. Pompeii, at the foot of Vesuvius, was
totally overwhelmed by the first eruption of the
volcano ; the town was not burned, but buried
under the ashes, which fell from the mountain. It is
now partly uncovered, and a spacious amphitheatre
is visible ; in the streets are to be seen the tracks
of the wheels of the carriages ; and in the houses,
which are small, and half ruined, are figures of
various colours, white, blue, and green. It is,
nevertheless, two thousand years since it was destroyed. There is a separate street for the tombs,

in which I myself have seen ashes in an urn; formerly it was the custom to burn the bodies. Each family had a separate building, which served as a tomb for all the members of it. The receptacles of the great, and the mean, were distinguished from each other. Pompeii is four leagues from Naples, on the road to Vesuvius. This volcano is but half the height of Etna; but the ascent to it is very laborious, owing to the depth of the cinders, into which one sinks as far as the knee. In the neighbourhood are the lavas, which formerly destroyed Baiæ. It was at Baiæ that the cruel and perfidious Nero ended his days; his house, and the warm baths in it, are still shewn there. Close by is the grotto of Aniana, which is highly remarkable; the air is so pernicious, that if a dog be put into it, in five minutes he dies. Near it once stood a town, which was swallowed up in one night, and, the following morning, its site was occupied by a small lake, on which game are plentiful. The atmosphere about it is bad, and would cause death to any one compelled to remain there.

The evening of the 13th we quitted the Bay of Naples, in tremendous weather,—a storm of wind.

thunder and lightning; we were all in great dread, but the gale was in our favor, and on the 14th we came in sight of Gaeta, and arrived at Terracina, the first town of the Roman State.

Her Royal Highness caused application to be made to the Pope, for permission to land without performing quarantine, and we proceeded to Capo d'Anzi. The answer of his Holiness reached us the morning of the 15th, and we landed immediately.

Since the 13th of July we had not set foot upon terra firma, but had been continually mewed up in our vessel. During the whole of the time, we had not had one day of weather perfectly favorable; ever either the wind was contrary, or fell calm; and, in this manner, we had experienced many disappointments.

From Jaffa to Capo d'Anzi it is fourteen miles in a direct line (quatorze milles, in original, in which there is evidently an omission), but when the wind is unfavorable, it is necessary to tack, and make six miles, in order to get forward three; and,

at times, after having made one hundred miles, the
vessel is driven quite back again.   Whilst going to
Jaffa, we had the wind constantly in our favor, because it blows, during eight months, in the same
direction; and for the same reason, when we were
on our return, it was contrary.   It changes in September only.

The evening of the 15th we arrived at Rome.
It is still a fine city, though no longer so celebrated
as in ancient times, when it ruled the whole world.
Rome is rich in magnificent palaces, of an imposing aspect, beautiful statues and fountains, and
has two mighty columns, on which are represented,
in basso-relievo, the exploits of the ancient Romans.
The church of St. Peter is the finest in the world,
and strikes the visitor with astonishment the moment he enters: in it are lofty columns of bronze,
in great number, and tombs of the ancient Kings
and Emperors of Rome; and in the midst of the
church are preserved the bodies of St. Peter and
St. Paul, who suffered martyrdom for their religion,
in Rome.   The tombs are surrounded by a multi-
tude of lamps, kept constantly burning.   In the
same edifice is a bronze statue of St. Peter, holding

in his hands the keys of Paradise: the Catholics adore it; and one of the feet has been so often kissed by the devotees, that it is quite worn. The square or place in front of the church is magnificent. On either side is a portico, ornamented with the statues of all the saints; those of our Saviour, and his twelve Apostles, are upon the church. On each side of the square is a beautiful fountain.

The museum of Rome is splendid; it requires three hours to make the circuit of it, walking quick. Rome is on the Tiber, which passes through the town, and is crossed by a fine bridge.

On the 16th her Royal Highness introduced us to the Pope, at his beautiful palace on Monte Cavallo, where we had the honor of kissing his hand. The Catholics kiss his slipper, in token of adoration; and it is esteemed a high favor when he presents his hand instead of his foot.

There are still, in Rome, many ancient temples. The Capitol is strikingly magnificent, and adorned with the busts of the Roman Emperors, and Consuls.  It was there that public meetings were held.

We departed from Rome the evening of the 17th, and on the 18th made a very short stay at Viterbo. During the night we passed through Sienna, the town in which the Italian language is spoken in all its purity.

On the 19th we went through Florence, seated on the Arno.  It is a lovely town; the houses are handsome, the streets wide and clean, and the peasant girls prettier and more becomingly dressed than in other parts of Italy.

On the 20th we passed through Bologna, a fine town, with porticos on both sides the streets: the same day we passed through Modena, Reggio, Parma, Piacenza, Lodi, Marignan, and Milan; and on the 21st arrived at our Villa d'Este; thus happily terminating our journey.  The Princess, as a token of her gratitude for her prosperous journey, gave seventy-five louis to the poor in Rome.

We are looked upon as people out of the com-

K

mon cast ;                    far as ourselves, and
seen so much.

I hope we shall never lose t e recollection of it ;
and oh! may we never be  .indful of the visible
protection which an all-merciful God has vouch-
safed to us, and may we, throughout the course
of our lives, testify our sense of his mercies.
Amen.

This small Journal I      en written in great
haste, and merely to       little amusement to
our good mother, in leading her through the places
we have visited.

The Journal was received at Colombier in November, 1816, and i        ract copy of it.

# NOTES.

[The following Notes are drawn from the source named in the
Introduction, and are more minute in their details than the
corresponding descriptions in the preceding Journal; they
contain likewise the relation of some circumstances which in
it are passed over unnoted.

That which immediately follows refers to the landing of her
Majesty at Tunis.]

### NOTE (a). Page 13.

" HER Royal Highness, wearied with the perpetual rock-
ing of the vessel, resolved to brave the perils of the waves,
in order to pass the night on terra firma. We landed at the
Goletta, whence the city is fifteen miles distant; this
distance may be travelled either by land or water, there
being a species of salt-water lake, which runs nearly up to
the houses. The ruins of Carthage extend (it is said) the
whole length of the lake. We took up our residence in the
house of the English Consul; but, two days after, the Bey
made an offer to the Princess of a magnificent palace, which

K 2

had not as yet been occupied, I was not even entirely fitted up. Her Royal Highness accepted it, and went thither with all her suite; she was received and treated with the honours due to her merit and her birth, having constantly a guard of honour at her command, composed of the chief officers of the Bey's household, by whom she was accompanied whenever she went abroad."

-------

### Note (b). Page 14.

" Notwithstanding all these precautions, there are always some who find means to deceive the watchfulness of their husbands. Ever on the look ( from their barred apertures, they observe the Christians who pass beneath, in comparison with whom the Turks must certainly suffer infinitely; the wives have a decided liking for the Christians, and their preference is perfectly pardonable. If they perceive a Christian pass frequently, they take care to prepare a little note, which they throw down t his feet: frequently it remains unnoticed; the lady then gains her female duenna by presents; she goes in pursuit of their favourite, solicits, nay, conjures, and facilitates oducing himself into the house. Woe to those curious or indiscreet persons, who cannot resist the temptation! whatever pains they may take to disguise themselves as Turks, there are very few who, sooner or later, are not discovered, and so incur the penalty of their folly, which is the loss of their heads, without even five minutes respite. As to the lady, she is tied up in a sack, and thrown into the sea. Sometimes, nevertheless, by their artifices, the *women* contrive to conceal their intrigues from their inhuman and vindictive husbands."

NOTE (*e*). Page 16.

" On the 6th her Royal Highness went to pay a visit to the Bey, at his country palace, about three miles distant from the town. We were in five carriages, and had about forty officers on horseback as an escort; they were dressed in different modes, but so fantastically, that they had the appearance of imaginary rather than of real beings. Some wore head dresses, exactly such as were in fashion eighty years ago; others had white handkerchiefs fastened to their heads, and cloaks of different colours, made like mantillas, on their shoulders, all wearing heavy wooden boots. We were greatly amused with the setting out of this grotesque band; but were struck most forcibly, by the contrast of their ridiculous costumes with the beauty of the horses on which they were mounted, and their saddles of red velvet, embroidered with gold, and ornamented with precious stones. The address and activity they display in the management of these fiery animals, is astonishing. During our short journey they went through a curious evolution, with a view to amuse the Princess; part of them galloped a quarter of a league in advance, then, returning with the rapidity of lightning, loaded their carbines and fired them, carrying on a mock fight with each other. It was surprising to see their horses at full speed, the bridle thrown on their necks, gallop, or rather cleave the air, without swerving from the path; and the riders, at the same moment, without any manner of support, manage their carbines so actively, and fire them with so much skill. It must be allowed they are unrivalled in this style of warfare, but in other respects they are mean and cowardly. We arrived at the palace of the Bey, surrounded by an immense crowd; the cannons of the fortress having announced our arrival, the two princes and the chief minister came out to receive her Royal Highness. After traversing many courts and antechambers, we came into the presence of the Bey, who was seated on cushions, and encircled by his ministers and principal officers: he received the Princess with great politeness, and her Royal Highness presented to him the whole of her suite. After a short conversation, through the medium of an interpreter, he inquired whether she had a desire to see his seraglio; the Princess having expressed her assent, he gave her his hand, and she beckoned to us to follow her. As for the gentlemen, notwithstanding their excessive curiosity, they were under the necessity of remaining at the door, and awaiting us. The first wife of the Bey came to receive the Princess, in a sort of circular court, in the centre of the apartments; we were then led into a spacious and magnificent chamber, covered with mirrors, in which were a number of women of all ages, clothed without the least taste, but with great splendour; they were loaded with gold, diamonds, and precious stones, from head to foot, and being without stockings, many of them had a diamond chain round the ancle; the fingers, and even the thumbs, were loaded with rich rings, and the tips of them stained black.

" We remarked that the greater number of the women were dark, and that, in their kind, they were much more beautiful than the fair ones, who were not above mediocrity. The Princess, the Bey, and his favourite wife, were seated on cushions, and black slaves presented them with beautiful napkins embroidered with gold; we were perfumed with the finest essences of Barbary in such profusion, that the scent almost overcame us:—afterwards, a collation was served, such an one as could scarcely have been provided at the most magnificent European fête. It was prepared by a beautiful Italian lady, the wife of the first physician to the Bey; she, also, did the honours of it. After the collation, was introduced the first musical corps of the court, consisting of six women, the youngest of whom was more than sixty. One was lame, another one-eyed, a third blind, and similarly with the others, and all were so immoderately fat, that they could with difficulty move. It was really amusing to see these youthful beauties enter under the charge of an eunuch.

They placed themselves on the floor, and commenced
playing a sort of                          :afened the ears; such,
however, was the best display of music of the court of
Tunis.   The air finished; after a short prelude, one of
these                          enormous mouth, and
regaled us with the tones of a voice so hoarse and discordant,
that it would be injustice to compare it to any other than
that of an owl, screaming at night, on the tower of some
ruined castle; and it was more than requisite to remember
that we were in the presence of two sovereigns, to enable us
                          ; more especially, as the Princess
had the ı                          attention, and bestowed
                          ırmonious voice of the
                7      y      :lighted with her com-
plaisance, and assured her            vas his most delightful
resource in his moments of ennui and dissatisfaction.   The
two P                          hroughout, then begged
her Royal Highness to condescend to visit their seraglio.
We found it much more numerous t ıan that of their father,
but by no means so rich.   7      were many women, of
different nations,                  :d off from their parents
while yet young.   ·.      hapless victims, once immured,
never walk forth more; they live ıere, and there they end
their days.   A stranger never meets their eye; consequently,
they were so delighted to see us, that they were at a loss how
to express their excessive joy.   Some of them spoke Italian,
but not very well; great part were seated on cushions, and

were so immoderately fat, as to be unable to rise without
assistance; these were the most admired, and to them all
the homage was paid. Prince Mustapha, entering unex‑
pectedly, caused the same movement among them, as would
a wolf in the fold. All were cast down and trembling, but
taking courage in some measure afterwards, they went one
after the other, with the most profound submission, to kiss
his hand; not according to our custom, but on the palm,
for such is the fashion of the Turks. Whilst these
unfortunate slaves thus discharged their duty, their tyrant
remained motionless as a statue, without even deigning to
bestow on them a glance of approbation or kindness.

" A collation was set before us, extremely well served, and
consisting of every rarity and delicacy; and we were again,
many times, sprinkled with perfumes. The ladies would
not suffer us to depart; and on her Royal Highness rising,
they pressed her to be seated again in such a suppliant
manner that she could not deny them; and it was not till we
had made a visit of five hours that we left them, and then
greatly to their sorrow. They accompanied us as far as the
court, making the most affecting gestures. O sweet liberty,
said I, on coming out, how inestimable thou art! These
unfortunates are buried here alive, condemned to see nought,
save the sky, their room, and the barbarian who sacrifices
them to every caprice. Every moment uncertain of their
existence, they hold it at the will of him who detains them

L

in his power, and who bereaves them of it when they least expect. Her Royal Highness having taken leave of the Bey and all his court, we returned to Tunis in the same manner in which we left it."

———

NOTE (d). Page 20.

The causes and manner of the Princess's departure from Tunis are minutely described as follows :—

" Her Royal Highness purposed spending the month of April at Tunis; but the English fleet arriving there unexpectedly, Lord Exmouth came himself to request her to quit the shore, as the Bey appeared obstinately resolved to refuse the slaves demanded; and it was probable that he should be compelled to resort to extremities. Preparations were made for our departure with the utmost promptitude; and many boats, sent by the order of the admiral, were loaded with our *baggage*. The inhabitants of Tunis were in consternation, expecting every moment that the town would be fired upon by the fleet; and the precipitate departure of the Princess seemed to confirm their conjectures, which were, in truth, but too well founded; two hours only being allowed for reflection. The Bey could not persuade himself that the menaces were serious, and was very backward in giving a formal decision; until, learning that her Royal Highness was on the point of quitting the town, and that her baggage was already shipped, he was terrified by the promptitude of the resolution, and justly assigning as its cause, the danger which hung over him, he already imagined that he saw Tunis subjected to the horrors of a bombardment: the town, although well fortified, must soon have yielded to superior force.

" The Bey, aware that time was important, and the danger pressing, dispatched his prime minister to the Princess, praying her to obtain an interview with Lord Exmouth, as he was fully resolved to give up the slaves to him. Notwithstanding this arrangement actually took place, her Royal Highness persevered in her design of quitting Tunis; it appeared as if she foresaw the revolution which took place some time afterwards, and which would doubtless have been pregnant with mischief to her, had she unfortunately been present. The Bey, who had with his own hands put his brother to death, and procured the cruel murder of his nephews, as a means of establishing himself upon their throne, was in that revolution dispatched by his eldest son, who assumed his seat. The youngest fled to the Goletta, took possession of five brigs of war, and did not scruple to become a leader of corsairs, and to infest the seas, in company with his worthy comrades, committing the most horrible outrages.

" We embarked on the 22d, and with a very brisk wind passed in front of the fleet; each ship fired twenty-one rounds of cannon, in honour of the Princess of Wales; the flags were mounted, and the masts and yards manned with sailors dressed uniformly, the whole producing a very pleasing effect. Lord Exmouth sailed on the 23d, and we on the 24th, with a favourable wind."

---

Note (e). Page 22.

" The English consul having sent horses to convey us to the city, we set out at five o'clock in the evening, and took up our abode at the house of the French consul, which was the most commodious, and best furnished."

---

Note (f). Page 31.

" They are, in general, very tall, but without grace; their countenance is melancholy, and without expression; and their eyes are cast down, so that it is difficult to distinguish of what colour they are. Does this arise from diffidence, or modesty? we are told from neither, but merely from habit."

---

Note (g). Page 31.

After relating an instance of despotic cruelty, exerted by a Turk towards a Greek, she continues:—

" It was told to her Royal Highness that, for several years, three hundred of these unfortunate beings (Greeks) had been incarcerated in the prisons for debt, the greatest part of whom were languishing in weakness, and declining to the grave in anguish. The Princess, not belying her accustomed generosity, paid their debts, and restored them once more to the light; from which, without her, they would have been for ever shut out. The governor gave proof of *his humanity:* whilst receiving the money, he could not refrain from shewing excessive vexation at these poor creatures being released, and in freedom: he would, doubt-less, have preferred seeing them expire in anguish, through ill treatment. I should never conclude, were I to attempt to describe the excess to which this barbarity is urged, against a people who merit it so little; and who formerly gave laws and examples to the universe. It is difficult to conceive, how they can have so far degenerated; but, truly, there is nought so cramps the soul, and so prevents the spirit from assuming its level, and aiming at great and useful designs, as slavery."

NOTE *(h).* Page 32.

" The governor of Athens paid several visits to her Royal Highness, accompanied by a numerous court, and a guard of honour, which had a most fantastical appearance; their uniform being incomplete, and their arms for the most part but clubs, cut in the country. The guard were on foot, and the governor on horseback; as throughout the whole of Greece, the use of carriages is unknown."

––––––

Note *(i).*  Page 32.

The following refers to Corinth :—

" The Bey sent a number of horses for the use of the Princess and her suite.  All his officers came, by his order, to meet her, and accompanied her to the palace, where she was received with great ceremony.  A suite of apartments had, for some time, been prepared for her use, in the most commodious manner that can be expected amongst the Turks.

" The following morning we made a visit to the seraglio. The wives are not numerous, but are prettier, and appear more happy and more free, than at Tunis.  The Bey married, about three years ago, a country woman, to whom alone *he has, since that time, attached himself.*  He treats her with regard, and may, in truth, be considered an exception to the general practice of the country ; being a model of constancy, where constancy was never known before.  The cause may be, that his wife is very beautiful ; and he himself appeared to us far more amiable than others of his nation. He paid. his respects to her Royal Highness daily, and neglected nothing that could render her stay in the place as agreeable as possible. There is nothing remarkable to visit. The castle is on a very elevated situation, and permission to visit it is rarely granted to strangers. This precaution led her Royal Highness to believe that there was certainly something curious in it, which they endeavoured to conceal from every eye; her curiosity was thus roused, and she requested leave to go through it, which was instantly granted to her. We went up to it, but found absolutely nothing more than the fortress. At the foot of the castle there are some columns remaining of a temple, which was dedicated to. Neptune; and close by is a tomb which is said to be that of the children of Medea, slain by herself, to punish Jason for his infidelity."

---

NOTE *(k).* Page 40.

" This news spread consternation throughout the suite, as it would have been difficult to choose five out of twenty-six; besides, every individual of the suite was anxious to go to Jerusalem: it was the object of the journey, and the hope of it alone had enabled us to support our fatigues with resignation and patience. It was hard thus to find our expectation deceived, at the very moment in which we depended on. its being realized. Her Royal Highness, always goodness

itself (*toujours la bonté même,* original), immediately formed
her determination, without explaining it to any one; she
gave orders to the captain to set sail, that same evening,
for St. Jean d'Acre, where we arrived on the 6th. The Princess went herself to the governor, and urged him to grant
permission to all the suite to travel to Palestine. He at first
started many difficulties. They were, however, gradually
overcome by the sight of some rich presents exhibited to
him, which operated on his avarice—a vice so powerful
among his fraternity that they cannot do other than yield to
it, even at the hazard of their lives and favour. Thus, to travel amongst the Turks, it is not only necessary to be well
provided with money, but also to be liberal of it; and it is
only with this metal, or with presents, that what is desired
can be obtained from them. The governor, not wishing that
the real motive which tempted him to deviate from his duty
should be known, told the Princess, through the medium of
his interpreter, that as he had received great obligations from,
and felt that gratitude was due to, the English, for the services
rendered to the city, he was resolved, at all hazards, to grant
this indulgence to their sovereign : he was even generous in
return, for he made her Royal Highness a present of five
linen tents, a zetique, similar to those used in Sicily, and as
many horses as were necessary for the journey; also an escort
of officers of the guard, guides to conduct us, and camels
to transport our baggage.

" On the 8th of July, at eight o'clock in the evening, we commenced our pilgrimage to the Holy Land, presenting the appearance of a little army—for our number exceeded two hundred. We were compelled to travel during the night, on account of the excessive heat during the day. The first night we were terrified with a view of the horrible and almost impracticable paths which we had to traverse; throughout they were choked with rocks and brakes, and were so confined that we were every moment in danger of being thrown down: our fear, also, was not likely to be diminished by the total want of every kind of habitation. We knew also that the desert was infested by robbers and banditti: against them, perhaps, our escort a little re-assured us; especially as the governor, fearing the power of the Princess, to whom he gave the title of Queen of England, had taken every precaution to prevent the possibility of insult being offered to her, fearing, with justice, that if it were otherwise, he should be the first to feel its effects. If an individual, without power, were to travel through this country, he would certainly be exposed to great danger, and probably would not quit it with life: indeed it is very rarely that Europeans are seen in the country. Many who have meditated this journey have renounced it, on a perspective of the dangers to which they would constantly be exposed; but the Princess of Wales, discouraged by no difficulties, and surmounting all, effected what she had so long anticipated. God has permitted her to accomplish her great enterprise."

M

Note (I),  Page 40.

" On the evening of the 9th we set out from Damascus,
and, after having travelled all night, arrived, at five o'clock
in the morning, at a plain, called Aér, where we pitched our
tents, and set out our mattresses on the ground. It was, however, utterly impossible for us to obtain any repose; the
burning sun pierced through in spite of the extreme thick-
ness of the linen; and a number of venomous insects got
under our tents, and stung us with such violence, that we
were swoln all over.  To remedy this inconvenience, we
thought of rubbing ourselves with bitter citrons; this plan
succeeded admirably, and the insects, disliking the thing
tormented us no more.  The earth beneath our feet was
glowing, and it was impossible to find coolness in any situation; the plain was perfectly dried up, and covered with
arid rocks; not a single tree, or plant, met our eye; while
a burning thirst devoured us, without a drop of water to
quench it; we scarcely could find enough to make a little
soup, and even that proved quite muddy, and filled with
small stones, which were not the most pleasant to the teeth.
We had wine, but from its temperature, it might have been
boiled over the fire.  We could not contrive what to procure
what to take to quench our thirst: happily, from time to time,
some gourds, called enguries, were found; the interior is
coloured, and yields much juice.  This was our chief nourishment, with the exception of a few cucumbers, which

were very scarce; and some dates, so withered, that elsewhere they would not have been touched. In the torment
of excessive thirst, all nourishment which is not liquid, is
disgusting; for it is much easier to abstain from eating, than
drinking. At length, after a terrific day, the caravan set
forward at six o'clock in the evening: the roads never appeared so bad to us as that night; exceedingly narrow; up
hill and down; at times filled with stones and brambles, so
interwoven, that the feet of the horses became entangled in
them, and they had much difficulty in extricating themselves.
Many of the caravan fell down from their camels, half
asleep, but by a species of miracle, no one met with any
more serious injury, than a few bruises, or a bleeding at the
nose."

---

### Note (m).  Page 50.

" Before the sun had appeared, and whilst it was still
possible to travel, we took the road to Jericho, which is
distant two leagues (from the Jordan). The road is over a
plain, on which nothing but a few noxious plants and brambles are met with. We passed at the foot of a mountain,
of terrific appearance; it is said to be that near which our
Saviour fasted forty days, and whither he was carried by the
evil spirit, when he tempted him, shewing him all the kingdoms of the world.

" I have heard from others of the suite, that the day spent at Jericho, was rendered, by the intense heat of the sun and sand, far more trying than any other, even of those spent in traversing the desert."

---

### NOTE (n). Page 51.

" The tents were pitched in order to shelter us from the rays of the sun, which were already very powerful, though, as yet, it was but six o'clock in the morning : throughout the whole day it was impossible to take any rest, or to sleep: never had the sun appeared to us so intense! its rays were flames, which pierced through our tents and scorched us."

**THE END.**

BARNARD AND FARLEY,
Skinner Street, London.

CPSIA information can be obtained at www.ICGtesting.com
Printed in the USA
LVOW10s1714140316

479091LV00019B/1247/P